MITCHELL BEAZLEY

TOURING IN WINE COUNTRY
BURGUNDY

HUBRECHT DUIJKER

SERIES EDITOR
HUGH JOHNSON

Contents

Foreword 7

Introduction 8

Viticulture and Wines 12
The grape varieties 14
The cuisine 16
How to use this guide 18

Chablis 20

Around Chablis 29

The Côte d'Or 32

Dijon 36

The Côte de Nuits 38

Marsannay-la-Côte 39
Fixin 40
Gevrey-Chambertin 41
Morey-Saint-Denis 43
Chambolle-Musigny 44
Vougeot 46
Vosne-Romanée 48
NUITS-SAINT-GEORGES 49
Prémeaux-Prissey 52
Ladoix 53
Hautes-Côtes de Nuits 54

The Côte de Beaune 58

Aloxe-Corton 59
Pernand-Vergelesses 60
Savigny-lès-Beaune 61
Chorey-lès-Beaune 63
Beaune 64
Pommard 70
Volnay 72
Monthélie 73
Auxey-Duresses 74
Saint-Romain 75

Touring in Wine Country
Burgundy
by Hubrecht Duijker

Fully updated by Gert Crum

First published in Great Britain in 1996
by Mitchell Beazley, an imprint of
Octopus Publishing Group Limited,
2–4 Heron Quays, London E14 4JP.

Reprinted 1997
Revised edition 2000
Reprinted 2002

Copyright © Octopus Publishing Group
Ltd 1996, 2000, 2002
Text copyright © Hubrecht Duijker
1996, 2000, 2002
Maps copyright © Octopus Publishing
Group Ltd 1996, 2000, 2002

Text adapted in part from *Burgundy – A
Wine Lover's Touring Guide* by Hubrecht
Duijker. First published 1993 by
Uitgeverij Het Spectrum BV

Executive Editor: Rebecca Spry
Editor: Hilary Lumsden
Executive Art Editor: Tracy Killick
Cartographic Editor: Zoë Goodwin
Index: Anne Barrett
Gazetteer: Sally Chorley
Production: Nancy Roberts
Cartography: Map Creation Limited
Design by Bridgewater Book Company
Illustrations: Polly Raines

Typeset in Bembo and Gill Sans

Printed and bound in by Toppan Printing
Company

Meursault	76
Puligny-Montrachet	78
Chassagne-Montrachet	80
Saint-Aubin and Gamay	81
Santenay	82
Maranges	85
Hautes-Côtes de Beaune	86

The Côte Chalonnaise   90

Northern Chalonnais	92
Bouzeron	94
Rully	95
Mercurey	96
Givry	98
Chalon-sur-Saône	100
Montagny	102

The Mâconnais   104

Northern Mâconnais	107
Uchizy	109
Cluny	112
Mâcon	114
Pouilly-Fuissé	116
Saint Véran	119

Beaujolais   120

Saint-Amour	123
Juliénas	123
Chénas	124
Moulin-à-Vent	125
Fleurie	126
Chiroubles	127
Morgon	127
Brouilly and Côte de Brouilly	128
Régnié	129
Southern Beaujolais	130

Gazetteer   136

Index   140

Foreword

Why is it that wine tasted in the cellar (or even in the region) of its birth has a magic, a vibrancy and vigour that make it so memorable?

It is easy to think of physical reasons. The long journey to the supermarket shelf cannot be made without some effect on a living creature – and wine is indeed alive, and correspondingly fragile.

It is even easier to think of romantic reasons: the power of association, the atmosphere and scents of the cellar, the enthusiasm of the grower as he moves from barrel to barrel...

No wonder wine-touring is the first-choice holiday for so many people. It is incomparably the best way to understand wine – whether at the simple level of its scenery and culture, or deeper into the subtleties of its *terroirs* and the different philosophies of different producers.

There are armchair wine books, coffee-table books, quick reference wine books... even a pop-up wine book. Now with this series we have the wine-traveller's precise, pin-pointed practical guide to sleuthing through the regions that have most to offer, finding favourites and building up memories. The bottles you find yourself have the genie of experience in them.

Hugh Johnson

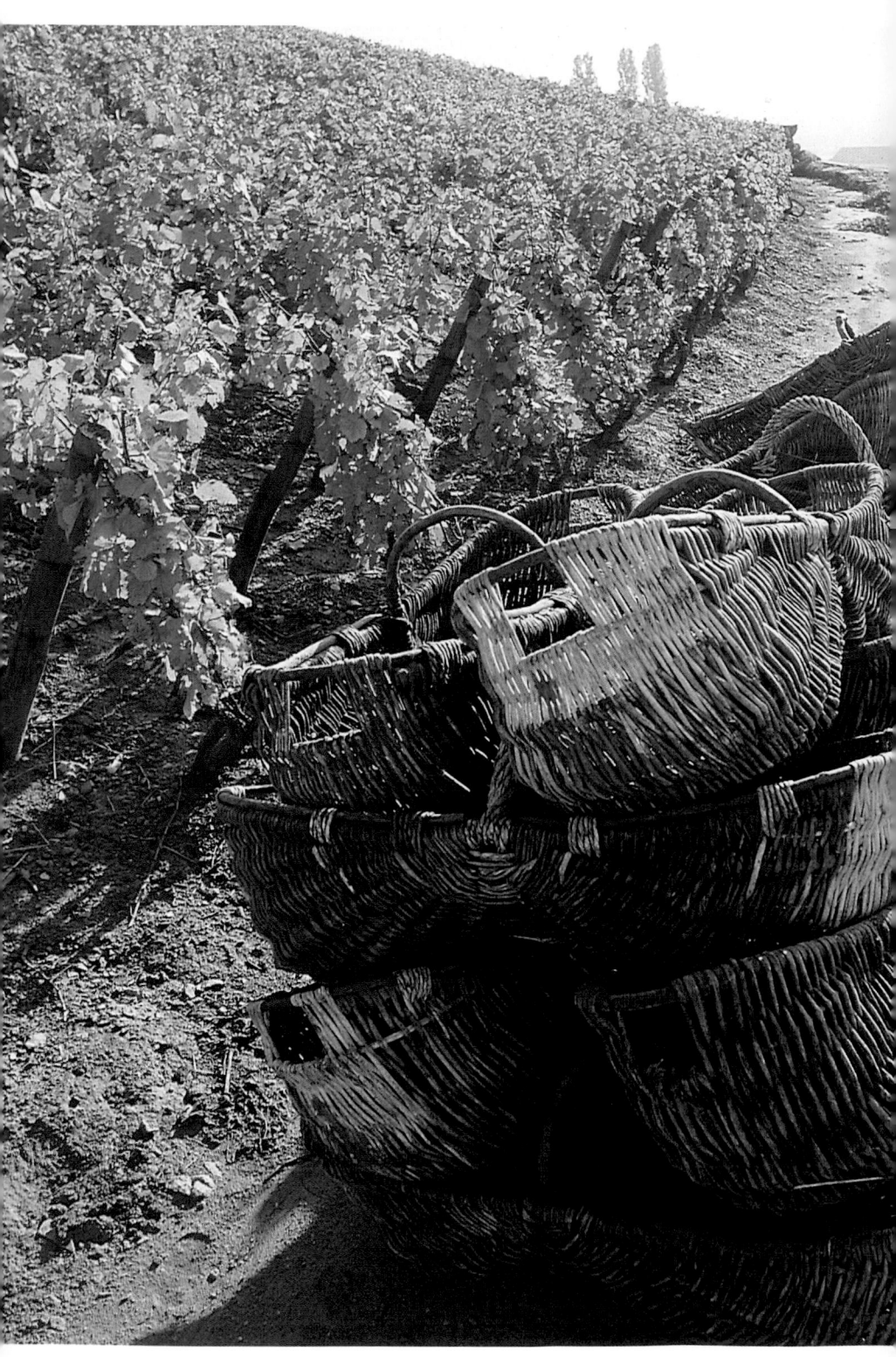

Introduction

To wine enthusiasts everywhere, the very name 'Burgundy' is inextricably linked with some of the finest wines known throughout the world. Yet it is quite possible to pass through this region and not know that you have been in wine country at all – let alone in the most renowned wine region of France. The Paris-Lyon *autoroute* sails disdainfully from the hills of the Morvan over the vines of Beaune, then plunges on south following the plain of the Saône, with the vineyard-covered hills to the west scarcely noticeable.

Take time to come off the main road, though, and the treasures that have made Burgundy's wines so famed will be discovered. The workaday side of Burgundy can be seen in a thousand cellars, most small and cramped workshops rather than Médoc-style *chais*. For this is the domaine of the smallholder, proprietors owning just a hectare (ha) or two, and these often made up of ten or more tiny patches in as many different vineyards. To own 10ha in Burgundy is to be a major figure in your village. In Bordeaux, such a holding would push a château well down the local pecking order (*see* page 12).

The region of Burgundy was once the richest of the ancient duchies in France, stretching right up through northern France into Flanders. The Hospices de Beaune, built in 1443 by Nicolas Rolin, chancellor to Philip the Good, is a fine example of the beautiful architecture reflecting this immense wealth. There is also a considerable amount of Flemish-style architecture throughout the region. Today, it consists of just five *départements* in eastern France: Ain, Côte d'Or, Nièvre, Saône-et-Loire and Yonne, with the amount of land under vine a relatively modest 40,000ha, small compared with the 100,000ha or so belonging to Bordeaux. The administrative

capital of Burgundy is the city of Dijon, but its wine capital is Beaune. Lying halfway between Chablis to the north and Villefranche, the heart of Beaujolais, to the south, it is the logical base for a serious exploration of the area.

Left Vintage in Corton-Charlemagne. Small plastic trays reduce the risk of damage to the grapes.

Above The enticing, old-fashioned style of Saint-Genioux de Sissoux is created by such small touches as this cheese list written in chalk.

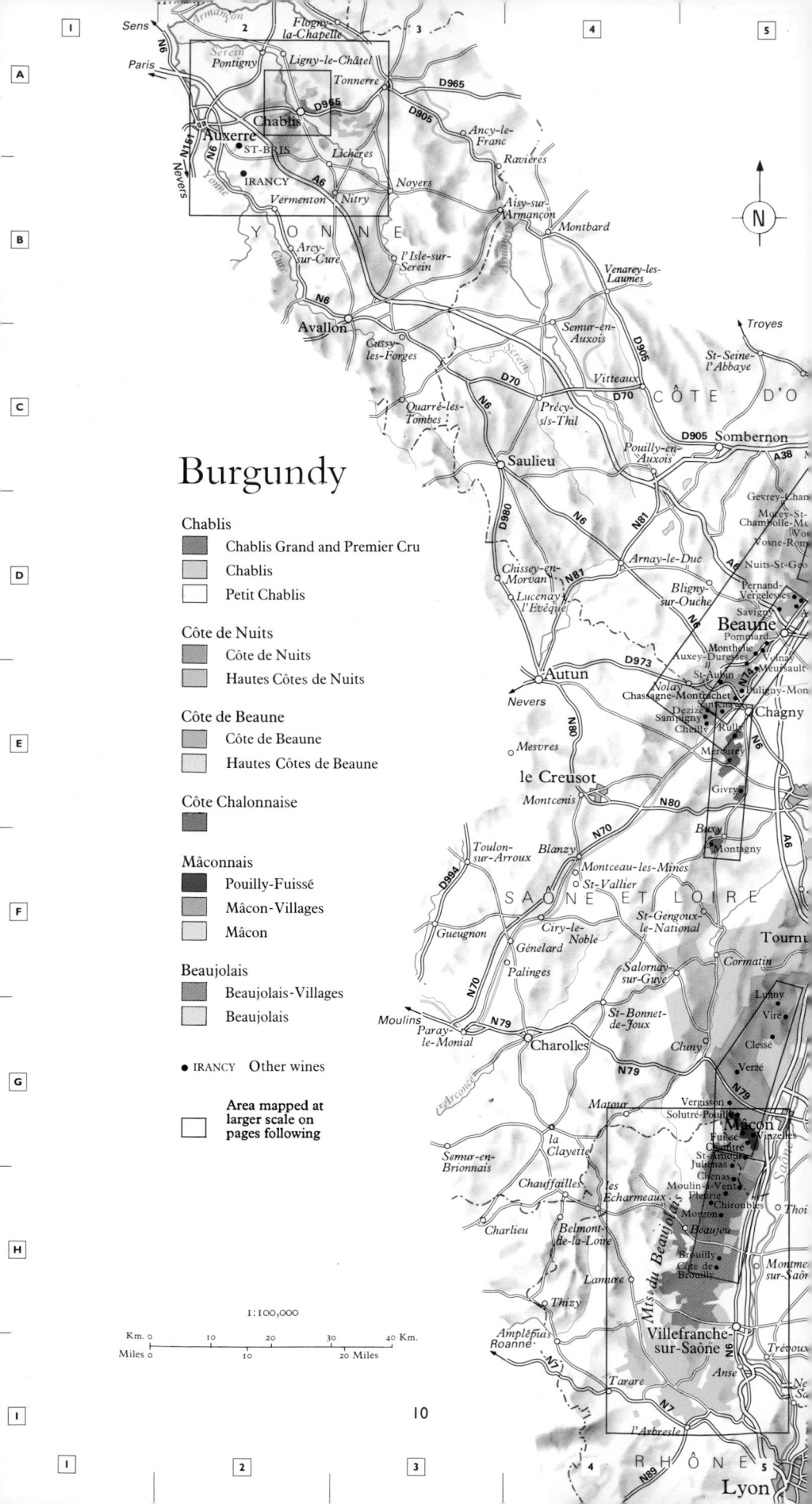

Burgundy

Chablis
- Chablis Grand and Premier Cru
- Chablis
- Petit Chablis

Côte de Nuits
- Côte de Nuits
- Hautes Côtes de Nuits

Côte de Beaune
- Côte de Beaune
- Hautes Côtes de Beaune

Côte Chalonnaise

Mâconnais
- Pouilly-Fuissé
- Mâcon-Villages
- Mâcon

Beaujolais
- Beaujolais-Villages
- Beaujolais

• IRANCY   Other wines

Area mapped at
larger scale on
pages following

1:100,000

Km. 0   10   20   30   40 Km.
Miles 0   10   20 Miles

Right Relaxing and enjoying Burgundy's many liquid delights could not be easier with such a wide choice of bars and restaurants. Simply check the listings for the town or village you wish to visit.

THE REGIONS

Each of Burgundy's regions, from Chablis in the north to Beaujolais in the south, offers something different, not only in terms of wine, but also of landscape and culture.

The heart of Burgundy however, both historically and qualitively, is the Côte d'Or. Here, the most illustrious wines, both red and white, are produced. The vineyards trace the eastern slopes of a low, broad mountain chain in a southerly direction, almost all within the *département* of the same name. The exceptions are those vineyards with the appellation Maranges, in the extreme south of the Côte d'Or, which are situated in the Saône-et-Loire *département*.

From here it is only a few kilometres (kms) to the northern-most vineyards of the next district, the Chalonnais, or Côte Chalonnaise. The wines, red and white, tend to lack the complexity of Côte d'Or wines, but offer good value for money. Sparkling Crémant de Bourgogne is also made here.

The undulating landscape of the Chalonnais changes seamlessly into the Mâconnais, which is again dominated by hills and valleys, especially to the south where the landscape becomes quite dramatic. Mainly white wines are produced, including the Mâconnais' most famous, Pouilly-Fuissé.

Finally Beaujolais, the largest district, starts in the Saône-et-Loire and continues down to the *département* of Rhône, just north of Lyon. It is the most romantic Burgundian district; in some sleepy villages, time seems to have stood still. Your journey will then be complete, and some mysteries of this magical region uncovered.

Viticulture and Wines

Winegrowing in Burgundy is unusual as the scale is so small, with plots of vines often spread across several vineyards. The reasons are historical. After the French Revolution and subsequent breakdown of religious and secular rule, the land was shared out and further divided by inheritance rights. Burgundy now has few estates larger than 25ha. This fragmentation is greatest in the Côte d'Or.

For many farmers, the lots are too small to make or bottle wine themselves. This is why the merchants – *négociants-éleveurs* – play such an important role in the Côte d'Or. They collect grapes, must or wine from small growers, assembling commercially viable quantities from single appellations.

In Chablis, the Chalonnais, Mâconnais and Beaujolais the emphasis shifts and *caves coopératives*, large groups of growers who pool their resources to make wines collectively, are common. In the Mâconnais, 90 per cent of all wines are produced in this way and most of it is handled by *négociants*.

WINE CATEGORIES

Getting to grips with the French appellation system is hard enough, but in Burgundy it is particularly complicated. On the basis of the grape varieties used (*see* page 14), French law recognises over 100 different appellations. They can be roughly divided into five categories:

Main picture *The harvest taking place in the Côte de Nuits – in this case, at the famous Domaine de la Romanée-Conti.*
Above *Removing particles in the wine (fining) by adding beaten egg whites. Bentonite clay is another substance useful for this process.*

Top right *During winter, the vines are pruned and the unwanted canes are gathered and burned.*
Right *High-tech fermentation vats in Beaujolais.*

Regional/Generic Wine
Made throughout Burgundy: red and white burgundy, includes Bourgogne Aligoté, Bourgogne Passe-Tout-Grains and sparkling Crémant de Bourgogne.

District Wine
Can be made only in the (sub)districts concerned such as Chablis, Côte de Beaune-Villages, Mâcon and Beaujolais.

Village/Commune Wine
From a single commune or a group of communes: for example, Gevrey-Chambertin (Côte d'Or), Pouilly-Fuissé (Mâconnais) and Fleurie (Beaujolais).

Premier Cru
Wines originating from a vineyard classed as Premier Cru. They are found in Chablis, the Côte d'Or and Chalonnais.

Grand Cru
The highest category. Grand Cru wines from the Côte d'Or are sold with the name of the vineyard alone – it has its very own appellation (Charmes-Chambertin, Corton-Charlemagne). Grand Cru wines from Chablis simply state Chablis Grand Cru along with the name of the vineyard.

CLIMATE AND SOIL
The soil throughout Burgundy has an enormous influence on the resulting wines and varies according to the region. In Chablis, limestone dominates and is well-suited to Chardonnay, as long as there is enough sun to ripen the grapes in these cool-climate vineyards. Add to this the variety of slopes – the Grand Cru vineyards are situated, some 150 to 200 metres (ms) high, on one stretch of southwest-facing slopes; most of the Premiers Crus face the other direction – it is easy to see how different the resulting wines can be. The calcium-rich soil continues into the Côte d'Or but it becomes a more complex geology, with layers of marl, clay and other soils present. Each soiltype influences factors such as drainage and soil temperature, affecting the ripening of grapes and ultimately the character of the wine itself. Limestone is still a feature of the Chalonnais, the Mâconnais and Beaujolais, but in this last region the soil can also be made up of decomposing slate. A subsoil of granite from ancient volcanoes also influences the flavour of these wines. Climate has an enormous influence. From the northernmost vineyards of Chablis, it is about 300kms to the southernmost point of Beaujolais. While Burgundy enjoys warm summers, it also suffers long, cold winters. Spring frosts and hail are a constant hazard, potentially devastating the crop. In Chablis, when frost threatens, heaters are often lit in the vineyards to warm the air above the vines. Sprinklers are also used to provide an insulating coating of ice that prevents the vines from freezing internally.

Travel south and the conditions become gradually milder. By the time you reach the Mâconnais there is already a slight Mediterranean touch to the air.

The grape varieties

Only a few grape varieties are grown in Burgundy and they are rarely blended. There are four main varieties:

Chardonnay

This is one of the world's most noble white grapes. It may have originated in Burgundy itself and is responsible for the region's best white wines. It produces a firm, full wine and can have a range of flavours, depending on how it is handled. In Burgundy, an elegant, minerally earthiness dominates the wines in contrast to the ripe, tropical flavours found in the New World. The wines age well whether or not oak barrels are used during production.

Pinot Noir

The greatest red burgundy is made from Pinot Noir – the only red grape variety grown in the Côte d'Or. Compared to Chardonnay, it is more difficult to grow, requiring particular climatic conditions: fairly cool, yet warm enough to ripen the grapes. The wines are elegant and accessible, often easy to drink when young, but maturing well. Soft, red fruits and a silky texture are typical of good Pinot Noir, and an earthy, gamey complexity is typical of good burgundy.

Left *The imposing product of a temperamental grape variety: red burgundy. Silky, reminiscent of soft, red fruits and slightly gamey; it is also very expensive to produce.*

Above *Chardonnay, the world's most famous grape variety, produces the region's finest white wines and the most sought-after dry white wines in the world.*

Main picture *Pinot Noir grapes: difficult to ripen, susceptible to many diseases, but producing exquisite, complex, long-lived wines.*

Gamay

Gamay, (full name Gamay Noir à Jus Blanc) is the red Beaujolais grape, producing all the region's red or rosé wines: light, fresh, fruity and easy to drink. Most is made to be drunk young, but some of the serious Cru Beaujolais can age well, taking on a fuller, more complex style. As well as the wines made from the Gamay variety alone, there is a blended wine, Bourgogne Passetoutgrains. This can be produced in the whole of Burgundy and consists of two-thirds Gamay and a third Pinot Noir.

Aligoté

A few of the best Aligoté wines come from the Chablis region, from the Hautes-Côtes and Bouzeron, a village in the north of the Chalonnais. The latter even has its own appellation: Bourgogne Aligoté de Bouzeron since 1997.

Other varieties

Pinot Blanc (which can give surprisingly good wines here), the kindred Pinot Gris, Sauvignon Blanc (Sauvignon de Saint-Bris), Sacy and Melon de Bourgogne are present in limited quantities, as are César and Tressot.

Above *Gamay, the grape variety responsible for all red Beaujolais and also found in parts of Mâcon. Luscious, sweet fruitiness is the hallmark of these wines.*

The cuisine

The people of Burgundy love the good life and always sit down to eat with the greatest of pleasure, whether at home or in a restaurant. Hundreds of restaurants flourish in this region and while some are luxurious and exclusive, the majority are simple and frequently used by the locals. A three- or four-course menu can, therefore, be surprisingly inexpensive. Outside the tourist villages you will only pay about FF100 – perhaps FF120.

Specialities

Traditional Burgundian recipes have been handed down from generation to generation, most of them making full use of the many fresh ingredients produced in the region, such as the famous beef from the white Charolais cattle, the raw hams from Morvan, crayfish, many types of salt-water fish, snails, mustard (from Dijon) and a large range of cheeses. Goat's cheese plays a particularly important role in the Mâconnais and Beaujolais and there are numerous versions to choose from. There is also a delicious variety called Montrachet and a delectable caraway cheese called Epoisses, which is sprinkled with the local spirit, Marc de Bourgogne. What is interesting, especially to the red-wine-with-cheese traditionalist, is that white burgundy often tastes just as good (and sometimes even better) drunk with the regional cheeses as red burgundy does.

Throughout Burgundy, many vegetables and fruit are grown, and soft fruits such as blackberries, raspberries and cherries are widespread. Many Burgundian winemakers also

Far left *Garlic, one of the most vivid images of Burgundian cuisine and, indeed, of France as a whole.* Left *Crème de Cassis, made in many villages in Burgundy, is the key ingredient for the popular blackcurrant-flavoured drink, Kir.*

Above *Goat's cheese in Burgundy comes in many shapes and sizes and is perfect with the region's wines.* Left *Snails — one of Burgundy's most famous delicacies — are often served as a starter, drenched with garlic butter and herbs.*

make the fruit liqueurs Crème de Cassis and Crème de Framboise, which, when mixed with white (and sometimes red) wine create the delicious apéritif known as Kir.

On the basis of the ingredients just mentioned, the Burgundian chefs prepare local specialities which taste just as marvellous as the accompanying wines. These include the nourishing *salade beaujolaise* with chicken livers and pieces of bacon, *œufs en meurette* (eggs poached in red, or sometimes white, wine), frog's legs, *jambon persillé* (chunky pieces of ham in a white wine jelly with parsley and garlic), *escargots de Bourgogne* (snails with garlic) and *andouillettes* – sausages for which numerous regional recipes exist. There are just as many variations of *coq au vin*, if only because of the numerous different types of wine. In every village in Beaujolais this dish is prepared with the local wine. *Poulet de Bresse* (also called *volaille*) often appears *à la crème* on the menu, with or without *morilles* mushrooms. *Boeuf à la bourguigonne* or *boeuf bourguignon,* which is served in countless restaurants, is beef cooked in red wine, with onion, pieces of bacon and mushrooms. *Jambon à la lie de vin* is ham braised in the wine lees (sediment) produced during fermentation. *Lapin rôti* (roast rabbit) is also a traditional dish, often with a mustard and cream sauce. *Rable de lièvre* (saddle of hare) and many types of game, including *sanglier* and *marcassin* (wild boar and young wild boar, respectively) are fairly common and ideal served with red wines from the Côte d'Or. The excellent beef from Charolais is frequently served as sirloin steaks with marrow and wine sauce. Blackberries and the liqueur made from them (Crème de Mûre) are often used in desserts such as sorbets and pies. Those who enjoy Burgundian cuisine and wines understand why the French critic Curnonsky described this area as 'a gastronomic paradise'.

How to use this guide

Above *An entrance to a vineyard in Mercurey, Côte Chalonnaise (see page 96) – a commune which produces a rich, supple red wine with good structure and a tiny amount of delicate white wine.*

This guide leads you through the length of Burgundy, starting in Chablis in the north and working its way southwards through the Côte d'Or, the Chalonnais and the Mâconnais to Beaujolais. Wine routes are suggested within each region, taking in every important wine village. Other places of interest are included, as well as suggested detours, scenic routes, views and walks. Hotels and restaurants are recommended, all with prices (hotel prices are usually for a double room). Some of the best and most welcoming wine producers or *négociant* firms are recommended for each village, often with the names of their best wines.

HOTELS
When reserving a hotel room, always ask for a quiet one and take note of loud church bells and popular, noisy cafés or bars. When making your reservation you will be informed of a final arrival time. If you intend to arrive later, telephone, or your room may be given away. It is wise to send or fax

written confirmation of a reservation. In many villages (such as in the Hautes-Côtes de Nuits), rooms in private houses are available, look for the signs *gîte* or *chambre d'hôte* or consult the list of addresses at the town hall or at the *syndicat d'initiative* (tourist office).

RESTAURANTS

Telephone restaurants in advance to be sure of a table, and to check that it is open on a particular day. Off season, many restaurants are open only three or four days a week.

Fixed menus often offer the best value for money and use the freshest produce of the day. In simple restaurants choose regional dishes – they will be better prepared and less expensive. Select regional wines and, if possible, wines from the village itself, as they will have been more expertly and critically chosen. A carafe of tap water is always free.

WINEGROWERS

It maybe difficult to get an appointment to see the most famous winegrowers, but the less well-known will generally welcome you with pleasure. Do not hesitate to show them this guide: someone who comes by recommendation and is truly interested in wines is usually more pleasantly received than a passing stranger. When tasting the wines it is normal to spit them out, but first ask where you can do this. Never tip but buy at least one bottle of wine as a token of appreciation (this is unnecessary if you have paid for the visit). French is generally the only language spoken, although many young winegrowers nowadays speak English.

CHOOSING WINES TO BUY

Choosing the best wines to buy in Burgundy is not easy given the number of growers and *négociants*. Price need not reflect quality, nor even the appellation. Widely varying wines can be produced from grapes grown in the same vineyard but by different owners. As winemaking methods also vary, so does the quality of the wine. Repute counts more than price or appellation.

PLACES OF INTEREST

Burgundy is steeped in history and cultural interest. Details of the most interesting places are included.

MAPS

Detailed wine maps showing commune appellation boundaries, Grands and Premiers Crus, and other vineyard boundaries are included, with suggested wine routes. These routes take in the most important villages and vineyards, but if you have time to explore further, then so much the better.

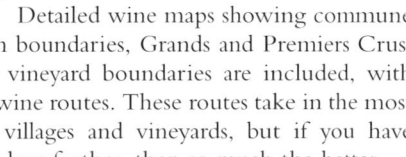

Chablis

The first great Burgundian vineyards you reach when driving south from Paris are those of Chablis, in the Yonne *département*.

It is only through historical coincidence that Chablis belongs to Burgundy (it was absorbed into the Duchy of Burgundy in 1477), because its location, climate and soil all suggest it could just as well belong to Champagne. The best vineyards of Chablis, like those of Champagne, contain a lot of limestone. In Chablis, the thick lime layer was formed by the fossils of countless shellfish, usually small oysters with a comma-like shell. The soil is Kimméridgian, named after Kimmeridge on the south coast of England, because a similar limestone layer is found there. It is the lime that is believed to give the wines of Chablis, exclusively white, their distinctive austere character. Wines made from Chardonnay are characterised by a pale colour, often with a green tinge, and a very dry, somewhat mineral-like, cool taste which can be succulent and fruity at the same time.

There are four categories of Chablis. The best wines, the Grands Crus, come from seven slopes directly to the north of Chablis: Blanchots, Bougros, Les Clos, Grenouilles, Les Preuses, Valmur and Vaudésir. They offer intense flavours, full of strength and character, and are at their best a few years after bottling. Somewhat lighter and less pronounced in character, but still with a marked identity, are the wines from the Premier Cru sites. These come from some 580ha divided among 30 different vineyards. Wines from these vineyards may be sold under the name of the individual vineyard, or under the name of a group of vineyards, the latter being more common.

Left *The soft, undulating lines of the Chablis landscape, with the pale Kimméridgian soil that gives the wines such distinctive character.*

Above *This sign is typical of those used to indicate a winemaking domaine. Most producers are clearly signposted in this way.*

Chablis

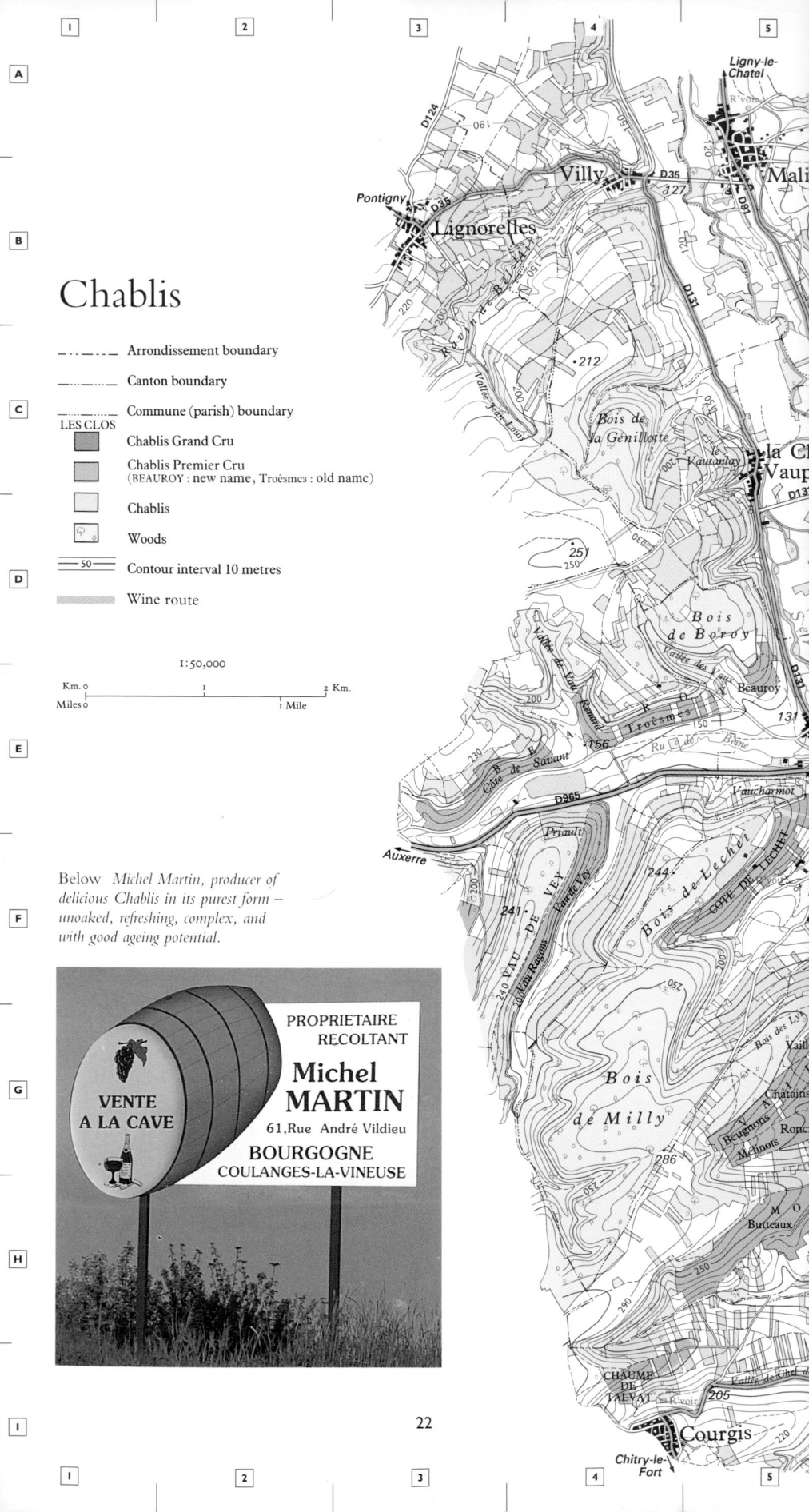

----·---- Arrondissement boundary

----·····--- Canton boundary

----·----- Commune (parish) boundary

LES CLOS

Chablis Grand Cru

Chablis Premier Cru
(BEAUROY : new name, Troësmes : old name)

Chablis

Woods

═══50═══ Contour interval 10 metres

Wine route

1 : 50,000

Km. 0   1   2 Km.
Miles 0   1 Mile

Below *Michel Martin, producer of delicious Chablis in its purest form – unoaked, refreshing, complex, and with good ageing potential.*

By far the largest number of wines are sold as straight-forward Chablis; in fact, twice as much wine is made from grapes grown outside the Grand Cru and Premier Cru vineyards. Quality can vary greatly, from fruity and clean to flat and aggressive – disappointing, especially considering the high prices Chablis often demands. Finally there is Petit Chablis, a wine which is increasingly modest, both in quantity and quality, and in which the characteristics of a true Chablis are hard to find.

CHABLIS AND ITS IMMEDIATE AREA

The town of Chablis is 12kms from the A6 Autoroute du Soleil (exit Auxerre–Sud). The winding road runs through Beines, which has an ancient medieval church. On the north side is a large man-made lake that protects the surrounding vineyards against night-time frosts by retaining some warmth from the

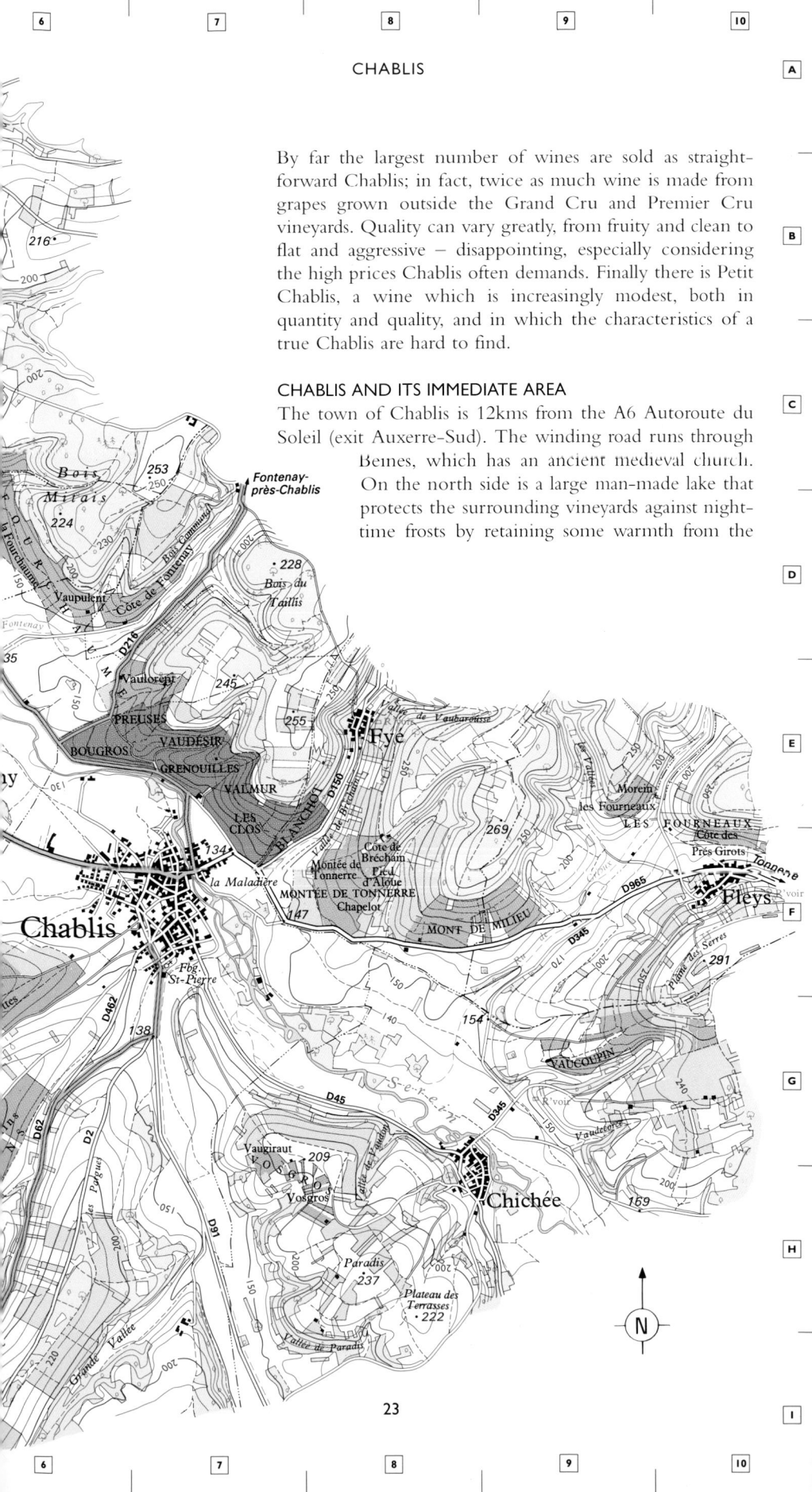

Right *Gougères, cheese-flavoured choux pastry puffs, are often served with wine throughout Burgundy.*

CHABLIS

HOTELS

Hostellerie des Clos
Tel: 03 86 42 10 63
The best hotel and restaurant of the district. Rooms start at around FF250. In the light, large dining room, you can eat very well. The least expensive set menu (around FF165) offers particularly good value for money. Wide wine selection. The owner, Michel Vignaud, is the cook.

Ibis
Tel: 03 86 42 49 20
Functional two-star hotel to the southwest of Chablis. About 40 rooms with modern furnishings from about FF275.

Les Lys
Tel: 03 86 42 49 20
Functional, two-star hotel. Around 40 modern rooms starting at about FF225.

Le Relais Saint-Vincent
Tel: 03 86 47 53 38
Peaceful, small hotel at Ligny-le-Châtel; ten attractive rooms starting at FF200. Also has a restaurant.

RESTAURANTS

Auberge du Bief
Tel: 03 86 47 43 42
At Ligny-le-Châtel, on a corner near the church on the river-bank. Traditional local dishes as well as more refined cuisine. Popular with the locals. Menus from FF155.

Le Chablis-Bar
Situated in the high street, here you will find some delicious Chablis and learn out about interesting local places from the *patronne*.

Le Syracuse
Tel: 03 86 42 19 45
Inexpensive and tasty regional dishes, for example, *andouillettes grillées* and *coq au Saint-Bris*. Excellent wine list.

Le Vieux Moulin
Tel: 03 86 42 47 30
This restaurant is located in an old watermill (Rue des Moulins, across from l'Obédiencerie). Regional cuisine, also *grillades*. Good wine list, reasonable prices (menus starting at FF100). Part of the Les Lys hotel.

RECOMMENDED PRODUCERS

Domaine J Billaud-Simon (Chablis)
Important estate owning many vineyards on the sought-after right bank of the Serein River, including plots in four Grands Crus. Technically very sophisticated.

Domaine Jean-Marc Brocard (Préhy)
According to Jean-Marc Brocard there are 'wines made from grapes and wines made from roots. The former get everything they need from the air, the latter find their truth in the soil'. This is how he is able to produce a whole range of Chablis with the typical taste of their *terroir*. The wines are not aged in oak.

sun's rays; this, in effect, creates a warmer microclimate by warming the air around the lake and preventing the dramatic night-time temperature fluctuations which can cause such severe frosts. Chablis itself is a small, quiet town, built around a main square. North of this square is the Romanesque-Gothic church of Saint-Martin. The doors of the church are covered with horseshoes, nailed on as offerings by pilgrims asking the saint to revive their tired horses.

The River Serein flows along the northeastern side of Chablis. In an old street, the Rue des Moulins, you will find l'Obédiencerie, a 15th-century building originally belonging to monks, which has an ancient wooden wine press. The building is now owned by the large Chablis producer, Domaine Laroche (visits by appointment). In the Rue de Chichée you will find Chablis/Auxerrois department of the Bureau Interprofessionnel des Vins de Bourgogne. You can also come here for further information. It is situated in a magnificently restored complex of medieval buildings known as Le Petit Pontigny. It used to belong to the great Cistercian abbey of Pontigny (12kms northwest of Chablis).

Chablis doesn't have many old streets, because it was badly damaged by bombs during the Second World War. However, the towers of the Porte Noël are reminders of a time when Chablis was walled and, thanks to the wine production, considerably prosperous. In the southern part of the town is the 12th-century church of Saint-Pierre, which is classified as a historic monument. Don't miss the fantastic view from the Panorama des Clos. Cross the River Serein to the east bank and follow the road straight on to the T-junction. Turn right here onto the D965 and take the first left. Climb uphill past the Grand Cru vineyards on your left until you reach the viewpoint from the woods.

Unlike other wine regions of France, Chablis does not have a signposted wine route, but the following will provide a good introduction to the area. From the centre of Chablis, cross the Serein to the east bank and turn left onto the D91, going north along the river-bank towards Maligny. On the slopes to the right are the best vineyards of the district, the Grands Crus. You may want to make a small diversion by turning right onto the D216 to Fontenay-près-Chablis to see the 11th-century church there. Return to the D91 and drive for about 7 km to the village of Maligny. To the left, on the way, you'll pass the water pump station which plays an invaluable role when frost is a danger to crops (*see* page 13). The stretch of vineyard on the right hand side is the Premier Cru of Fourchaume.

In Maligny itself is the château, situated in a large park, and currently being lovingly restored by winegrower Jean Durup. In the centre, by an old market hall, is the medieval church of Notre-Dame, which is worth a visit. Another 3.5 km along the D91 is Ligny-le-Châtel, with a striking church featuring a Romanesque nave, a Renaissance-style chancel and many religious works of art. Cross back over the River Serein and take first left to Pontigny to visit its famous 12th- to 13th-century monastery. This was the largest Cistercian church of its time in France, and one of the first Gothic

La Chablisienne (Chablis)
Large cooperative with about 280 members. The wines are of reliable quality and are usually good value.

Domaine du Chardonnay (Chablis)
Established in 1987 by three young growers. Reliable, fruity Petit Chablis, Chablis and Chablis Premiers Crus.

René et Vincent Dauvissat (Chablis)
Traditional estate producing delicious wines, among the best of the district. The range includes two Grands Crus and three Premiers Crus.

Jean-Paul Droin (Chablis)
This company produces more than ten types of Chablis, almost all of good to excellent quality. The four Grands Crus are particularly worth trying.

Domaine de l'Eglantière (Maligny)
The largest privately owned wine estate in Chablis (110ha), created by the dynamic Jean Durup. In spite of the considerable quantity made, the wines – mainly Chablis and Premiers Crus – are outstanding. These wines are not aged in oak.

Domaine Corinne et Jean-Pierre Grossot (Chablis)
Magnificent wines, from Chablis *tout court* including Fourchaume, Les Fourneaux and Mont de Milieu.

Domaine Laroche (Chablis)
This estate owns a fine tasting centre in Chablis itself, and the old l'Obédiencerie building. The wines are made in a modern complex south of Chablis. Expensive but of consistently high quality and simply labelled 'Laroche'.

Domaine Long Depaquit (Chablis)
Previously famous domaine belonging to the house of Albert Bichot. Looks as if it is gradually regaining its former glory. The special wine is La Moutonne, a *clos* in the Grand Cru Vaudésir.

Domaine de la Maladière (Chablis)
Large, prestigious domaine, taken over by the Henriot group (Champagne) in 1998. 65 ha, of which 15.5ha are in the Grands Crus, 19.5ha are in the Premiers Crus and 29ha are Chablis. The best wines are fermented and matured in oak vats.

Domaine des Malandes (Chablis)
Memorable, high-quality wines, fermented and aged in tank, not oak. Among the best are the Premiers Crus Côte de Léchet, Fourchaume, Montmains, Vau-de-Vey and the Grands Crus Les Clos and Vaudésir.

Domaine des Maronniers (Préhy)
The conscientious Bernard Légland produces first-class wines. Unoaked.

Louis Michel & Fils (Chablis)
Old family estate offering fresh, complex, unwooded wines which age wonderfully well. You can taste them in the 17th-century cellar.

J Moreau & Fils (Chablis)
Famous wine-selling firm which now

Left *Intricate ironwork on a wine producer's gateway in Chablis. For centuries, wine production has been a great source of wealth for the region, reflected in details such as this.*

Right *Chablis was badly bombed during the war, but several historical buildings remain by the River Serein in the centre of the town.*

belongs to the large Bourgogne wine merchants Boisset (Nuits-Saint-Georges)

Domaine Louis & Anne Moreau (Beines)
It is important to distinguish between the wine dealers J Moreau & Fils and this domaine. From 2002, harvest at this magnificent property will return to Christian and Jean-Jacques Moreau. It covers 20ha, of which more than 10ha are Grands Crus, including Le Clos des Hospices, and almost 8ha are Premiers Crus. For the moment, Louis Moreau (son of Jean-Jacques) and his wife Anne still have their domaine in Beines where they produce stylish wines. The Moreaus disapprove of oak-ageing for Chablis wines of any kind because they feel it does not suit the lively, mineral character of the wine.

Domaine Gilbert Picq et Ses Fils (Chichée)
Gilbert is now retired and the 13-ha domaine is now managed by Didier Picq and his brother and sister. Beautiful, stylish wines; good Chablis Vieilles Vignes.

Domaine Pinson (Chablis)
Traditional methods are followed here; thus the wines are matured in wooden casks. Wonderful, quite full Les Clos, and a similarly splendid Mont de Milieu.

François et Jean-Marie Ravenau (Chablis)
Now established as Domaine François Ravenau, the estate is managed by Jean-Marie and his brother Bernard. Superb wines that need ageing. This is probably the best domaine in the Chablis region, partly due to its low output.

A Regnard & Fils (Chablis)
Property of Patrick de Ladoucette; producing fine, if rather expensive, wines.

Domaine Sainte Claire (Préhy)
Owned by Jean-Marc Brocard. Wines include the Premiers Crus Montmains, Vaillons, Vau Lignau, and the Grand Cru Valmur and all deserve attention.

Simonnet-Febvre (Chablis)
Small, serious company which acts as a broker for several merchants in Beaune. It also handles red and rosé Irancy wines.

Gérard Tremblay (Poinchy)
Modern cellars; fresh, clear-tasting wines such as Valmur Grand Cru and Fourchaume Premier Cru.

Domaine de Vauroux (Chablis)
Wines of character and quality.

Domaine de Vaudon (Chablis)
The house of Joseph Drouhin in Beaune is one of the largest Chablis producers. Owns many vineyards in this region, including the Domaine de Vaudon, which has three Grands Crus and five Premiers Crus.

Domaine Vocoret (Chablis)
Large winegrowing estate covering about 50ha, run by Patrice Vocoret. Vast range of good wines, including Chablis, Chablis Premier Cru and Chablis Grand Cru.

buildings in Burgundy. Thanks to these monks, winegrowing around Chablis flourished as long ago as the Middle Ages.

Drive back to Chablis on the D131 towards Villy. Try to stop briefly in La Chapelle-Vaupelteigne to look at the old chapel and splendid view. In the next village, Poinchy, turn right onto the D965 to Milly. Here, there is a medieval chapel with a fine sculpture of a kneeling monk. The local château dates from the same period. The village of Milly is situated at foot of the Premier Cru vineyard, Côte de Léchet and from the top of the vineyard there is a magnificent view over Chablis. Return via Poinchy, and turn right to get onto the D131, which takes you back into Chablis.

To the south of Chablis, the churches of Courgis and Préhy are worth a detour. Courgis sits on a hill and has interesting castle ruins; Préhy has a fine view across the vineyards; the village church is surrounded by vines.

AROUND CHABLIS

HOTELS
Le Relais Saint-Vincent
Ligny-le-Châtel
Tel: 03 86 47 53 38
Quietly located, small hotel with pretty rooms (15) from FF250. Large breakfast. Also has a restaurant which serves good to very good regional dishes. The cheapest menu costs less than FF100.
Domaine de Montpierreux
Venoy
Tel: 03 86 40 20 91
Near the Auxerre-Sud exit on the *autoroute* is a romantic little château from 1860. Offers beautiful, tastefully furnished rooms as *chambres d'hôtes*.

RESTAURANTS

Les Vendanges
Coulanges-la-Vineuse
Tel: 03 86 42 21 91
Simple village café and restaurant. For less than FF100 the most ravenous hunger can be satisfied. A few rooms.
Auberge du Bief
Ligny-le-Châtel
Tel: 03 86 47 43 42
Situated on a bend near the church by the river's edge. Serves both regional cuisine and more sophisticated dishes. Menus from about FF175.
Auberge La Beursaudière
Nitry
Tel: 03 86 33 69 69
South of Chablis. An excellent restaurant in pleasant rural surroundings. The regional specialities are particularly good, and menus start from FF100. Excellent wine cellar. Large terrace.
Le Saint-Bris
Saint-Bris-le-Vineux
Tel: 03 86 53 84 56
Two pretty dining-rooms where you can eat very well for surprisingly little money. Even the Sunday *à la carte* menu costs less than FF90. This pleasant restaurant is situated right next to the church.
Auberge du Château
Val-de-Mercy
Tel: 03 86 41 60 00
Small and attractive with a few rooms. Just south of Coulanges-la-Vineuse.
Le Moulin de la Coudre
Venoy
Tel: 03 86 40 23 79
Leave the *autoroute* at Auxerre-Sud and follow the road towards Chablis; you will immediately see the signboards pointing the way to this pretty restaurant run by Jean-Pierre Vaury. Pleasantly situated along the bank of a little stream. The Moulin uses mainly regional produce. Excellent wine list. Menus from FF105 to FF297.
Auberge des Tilleuls
Vincelottes
Tel: 03 86.42.22.13
Vincelottes is situated between Chablis and

AROUND CHABLIS – AUXERRE AND IRANCY

Just outside the district of Chablis in the Auxerrois region, there are four principal communes: Saint-Bris-le-Vineux, Chitry, Irancy and Coulanges-la-Vineuse, the first two producing mainly white wines (Crémant de Bourgogne and Bourgogne Aligoté) and the latter two mainly reds.

The most important wine municipality is Saint-Bris-le-Vineux where the wine speciality is, rather surprisingly, Sauvignon de Saint-Bris, a lively, aromatic wine made from the white grape variety Sauvignon Blanc. This grape has been growing here since the mid-19th century, when it was used as part of a blend. Now it is vinified separately and has VDQS status. Sauvignon de Saint-Bris is often bought by wine-lovers in search of an alternative to the illustrious, more expensive Sauvignon wines from Sancerre and Pouilly Fumé; the wines are a little lighter in style.

Right *Tending vines near Chablis.*
At times, viticulture appears barely
different from other kinds of farming.

Vézelay, near Irancy, on the banks of the
Yonne. A pretty *auberge* with a beautiful
terrace. The *jambon à la chablisienne* is
recommended. Menus from FF138.
Les Vendanges
Tel: 03 86 42 21 91
Simple village café and restaurant. For
less than FF100 you can satisfy even the
biggest hunger. It also has a few rooms.
At Coulanges-la-Vineuse.

RECOMMENDED PRODUCERS

Caves de Bailly (Bailly)
Excellent sparkling wines are produced
here in large underground cellars along
the Yonne. These Crémants de Bourgogne
are at the top of their class.
Domaine Bersan & Fils
Large domaine with pure, fragrant wines,
among which are the local Sauvignon,
Bourgogne Aligoté and white Bourgogne.
Futuristic cellar, outside the village.
Robert et Philippe Defrance
Fresh, fruity white wines.
Domaine Fort
Superior Sauvignon Blanc; attractive Irancy.

Below *The style of these tall,*
gabled buildings in Auxerre's Place
Saint-Nicholas reflect the northern
location of the town itself.

From the village of Chablis, drive south on the D91 and
turn right after only 1km onto the D62 to Courgis.
Continue on through Chitry, which has a fortified church,
to Saint-Bris-le-Vineux, a small village nestling on the side
of a low hill. There are winegrowers' signs everywhere and
many of them have fascinating ancient cellars dating from
as far back as the 10th century. The local church, built in
the 13th century, is particularly imposing.

Take time to visit the Caves de Bailly in the hamlet of
Bailly, just outside Saint-Bris. This is an enormous cellar
hewn out of a limestone quarry where thousands of bottles
of the company's Crémant de Bourgogne are stored. It was
stone from this quarry that was used to build the Panthéon
in Paris, as well as many other notable buildings.

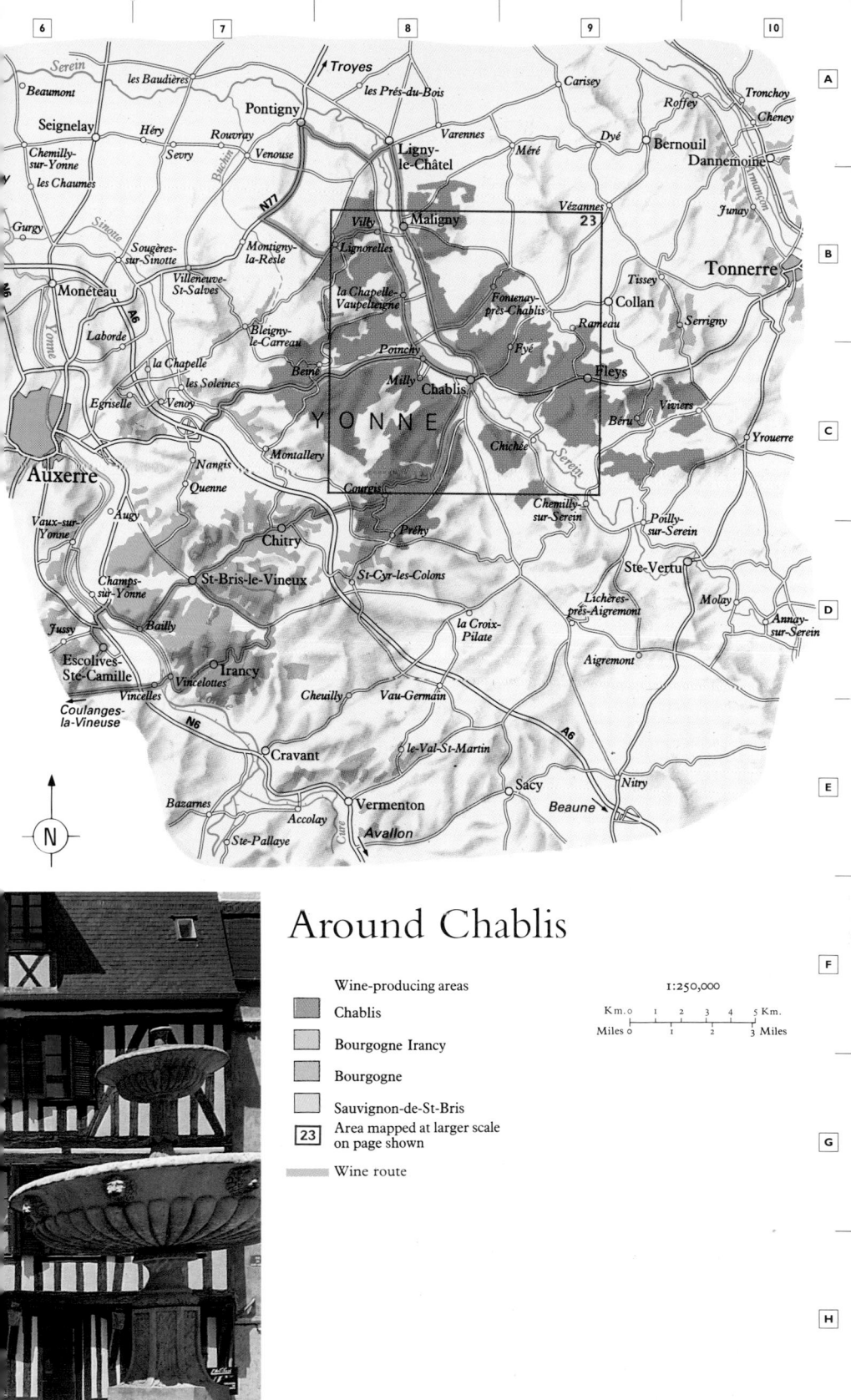

Around Chablis

Wine-producing areas

- Chablis
- Bourgogne Irancy
- Bourgogne
- Sauvignon-de-St-Bris
- 23 Area mapped at larger scale on page shown
- Wine route

1:250,000

Km. 0   1   2   3   4   5 Km.
Miles 0   1   2   3 Miles

MEPRIMVM MOTAT CŒLVM ∴EA REGVL
SITVA SIT CŒLVM REGVLA TV

Above and right *Views of the town of Auxerre.*
Far right *Irancy, one of France's most beautiful wine producing regions.*

Ghislaine et Jean-Hugues Goisot
Elegant Sauvignon and Bourgognes from Saint-Bris. You can also taste the wine in the 11th- and 12th-century cellars.
Domaine des Remparts
One of the most famous local wine-growing estates, owned by André, Patrick and Jean-Marc Sorin. First-class Bourgogne Aligoté; Sauvignon de Saint-Bris.
Luc Sorin
High-quality Bourgogne Aligoté, Sauvignon de Saint-Bris and Bourgogne Irancy.

From Saint-Bris, take the D956 south, turning right at the signpost for Irancy after about 1km. The local wine, Bourgogne Irancy, is made from Pinot Noir but also contains a small amount of the little-known red grape César which, it is thought, may have originated here. The César contributes colour, tannin and backbone to the lighter Pinot-based wines, distinguishing Bourgogne Irancy from the mass of rather nondescript Bourgognes Rouges made all over the region. Irancy sits at the very centre of a large amphitheatre of vineyards and is one of Burgundy's most beautifully located villages.

Continue straight on to Vincelottes, crossing the River Yonne there and driving straight on along the D85 to Coulanges-la-Vineuse. This village, situated on a hill and surrounding an eye-catching 18th-century church with a tall, pointed tower, also produces light red wines made entirely from Pinot Noir. The village has a small Musée de la Vigne; ask for admittance or make appointments either at the town hall or at the bar-restaurant Les Vendanges.

IRANCY

RECOMMENDED PRODUCERS

Léon Bienvenue
Leading grower who gives his red Bourgogne Irancy at least a year's ageing in cask.

Bernard Cantin
The mayor of Irancy and also producer of elegant, fruity wines.

René Charriat
Producer of a fairly light-coloured Irancy with a good level of alcohol.

Robert Colinot & Fils
This producer's red Irancy usually profits from a little bottle-age.

Roger Delalogue
Small grower with vaulted cellars where the red wines are kept in cask. Agreeable red and rosé Irancy for those who like light wines.

Jean Podor
Supple red Irancy. It has some depth in warm, sunny years.

COULANGES-LA-VINEUSE

RECOMMENDED PRODUCERS

Raymond Dupuis
One of the district's best growers. The red wine has fruit and charm and is reasonably rounded.

André Martin & Fils
If the sun cooperates, the red wine from this estate has the backbone to age for some years.

WINE FESTIVAL

On the weekend before November 11, Saint-Bris-le-Vineux usually celebrates the Fête du Sauvignon.

The Côte d'Or

The Côte d'Or is the heart of Burgundy. It lies along the irregular hillside which starts just south of Dijon and stretches for 50kms in a southwesterly direction, ending at Santenay. Almost the entire wine area is situated within the *département* of the same name; only a few communes in the extreme south, under the appellation of Maranges, belong to a different *département*, Saône-et-Loire.

The wine villages and their vineyards lie along the *route nationale* 74 (RN 74), which runs straight down through the Côte d'Or connecting Dijon with Chagny. It is a busy road that is sometimes difficult to avoid, but if you have the time, do try to take the smaller roads. In the north, for example, between Marsannay and Nuits-Saint-Georges, you can follow a peaceful parallel route to the west of the *route nationale*, which runs

through some of the most famous wine villages. A similar road runs further south between the villages of Pommard and Santenay.

The best vineyards are situated on the well-exposed, east-facing slopes, sheltered from westerly rain-bearing winds by the wooded escarpment that runs above them. The soil here is so diverse that often even neighbouring vineyards will have quite different soil characteristics. Added to this, the land is divided into extremely small plots, each owned by different growers. The result is that burgundy is produced by lots of growers, each making small amounts of a wide range of different wines. The quantities are often so small that it makes little sense for the growers to try to sell the wines themselves, which is why the shippers – the *négociants-éleveurs* – play such an important role. They buy these small parcels of wine, blend them and sell them under their own labels. Some growers do bottle and sell their own wines, and many have received international acclaim – and consequently charging high prices.

To make matters even more complicated, the quality of wine made by the growers varies quite considerably, even in the same year. It is therefore important to know the reputation of the winemaker rather than banking simply on the classification of the vineyard. A 'village' wine bearing just the name of its commune, but from a quality-conscious

Left *The Hôtel-Dieu in Beaune was built in 1443 by Nicolas Rolin.*

Above *Vineyards in Chambolle-Musigny, a commune producing a light, fragrant style of wine.*

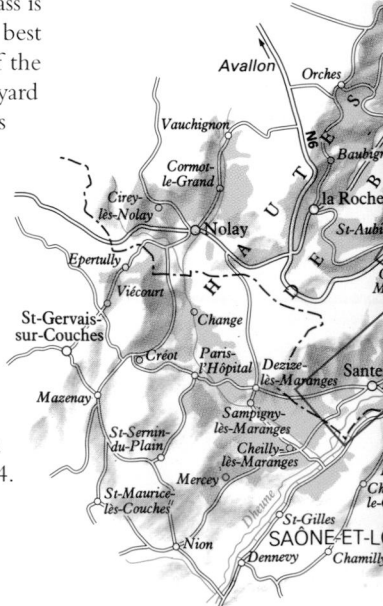

grower, may be better than a Premier Cru from a lax estate. The wines of the Côte d'Or are divided into four classes. The top category is **Grand Cru**, which applies to 32 individual vineyards, including Chambertin, Musigny, Clos de Vougeot and Montrachet. Wines made from these vineyards are sold under the vineyard name, with no mention of the commune in which they are situated. The next class is **Premier Cru**, which includes over 300 of the best vineyards. These wines are marketed under the name of the commune, followed by the name of the relevant vineyard (same type size) or simply 'Premier Cru' if the wine is made from grapes from more than one vineyard.

The third class is **village** or **commune**, such as Gevrey-Chambertin, Volnay or Meursault. These wines can be sold with their vineyard names appearing in smaller type beside the name of the commune. This category includes the Côte de Nuits-Villages and Côte de Beaune-Villages appellations which cover a number of wines from several bordering villages in the Côte de Nuits and the Côte de Beaune. The fourth category includes **regional** wines – Bourgogne, Bourgogne Aligoté, etc. These wines often come from the flatter land to the east of the RN74.

Above *A traditional panier used by grape-pickers here at the Romanée-Conti estate, with an essential pair of secateurs to remove the bunches from the vine.*

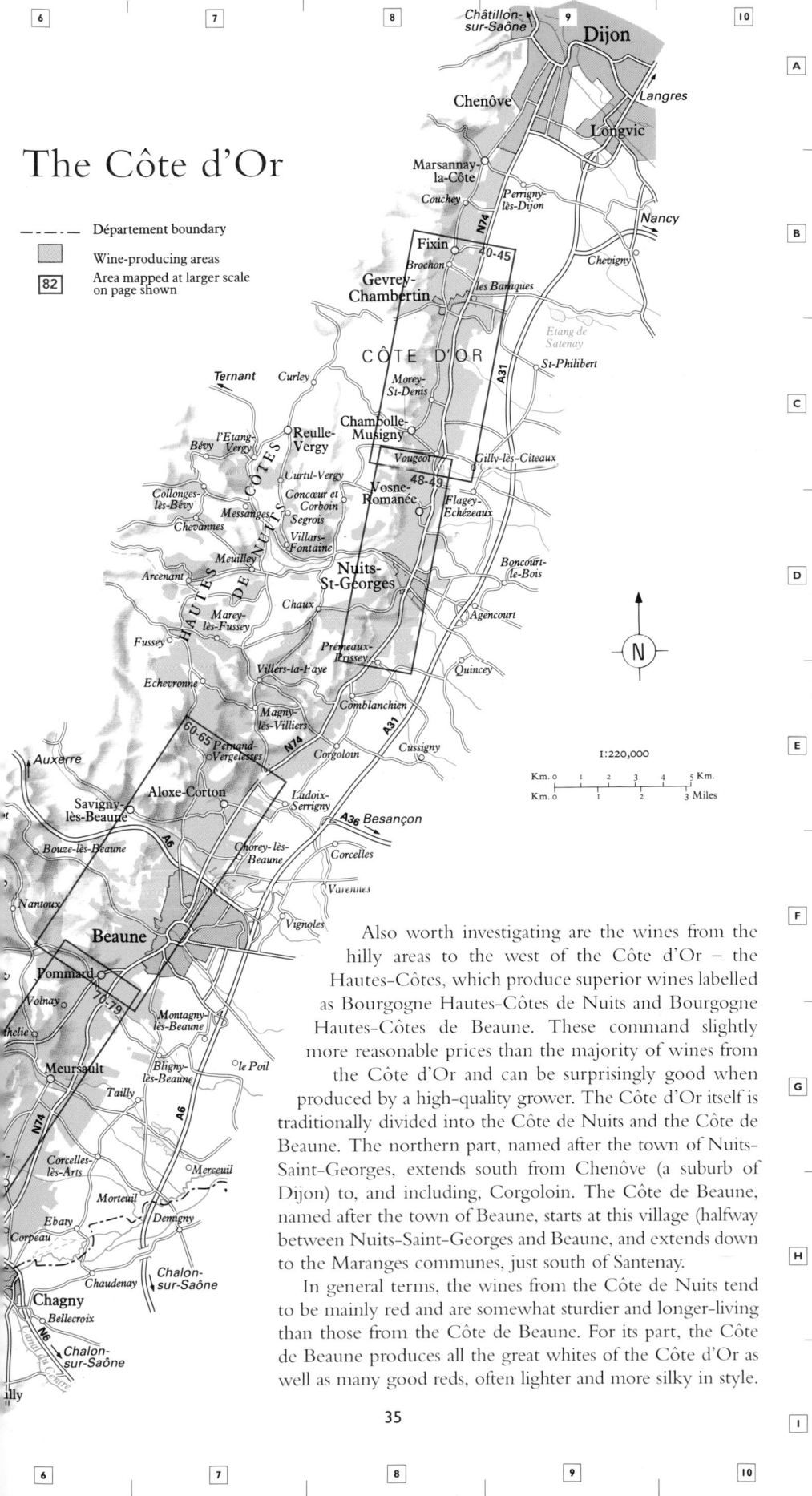

The Côte d'Or

- - - - - Département boundary

Wine-producing areas

82 Area mapped at larger scale on page shown

Châtillon-sur-Saône
Dijon
Chenôve
Langres
Longvic
Marsannay-la-Côte
Couchey
Perrigny-lès-Dijon
Nancy
Fixin
40-45
Brochon
les Baraques
Gevrey-Chambertin
Etang de Satenay
CÔTE D'OR
St-Philibert
Ternant
Curley
Morey-St-Denis
l'Etang-Vergy
Reulle-Vergy
Chambolle-Musigny
Bévy
Vougeot
Gilly-lès-Cîteaux
Curtil-Vergy
48-49
Collonges-lès-Bévy
Concœur et Corboin
Vosne-Romanée
Flagey-Échézeaux
Messanges
Segrois
Chevannes
Villars-Fontaine
Meuilley
Boncourt-le-Bois
Arcenant
Nuits-St-Georges
Chaux
Agencourt
Marey-lès-Fussey
Fussey
Prémeaux-Prissey
Quincey
Echevronne
Villers-la-Faye
Magny-lès-Villiers
Comblanchien
Auxerre
Pernand-Vergelesses
60-65
Corgoloin
Cussigny
Savigny-lès-Beaune
Aloxe-Corton
Ladoix-Serrigny
Besançon
Bouze-lès-Beaune
Chorey-lès-Beaune
Corcelles
Nantoux
Varennes
Vignoles
Beaune
Pommard
70-79
Volnay
Montagny-lès-Beaune
Meursault
Bligny-lès-Beaune
le Poil
Tailly
Corcelles-lès-Arts
Merceuil
Morteuil
Ebaty
Demigny
Corpeau
Chalon-sur-Saône
Chaudenay
Chagny
Bellecroix
Chalon-sur-Saône
HAUTES CÔTES DE NUITS

1:220,000

Km. 0 1 2 3 4 5 Km.
Km. 0 1 2 3 Miles

N

Also worth investigating are the wines from the hilly areas to the west of the Côte d'Or – the Hautes-Côtes, which produce superior wines labelled as Bourgogne Hautes-Côtes de Nuits and Bourgogne Hautes-Côtes de Beaune. These command slightly more reasonable prices than the majority of wines from the Côte d'Or and can be surprisingly good when produced by a high-quality grower. The Côte d'Or itself is traditionally divided into the Côte de Nuits and the Côte de Beaune. The northern part, named after the town of Nuits-Saint-Georges, extends south from Chenôve (a suburb of Dijon) to, and including, Corgoloin. The Côte de Beaune, named after the town of Beaune, starts at this village (halfway between Nuits-Saint-Georges and Beaune, and extends down to the Maranges communes, just south of Santenay.

In general terms, the wines from the Côte de Nuits tend to be mainly red and are somewhat sturdier and longer-living than those from the Côte de Beaune. For its part, the Côte de Beaune produces all the great whites of the Côte d'Or as well as many good reds, often lighter and more silky in style.

DIJON

HOTELS

Wilson
Place Wilson
Tel: 03 80 66 82 50
This hotel, built in the 17th century as a coaching inn, has comfortable rooms from around FF400. See restaurant Thibert.

Chapeau Rouge
5 Rue Michelet
Tel: 03 80 30 28 10
Luxurious hotel with highly rated restaurant (one Michelin star). 30 rooms from around FF650.

Parc de la Colombière
49 Cours Parc
Tel: 03 80 65 18 41
Rooms starting at around FF300. Pleasant outdoor seating area.

Dijon

The most direct route from Chablis to Dijon is to return to the A6 motorway from Chablis and, heading south for approximately 100kms, leave the motorway at Pouilly-en-Auxois and take the A38 east to Dijon. For those with more time to amble across the countryside, there is a more scenic route: from Chablis, take the D965 to Tonnerre and then turn south onto the D905. This road meanders along the River Armançon to Montbard, then along the River Brenne before joining the A38 just outside Dijon. Turn left onto the A38, heading east into the town centre. From Tonnerre to the A38 is about 130kms.

Despite having somewhat unattractive suburbs, the centre of Dijon is still very pretty. After a large fire in the 12th century, it was rebuilt by the Burgundian Duke Hugo II,

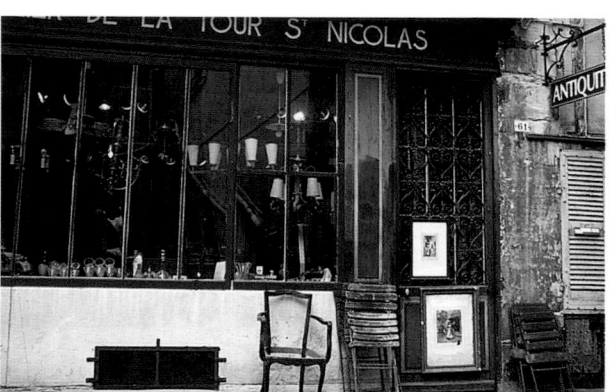

Above *Dijon's rich heritage makes it a great stopping-off point en route to the vineyards further south, for antiques shopping or simply admiring the architecture.*

Above left *Rue de la Liberté, and left, Rue Verrière. Timbered buildings in the city centre are a reminder of Dijon's prosperous past.*

and remains of this period can still be found. Dijon's greatest days of prosperity, however, were between 1364 and 1477, when four successive dukes of Valois – one of whom was Philip the Bold – turned the city, politically and culturally, into one of the most important centres of Europe.

There was a second affluent period between the 16th and 18th centuries. The princes of Condé were the governers and prosperous citizens enriched Dijon with marvellous buildings.

Religion has always been important in this city, with at least six churches in the city centre. The cathedral of Saint-Bénigne is the oldest. Its crypt dates from the 11th century and the rest of the architecture is mainly 13th century. Dijon has eight museums, one of which – the archeological museum – is situated in the former monastery buildings by the cathedral.

Also notable is the Gothic Notre-Dame, which has a wonderful façade. Insid, among other artefacts, is a 12th-century wooden Black Virgin statue. The church of Saint-Michel, on the same square, is also worth a visit.

The most beautiful parts of the city are found in the walks between the churches. The pedestrianised Rue de la Liberté is the most important shopping street, with half-timbered houses and cafés where you can sit and simply watch the world go by. The role of wine in the region is reflected in the Place François Rude, whose fountain is decorated with a figure treading grapes. Leading off this is the Rue des Forges, full of beautiful houses, all reflecting the prosperity of the town. Further riches can be found at the Place de la Libération, where the impressive Palace of the Dukes of Burgundy and the States General of Burgundy is situated. The building now houses the town hall and the Museum for Fine Arts, regarded by many as the best art gallery in France outside Paris.

Also near here is the Musée François Rude, where you can admire works by the sculptor Rude, who was born in Dijon. This museum is situated in part of the former abbey of Saint-Etienne (not far from the previously mentioned church of Saint-Michel).

If you really fall under the spell of the venerable riches of Dijon, then you can also dine in an historic ambiance, because at 18 Rue Sainte-Anne is the restaurant La Toison d'Or, which has a small museum. The collection includes ancient wine utensils as well as scenes from French history recreated with models. What's more, the food is delicious (menus start at about FF140; tel: 03 80 30 73 52).

Below *Pain d'épices (spiced bread), often made with honey and highly popular throughout France.*

RESTAURANTS

Thibert
10 Place Wilson
Tel: 03 80 67 74 64
Highly-rated restaurant, part of the Hôtel Wilson. High-standard cuisine and comprehensive wine list. Menus from FF140 to FF450. Closed August 1 to 23.

Jean-Pierre Billoux
Le Pré aux Clercs
13, place de la Libération
Tel: 03 80 38 05 05
One of the best chefs in Dijon has been forced to move. But Jean-Pierre Billoux has maintained his identity and class in his new establishment, in the former Place Royale. Excellently prepared dishes and an extensive wine list with a very personal selection. Menus from FF180 to FF500.

Ma Bourgogne
1, boulevard Paul Doumer
Tel: 03 80 65 48 06
Everything here is simple, fresh and well prepared. The prices too are very reasonable. This restaurant run by its chef Bernard Minot is popular among the local inhabitants of Dijon. A good but slightly out-of-the-way eating place. Menus from FF120 to FF180. Closed on Saturdays.

La Dame d'Aquitaine
23 Place Bossuet
Tel: 03 80 30 36 23
Quaintly located restaurant in a 13th-century crypt. Menus start at around FF130. Restaurant is closed on Sundays and Monday lunchtimes.

The Côte de Nuits

The Côte de Nuits stretches from Marsannay down to Corgoloin. This part of the Côte d'Or is red wine country; white is a rarity here. At the northern end of the Côte de Nuits, the firmest, longest-lived and most velvety red burgundies are made. Time is rewarded by complex elegant wines, with an incredible depth of flavour.

Leaving Dijon from the south of the city, travel south on the N74 towards Chenôve. Legend has it that, in 1648, the wines of Chenôve fetched higher prices than those of Gevrey, perhaps partly because of the famous Clos du Roi vineyard which was owned by the Duke of Burgundy.

From Chenôve, instead of returning to the busy N74, take the D122 Route des Grands Crus, which runs in a southerly direction just west of the N74 and parallel to it. This winds a much more peaceful and scenic route through the villages between Chenôve and Nuits-Saint-Georges.

MARSANNAY-LA-COTE

Like Chenôve, Marsannay-la-Côte has become a commuter town because of its proximity to Dijon. It has lost many of its vineyards, although vines still cover a fifth of the land.

The tiny town centre is worth a stop for refreshments and some fresher air after Dijon's busy city centre. There are two bars in the church square where you can quench your thirst: Café de la Place, owned by Christian Bouvier, and Café des Sports, also known locally as 'Chez Marianne'.

Here, and in the local restaurants, you can savour the most famous rosé of Burgundy: Rosé de Marsannay. The wine, first made by Joseph Clair in 1919, is produced from vinifying Pinot Noir grapes as if they were white. The last pressings yield a pink-tinged juice which gives the wine its pink-grey colour. However, the village was granted its own

Left Clos de Vougeot. The monks of Cîteaux wisely divided it into three cuvées according to the quality of the soil. The cuvées: des Papes (upper part), des Rois (the middle) and des Moines (bottom).

appellation for red and white wines in 1987, a move which may result in less rosé being made in the future. Even now, the accent is really on red wine, which accounts for three times the volume of rosé.

Above The Grand Cru Latricières Chambertin – an extremely elegant and lacy wine, as its name suggests.

FIXIN

The charming village of Fixin is situated just 3kms south of Marsannay on the D122 Route des Grands Crus. Before Marsannay acquired its own appellation, Fixin was the first appellation contrôlée south of Dijon. This is the beginning of the *vrai* Côte de Nuits – mainly concentrated red wines benefiting from some years of bottle-age.

Formerly called Fiscentix, the dukes of Burgundy had a summer residence here with its own vineyard. The 12th-century hunting lodge, later given to the monks of Cîteaux, still exists and is now a wine estate, the Clos de la Perrière, and Fixin's most famous Premier Cru vineyard.

Right next to the Clos de la Perrière is Fixin's other Premier Cru vineyard, the Clos du Chapître. Also notable is the Clos Napoléon, which borders the Parc Noisot. Situated against a wooded hill above Fixin, these gardens were created in 1837 by Claude Noisot, an old commandant of the imperial guard, in hommage to Napoleon. A replica of the house in which the exiled emperor lived on Saint-Helena was built and this now houses Napoleonic memorabilia.

Fixin and the neighbouring hamlet of Fixey have beautiful churches with the traditional multicoloured spires. There is also a small museum of wine artefacts in the 17th-century cellar of Domaine du Clos Saint-Louis.

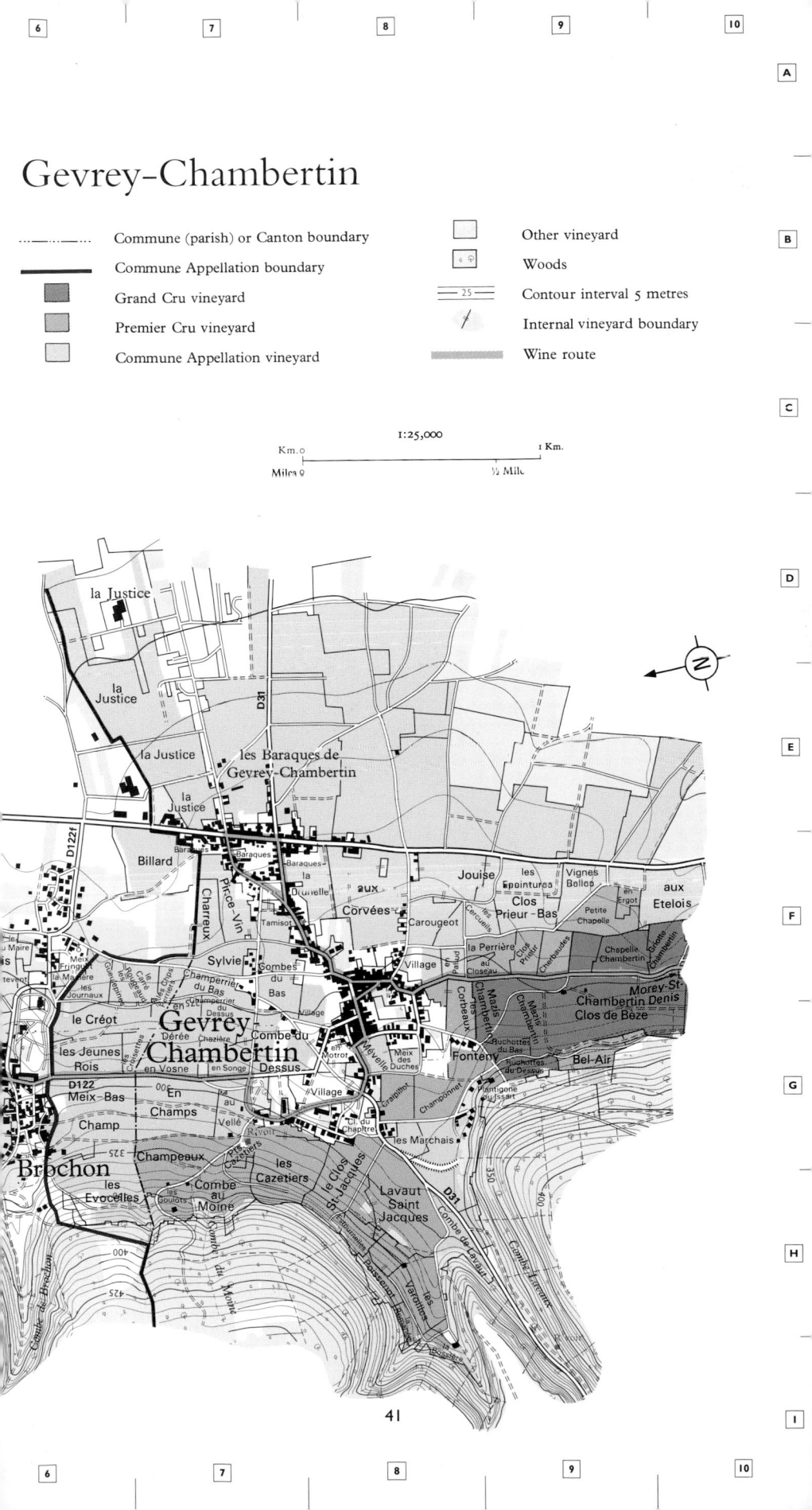

Gevrey-Chambertin

·········· Commune (parish) or Canton boundary	Other vineyard
—— Commune Appellation boundary	Woods
Grand Cru vineyard	Contour interval 5 metres
Premier Cru vineyard	Internal vineyard boundary
Commune Appellation vineyard	Wine route

1:25,000

Km.0   1 Km.

Miles 0   ½ Mile

la Justice

la Justice

la Justice

les Baraques de Gevrey-Chambertin

la Justice

Billard

Baraques

Baraques la Drumelle

Jouise

les Epointures

Vignes Ballon

aux Etelois

Pince-Vin

aux Corvées

Clos Prieur-Bas

en Ergot

Charreux

Tamisot

Carougeot

Petite Chapelle

Chapelle Chambertin

Sylvie

Combes du Bas

la Perrière au Closeau

Clos Prior

Chezbaudes

Morey-St Chambertin Denis Clos de Bèze

Champerrier du Bas

Village

Mazis Chambertin

Bel-Air

le Créot

Dérée Chazière

Combe du Dessus

en Motrot

Meix des Duches

Fonteny

Ruchottes du Bas

Ruchottes du Dessus

les Jeunes Rois

en Vosne en Songe

Dessus

Village

Craipillot

Champonnet

Antigone du Issart

Gevrey Chambertin

D122 Meix-Bas

En au Velle

Champs

au Chapitre

les Marchais

Champ

Champeaux

les Cazetiers

les Cazetiers

le Clos St-Jacques

Lavaut Saint Jacques

Brochon

les Evocelles

Combe au Moine

41

MARSANNAY

HOTELS

Au Chardonnay
Tel: 03 80 51 37 23
Five spacious, comfortable rooms full
of atmosphere in a former *cuverie*,
offered here as *chambres d'hôtes*.
Friendly hosts speaking fluent English.
Heated swimming pool. Bicycles can
be rented. Prices about FF500.

RESTAURANTS

Les Gourmets
Tel: 03 80 52 16 32
Celebrated, busy restaurant. Varied wine
list. Menus start at about FF150.
La Renardière
Tel: 03 80 52 16 41
Regional dishes. Menus under FF100.

RECOMMENDED PRODUCERS

Domaine Charlopin-Parizot
Good, notable wines.
Bruno Clair
Four delicious Rosés de Marsannay
produced. Traditional reds are admirable.
Domaine Huguenot Père & Fils
Decent, slightly oaked, intense
burgundies. Also a pleasant rosé.

FIXIN

RESTAURANT

Chez Jeanette
Tel: 03 80 52 45 49
Regional dishes. Three set menus under
FF150. Also has rooms.

RECOMMENDED PRODUCERS

Vincent et Denis Berthaut
Traditional wines needing age. The best
are the Fixin Premier Crus.
Domaine Pierre Gelin
Solid reds, more rustic than sophisticated.
Manoir de la Perrière
The building on this estate was built by the
monks and boasts some great cellars and
an ancient wine press.

GEVREY-CHAMBERTIN

HOTELS

Les Grands Crus
Tel: 03 80 34 34 15
Peaceful location, rooms from FF380.
Arts et Terroirs
Tel: 03 80 34 30 76
16 rooms (from FF280), a permanent
exhibition of regional artists, and an
exquisite garden. Bicycles are also available.
Aux Vendanges de Bourgogne
Tel: 03 80 34 30 24
Completely refurbished rooms (from
FF229). Food is good and well prepared.
Menus from FF75. Wine list is a dream.

Above and right *Two images of
Gevrey-Chambertin: a traditional
cellar and a chapel amongst vines.*

GEVREY-CHAMBERTIN

The village of Brochon lies just 0.5kms south of Fixin, with its neighbouring village of Gevrey-Chambertin a further 1.5kms south along the D122 Route des Grands Crus (13kms south of Dijon).

It is thought that vines first started growing along the hillside between these two villages during Roman times. Certainly the Roman presence in this area has been confirmed by the excavation of sculptures from the period.

The vineyards on the slopes to the right of the road south of Brochon are Premiers Crus, while a series of Grand Cru vineyards extend to the right and left of the D122, directly south of Gevrey-Chambertin.

The locals will tell you that the Clos de Bèze was the first field in the region to be planted with grapevines in the 7th

century by the monks of the Abbey of Bèze. A farmer, called Bertin, later planted a plot of land next to it, *le champ de Bertin,* and the wines from his vineyard enjoyed just as good a reputation as those of the Clos de Bèze – hence the vineyard came to be called Chambertin-Clos de Bèze. The village of Gevrey added the illustrious word 'Chambertin' to its name by royal decree in 1847. No other village in Burgundy now has as many Grands Crus.

The other Grands Crus in the village are: Chapelle-Chambertin, Charmes-Chambertin (by far the largest), Griotte-Chambertin, Latricières-Chambertin, Mazis-Chambertin (also spelled Mazys and Mazi) and Ruchottes-Chambertin. In terms of quality, the three most interesting of these Grands Crus are Griotte, Latricières and Mazis.

In the village itself is the 10th-century castle, with its angular towers and vaulted wine cellars, restored by the monks of Cluny. The church of Saint-Aignan is also interesting to visit with its beautiful wood carvings and decorated tombstones.

MOREY-SAINT-DENIS

The next village along the D122 is Morey-Saint-Denis. It is about 3kms south of Gevrey-Chambertin and the road passes directly through the Grand Cru vineyards of Clos de Bèze, Chambertin and Latricières. The first vineyard to fall within the appellation boundary is the Grand Cru Clos de la Roche, to the right of the road. The village's other famous Grand Cru vineyard, Clos de Tart, lies on the south side of the village. This vineyard is exclusively owned by Mommessin and the cellars are worth a visit to see their excellently preserved 12th-century presses.

RESTAURANTS

Les Millésimes
Tel: 03 80 51 84 24
First-class cooking and amazing cellar with some 49,000 bottles. Menus from FF335.

La Rôtisserie du Chambertin
Tel: 03 80 34 33 20
Stylish restaurant, located in a cellar, reached through a small museum. Sophisticated regional cuisine and superb wine list. Menus from FF210. Plus bistrot serving excellent food for FF150 upwards.

Sangoy Côté Cour
Tel: 03 80 58 53 58
Interior may lack atmosphere, but the cuisine and wines are exciting; this is not surprising, given that it is linked to Les Millésimes. Menus of FF75, FF125 and FF175.

RECOMMENDED PRODUCERS

Domaine Bachelet
Great wines at all quality levels.

Philippe Batacchi/Domaine Clos Noir
Sound, fragrant red wines.

Lucien Boillot et Fils
Good wines: Nuits-Saint-Georges and Volnay.

Pierre Bourée Fils
Small company; solid wines made to last.

Alain Burguet
Charming, balanced well-made wines.

Camus Père & Fils
Great range of sites. Implicit belief in *terroir*.

Domaine Pierre Damoy
Owns largest single share of Clos de Bèze.

Domaine Drouhin-Laroze
Distinguished estate. Pure, fairly light-coloured wines. Drink relatively early.

Philippe Leclerc
Top wines: body and new oak, age well.

Domaine Maume
Dark, lingering, intense, flawless wines.

Domaine Denis Mortet
Balanced, firm wines, full of fruit.

Naigeon-Chauveau/Domaine des Varoilles
Good-value village wines. Also Domaine des Varoilles.

Joseph Roty
Perfectionist winemaking. Refined and expressive wines.

Domaine Armand Rousseau Père & Fils
Traditional classy wines with individuality.

MOREY-ST-DENIS

HOTEL

Castel de Très Girard
Tel: 03 80 34 33 09
Good-sized rooms with character from FF300. Menus from FF95 to FF220. Wide range of wines; great choice of half-bottles.

RECOMMENDED PRODUCERS

Domaine Pierre Amiot et Fils
Distinguished wines, firm, elegant, subtle and yet deeply flavoured.

Domaine Arlaud Père et Fils
Classic red wines, top-quality.

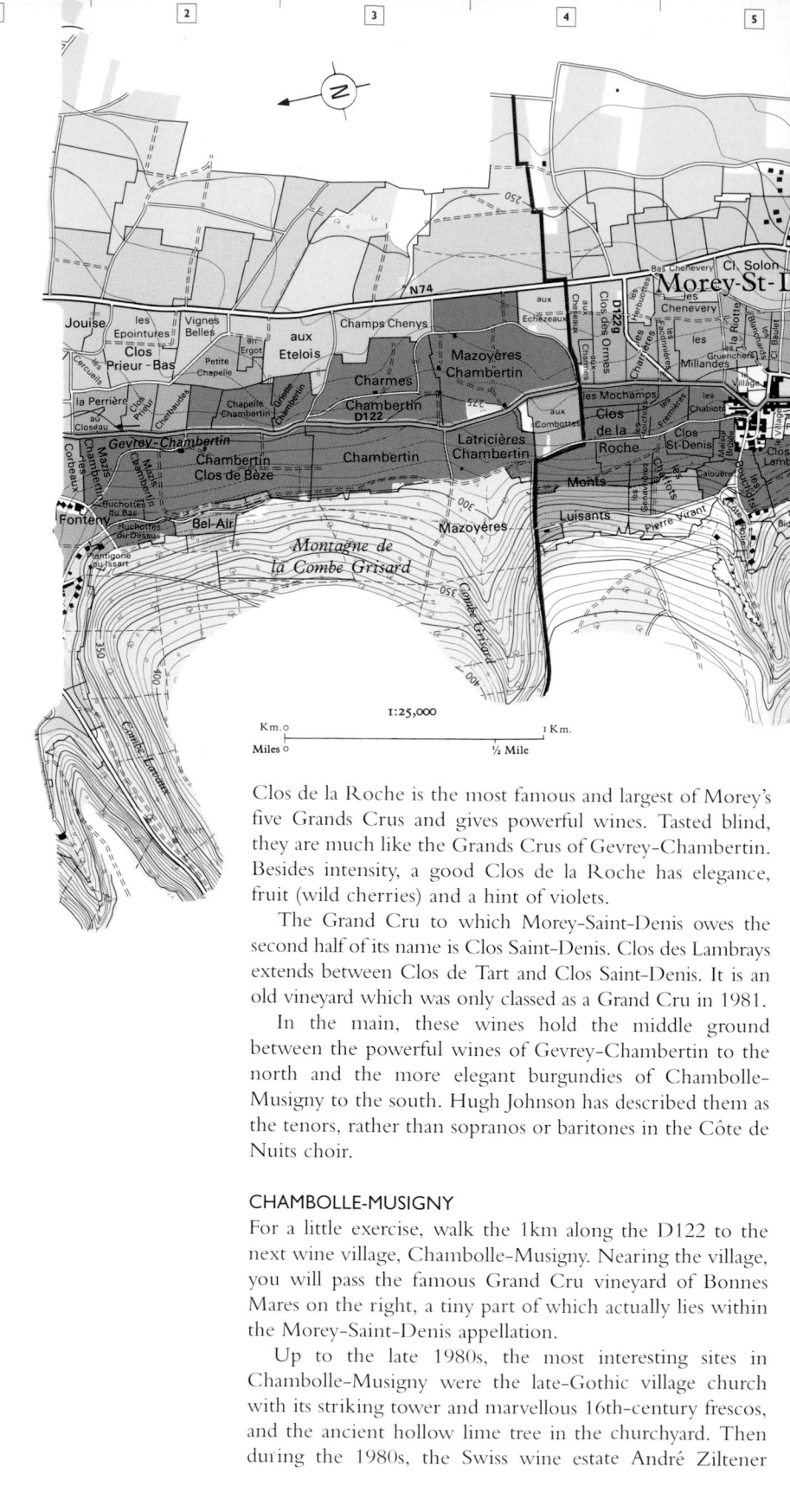

1:25,000

Km.0 ————————— 1 Km.

Miles 0 ————————— ½ Mile

Clos de la Roche is the most famous and largest of Morey's five Grands Crus and gives powerful wines. Tasted blind, they are much like the Grands Crus of Gevrey-Chambertin. Besides intensity, a good Clos de la Roche has elegance, fruit (wild cherries) and a hint of violets.

The Grand Cru to which Morey-Saint-Denis owes the second half of its name is Clos Saint-Denis. Clos des Lambrays extends between Clos de Tart and Clos Saint-Denis. It is an old vineyard which was only classed as a Grand Cru in 1981.

In the main, these wines hold the middle ground between the powerful wines of Gevrey-Chambertin to the north and the more elegant burgundies of Chambolle-Musigny to the south. Hugh Johnson has described them as the tenors, rather than sopranos or baritones in the Côte de Nuits choir.

CHAMBOLLE-MUSIGNY

For a little exercise, walk the 1km along the D122 to the next wine village, Chambolle-Musigny. Nearing the village, you will pass the famous Grand Cru vineyard of Bonnes Mares on the right, a tiny part of which actually lies within the Morey-Saint-Denis appellation.

Up to the late 1980s, the most interesting sites in Chambolle-Musigny were the late-Gothic village church with its striking tower and marvellous 16th-century frescos, and the ancient hollow lime tree in the churchyard. Then during the 1980s, the Swiss wine estate André Ziltener

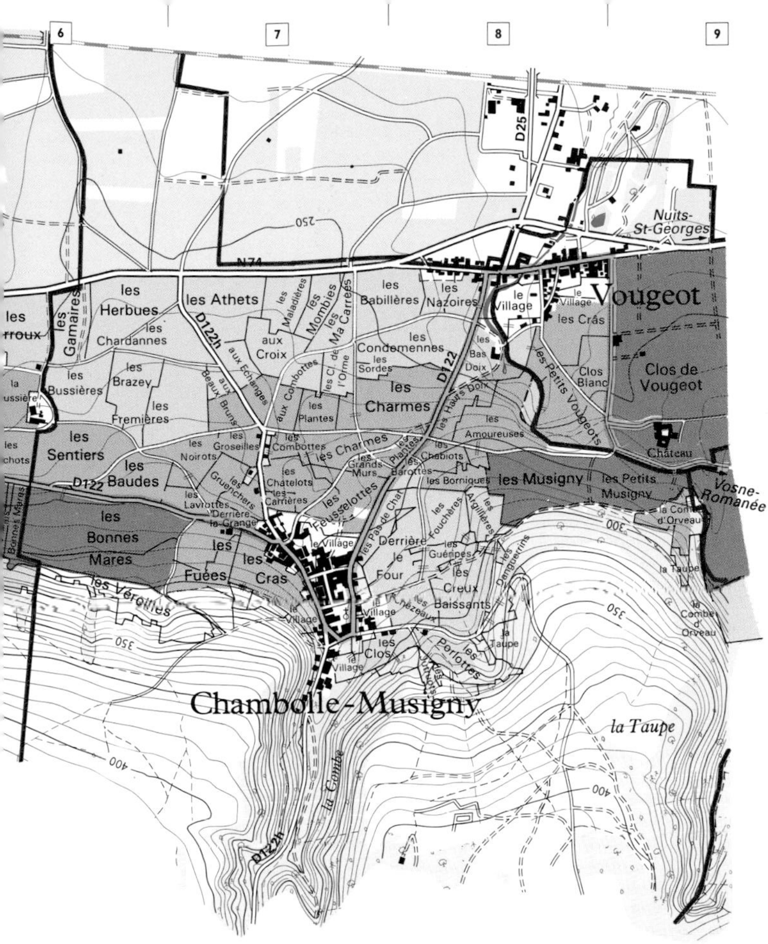

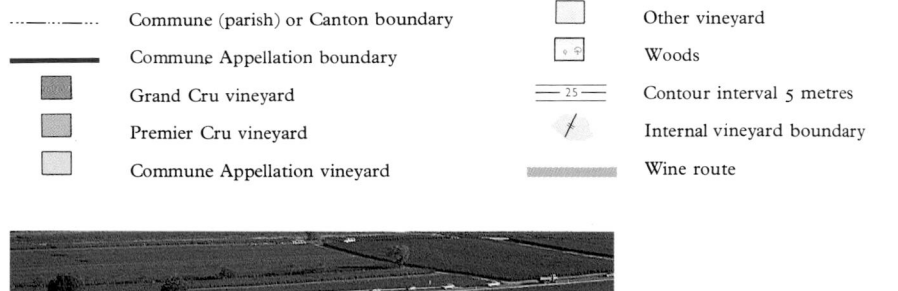

Morey-Saint-Denis

...—.—...	Commune (parish) or Canton boundary	☐	Other vineyard
▬▬	Commune Appellation boundary	☐	Woods
▨	Grand Cru vineyard	═25═	Contour interval 5 metres
▨	Premier Cru vineyard	╱	Internal vineyard boundary
☐	Commune Appellation vineyard	▬▬▬	Wine route

Left *Morey-Saint-Denis has clay and limestone soils and produces some of Burgundy's darkest, most long-lived red wines; also rare white.*

Above *Clos de Tart in Morey-Saint-Denis, a wine which has great depth of colour and flavour and considerable ageing potential.*

Domaine Dujac
Firm wines: graceful, elegant, with new oak.
Domaine des Lambrays
Great improvement since new ownership in 1979. The result is a noble wine with vanilla aromas and intense fruit. Grand Cru was granted in 1981.
Georges Lignier et Fils
Fruity perfumed wines with a touch of oak, vanilla and firm tannin.
Domaine Hubert Lignier
Fine wines at all levels.
Domaine Ponsot
Concentrated reds: Vieilles Vignes wines are the stars. Also white Morey-Saint-Denis.
Domaine B Serveau et Fils
The Premiers Crus in particular develop into softly fruity, velvety wines.
Clos de Tart
Renowned Grand Cru Clos de Tart smells of raspberries, strawberries and new oak.
J Taupenot-Merme
Delicious wines. Charmes-Chambertin is best, but try the Morey-St-Denis.

CHAMBOLLE-MUSIGNY

HOTEL
Château André Ziltener
Tel: 03 80 62 41 62
Small, luxurious hotel. Prices from FF1,100.

RESTAURANT
Le Chambolle-Musigny
Tel: 03 80 62 86 26
Reasonably-priced restaurant serving local specialities and wines. Menus from FF80.

RECOMMENDED PRODUCERS
Domaine Bertheau
Traditional producer; wines keenly priced.
D Moine-Hudelot
Characterful wines from good vineyards.

renovated a local castle, renaming it Château André Ziltener. It is now a luxury hotel and the cellars have been made into a museum (open seven days a week).

The light, lime-bearing soil gives the red wines of Chambolle-Musigny the finest structure of the entire Côte de Nuits. They are full of subtlety, but structured enough to age excellently. The very best come from the Grand Cru Le Musigny. Bonnes Mares, the other Grand Cru, is softer, less delicate, but still delicious. Feminine grace and delicacy are just as strongly present in the wines of Premiers Crus such as the aptly named Amoureuses and Charmes.

VOUGEOT

At Chambolle-Musigny, the D122 Route des Grands Crus turns sharp left, leading down in a southeasterly direction. The village of Vougeot is just 1km along the road. At the T-junction, take the right turn for the village centre. On the other side of the village, instead of following the D122, which joins up with the N74, take the road forking off to the right, the Chemin du Clos de Vougeot. This takes you back up past the unmistakable, world-famous Clos de Vougeot vineyard on the left.

The village of Vougeot consists of little more than an 800-metre long street with several short side streets. Every year it attracts many thousands of visitors, and this is due to the fame of the Clos de Vougeot vineyard, whose history spans some 700 years.

Above *The patterned landscape of the Clos de Vougeot vineyard, with the striking château in the background.*

Left *The cellar of the Clos des Lambrays, which was finally given Grand Cru status in 1981.*

Domaine J F Mugnier
Château de Chambolle-Musigny Musigny.
Domaine G Roumier
Fantastic, unbeatable, aromatic burgundies.
Hervé Roumier
Passionately made fruity red wines.
Domaine Comte Georges de Vogüé
One of Burgundy's great names.
The Musignys are the height of finesse.
Small amount of white made.

VOUGEOT

HOTELS

Domaine Bertagna
Tel: 03 80 62 86 04
This wine estate has a dozen rooms, with prices starting at about FF300.
Château de Gilly
Gilly-lès-Cîteaux
Tel: 03 80 62 89 98
Originally a 14th-century Cistercian abbey. Prices start at FF700. Good food in cellar restaurant from FF200.

RECOMMENDED PRODUCERS

Domaine Bertagna
Recent rise in quality. Rare white Vougeot.
Georges Clerget
Well-constructed, aromatic wines.
Michel Clerget
Tiny production. Wonderful les Charmes.
Alain Hudelot-Noëllat
Carefully vinified, formidable wines.
Bernard Munier (Gilly-lès-Cîteaux)
Elegant red wines.
Château de la Tour
Rich, fruity wine; occassionally lacks finesse.

VOSNE-ROMANEE

RESTAURANTS

Losset
Tel: 03 80 62 88 10
Inconspicuously sited by the church in Flagey-Echézeaux. Excellent, inexpensive regional food. Menus from FF140.
La Toute Petite Auberge
Tel: 03 80 61 02 03
Regional, well-prepared dishes, from FF85.

Surrounded by a stone wall, the vineyard covers about 50ha and is divided between 80 winegrowers who cultivate 100 different plots. It is therefore not surprising that the wines of Clos de Vougeot are so varied. The Clos de Vougeot is in fact Burgundy on a small scale, because nowhere else is it so clear that the reputation and winemaking ability of a producer are more important than the name or status of a plot of land. It is generally agreed, though, that the top of the slope has better soil and produces higher-quality wines than the bottom, which can get waterlogged.

As you drive up the Chemin du Clos de Vougeot, you pass the Château de la Tour on the left, a scaled-down castle built in 1890. It belongs to the single largest owner of Clos de Vougeot land, Domaine Château de la Tour. Situated almost at the top of the vineyard is the austere, 16th-century castle, Château de Vougeot, built by the monks of Cîteaux and, since 1944, the property of Les Chevaliers du Tastevin. This wine fraternity, founded in 1934 when the market for Burgundy wines was at a low, has been incredibly successful in promoting these wines worldwide. The Confrérie holds enrolment ceremonies, banquets and tastings in the castle throughout the year, but it is also a wine museum.

Next to the Clos de Vougeot, near the entrance to Château de Vougeot, is the Premier Cru Clos Blanc de Vougeot, where a good, fruity white wine is made. The road follows the edge of the Clos de Vougeot vineyard, past the château and on towards Vosne-Romanée.

VOSNE-ROMANEE

Continuing along towards Vosne-Romanée, be aware that you are approaching hallowed ground in terms of winemaking. On your left are the world-famous Grand Cru vineyards Les Grands Echézeaux and Echézeaux. These actually lie in the commune of Flagey-Echézeaux dividing Vougeot from Vosne-Romanée. At the T-junction, turn left down the hill and into the village of Vosne-Romanée.

No-one should visit Vosne-Romanée because of its architectural beauty, but the wine is another story. There are six Grands Crus within this municipality, some of them legendary around the world, and, although sometimes outrageously expensive, it is generally agreed that they represent Burgundy's finest wines, full of brilliant, concentrated flavour, perfect balance and magical finesse.

The most famous is La Romanée-Conti, marked by gravelly red soil and a large stone cross. The present owner

Right Pruning, shown here in the vineyards of the Romanée-Conti estate, is one of the most important vineyard tasks.

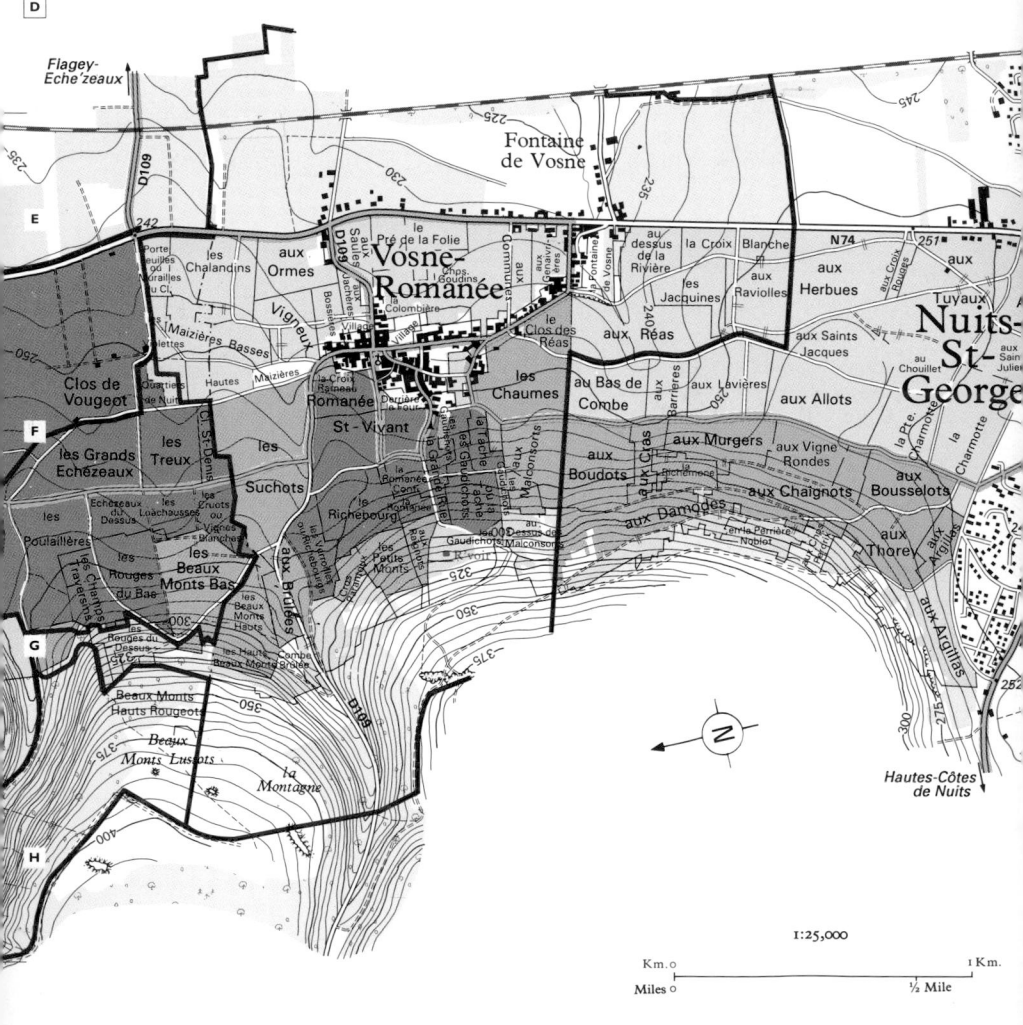

is the Domaine de la Romanée-Conti, established in 1942 and jointly owned by two families, Leroy and De Villaine.

The red wine La Romanée-Conti is exotically perfumed, richly nuanced, concentrated and complex with perfect balance. It needs at least ten years and then tastes both luxurious and satin-like. During the French Revolution, a document declared this to be the best wine, not only of the Côte d'Or vineyards, but of all the vineyards in France itself.

Another famous Grand Cru here is La Tâche, also owned entirely by the Domaine de la Romanée-Conti. This wine is somewhat earthier than that of La Romanée-Conti, and marvellously complex (spices, mushrooms, small red fruits, freshly mown grass). The other Grands Crus are: Le Richebourg (powerful, yet complex), La Romanée Saint-Vivant (stylish, elegant), La Romanée (intense, deep-coloured), and La Grande Rue (firm, fine) which was promoted to Grand Cru status in 1991.

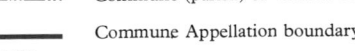
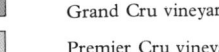
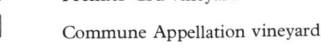

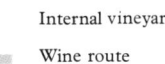

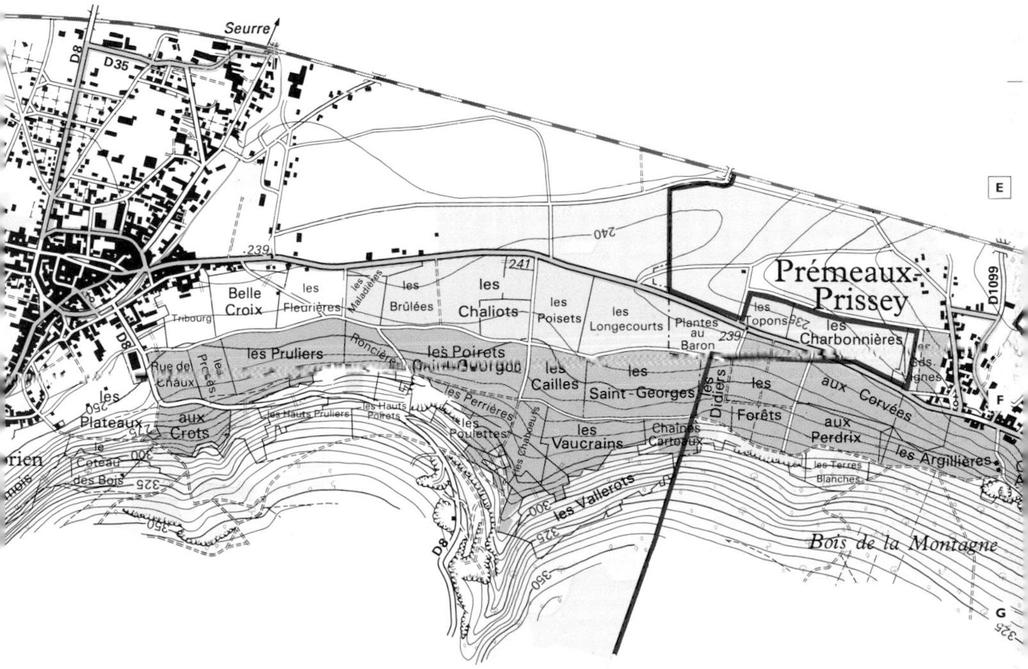

Nuits-Saint-Georges

·········· Commune (parish) or Canton boundary	Other vineyard
——— Commune Appellation boundary	Woods
Grand Cru vineyard	Contour interval 5 metres
Premier Cru vineyard	Internal vineyard boundary
Commune Appellation vineyard	Wine route

RECOMMENDED PRODUCERS
Robert Arnoux
Sometimes excellent, can be thin.
Select carefully.
Jean Grivot
Serious, high-quality wines. Recent Guy
Accad supervision.
Domaine Jean Gros
Top estate run by mother-and-son team.
Domaine Leroy
Organic methods, tiny yields. Fine,
age-worthy wines.
Domaine Méo-Camuzet
Rich, elegant wines. Can be drunk young.
Oak integrates well after a few years.
Mongeard-Mugneret
Structured wines with velvety fruit.
Domaine G Mugneret-Gibourg
Eight quality wines are made here, headed
by a superb Clos de Vougeot.
Gérard et René Mugneret
Reliable, unfiltered wines.
A Pernin-Rossin
The Guy Accad touch again – deep-purple
colour, intense bramble aromas, rich fruit.
Domaine de la Romanée-Conti
Not many wine estates are as famous as
this – with prices to match. Average age
of vines 45 years. New casks are used
although some wine is unoaked. Several
years' ageing always required.

NUITS-SAINT-GEORGES

HOTEL
La Gentilhommière
Tel: 03 80 61 12 06
On D25, west of Nuits. Rooms from
FF390. Lunch from FF140, other menus
from FF195.

RESTAURANTS
Caveau Saint-Ugezon
Tel: 03 80 61 21 59
Inexpensive menus and reasonably priced
wines. Good for lunch.
La Côte d'Or
Tel: 03 80 61 06 10
Refined cuisine. Special daily menu from
FF150, ordinary menu starts at FF270.
Large wine list. Also a hotel.
Le Sanglier
Tel: 03 80 61 04 79
Rural inn on D25. Inexpensive menus with
grilled meat dishes a speciality.

NUITS-SAINT-GEORGES
Nuits–Saint-Georges is often described as 'the nerve centre of Bourgogne', because of the large number of wine merchants who operate from there. From the church in Vosne-Romanée, leave the village by taking the road towards the vineyard slopes. Turning left at the T-junction, left at the next and right at the following one, will take you into Nuits-Saint-Georges.

The town is both the geographic and commercial centre of the Côte de Nuits. It is modern but maintains a historic atmosphere. The main street, rue Fagon, is named after the royal physician who cured Louis XIV with the town's wine.

The heart of Nuits is the Place de la République. It has a 17th-century clock tower (*beffroi*) housing an archaeological museum. On the west side of the town is the beautiful Saint-Symphorien church. On the south side, the Hospice Saint-Laurent has a remarkable statue of the Virgin Mary.

Just as in Beaune, vineyards have been donated to the hospitals of Nuits, and wines are auctioned shortly before Easter. They are mainly Premiers Crus from Nuits-Saint-Georges and their average quality is high. Wines from the north side of the town, nearest to Vosne, have a silky richness reminiscent of Vosne wines. Those from the south of Nuits, closer to Prémeaux, tend to be rougher and more vegetal, and need cellaring. The best-known Premiers Crus are Les Saint-Georges, Les Vaucrains, Les Pruliers and Les Porrets. Typical Nuits-Saint-Georges has a muscular flavour and firm tannins. Lighter types are also made, which are good when young, with supple fruitiness. Some white grapes are harvested, from which, among others, a luxuriant white called La Perrière is made.

For a unique tasting, visit Le Berchère, which is owned by Moillard and situated on the northern side of the town. Visitors can taste up to 20 wines, arranged by themes.

Nuits-Saint-Georges was also the base for the controversial consultant winemaker, Guy Accad, who had dozens of illustrious clients in the Côte d'Or. His aim was to make deeply-coloured, aromatic wines that age. His methods included careful soil analysis, restricted yields, super-ripe grapes and a cold, extended skin maceration before a long, cool fermentation. The results were successful: powerful wines that aged as desired and were in much demand.

The appellation Nuits-Saint-Georges also extends to the southern neighbouring municipality, Prémeaux.

Auberge du Moulin aux Canards
Aubigny-en-Plaine
Tel: 03 80 29 98 40
Near the abbey of Cîteaux; the *canard entier* is undoubtedly worth the detour – order when you book your table.

RECOMMENDED PRODUCERS

Marcel Rocquenet
Conscientious winemaking, attractive wines.
Jean Claude Boisset
One of the most influential *négociants* in Côte d'Or. Owns, among others, Lionel J Bruck, Jaffelin, Pierre Ponnelle, Ropiteau Frères and Charles Viénot.
Jean Chauvenet
Strong, stylish reds.
Robert Chevillon
Reliable quality.
Joseph Faiveley
Among the leaders in Burgundy. Well-structured, soundly balanced and generous reds; whites are fresh and of similar quality.
Domaine Henri Gouges
Recently big improvements have been seen; white La Perrière is rare and fragrant
Labouré-Roi
One of Burgundy's largest *négociants-éleveurs*. Excellent wines reflecting their commune styles.
Alain Michelot
A top estate. Aromatic wines with an elegant firmness and great purity.
Moillard
Has its own vineyards and is also a *négociant-éleveur*. Wines can be excellent, supple and generous.

PLACE OF INTEREST

From Nuits it is only 11kms to the abbey of Cîteaux (heading east). There, monks make delicious cheese.

Far left *Methusalahs of Romanée-Conti in cellar of the domaine.*
Mid left *The vines of Grands Echèzeaux.*
Left *Tools for training vines.*
Above *Grape pickers setting off to harvest at Romanée-Conti.*

PREMEAUX-PRISSY

 RESTAURANTS

Auberge de la Miotte
Ladoix-Serrigny
Tel: 03 80 26 40 75
18th-century former hunting lodge behind
the church in Serrigny. *Coq au vin, boeuf
bourguignon, cuisse de canard au baies de
cassis* and other regional dishes are served
at very reasonable prices. Menus start at
about FF75.

Les Coquines
Ladoix-Serrigny (Buisson)
Tel: 03 80 26 43 58
Situated on the *route nationale*, this
restaurant serves great food. The cooking
is inventive and attention has been paid to
the interior. Menus start around FF155.
Large wine list.

RECOMMENDED PRODUCERS

Domaine Bertrand Ambroise
This small estate produces delicious wines.
Domaine de l'Arlot
Established at the end of the 19th century
by Jules Belin. Bought by AXA Millésimes
in the second half of the 1980s, it has risen
again in full glory with its Nuits-Saint-
Georges Premier Cru Clos de l'Arlot,
white and red. Try also the Clos des
Forêts, and Saint-Georges Premiers Crus
and the Côte de Nuits-Villages.
Robert Dubois & Fils
Dynamic, highly skilled, progressive wine-
growing family producing richly coloured,
powerful, aromatic wines of a good
standard, such as the Côte de Nuits-
Villages, Nuits-Saint-Georges and Nuits-
Saint-Georges Les Poirets Saint-Georges.
Domaine Jean-Jacques Confuron
Quite a large estate, with a fine range of
vineyards, managed by Sophie and Alain
Meunier. Delightful wines from Nuits-Saint-
Georges and Chambolle-Musigny; Clos de
Vougeot and Romanée-Saint-Vivant.

*Above Harvesting in Burgundy
can be frenetic and exhausting work.
Left Vine pruning must be carried
out with extreme care to ensure
quality grapes for years to come.*

*Right A vine-covered outbuilding
at Clos de l'Arlot, one of the most
important properties of Nuits-Saint-
Georges.
Far right Nuits-Saint-Georges
with its vines in foreground.*

PREMEAUX-PRISSEY

To get from Nuits-Saint-Georges to Aloxe-Corton, you
cannot avoid using a stretch of the N74. Only the first section
of the route (about 10kms), between Nuits and Prémeaux-
Prissey, is surrounded by vineyards. It is worth taking a quick
detour at Prémeaux by turning left in order to view the small,
pretty church with its multicoloured roof.

By driving downhill and keeping to the right, you pass
the Château de Prémeaux, where there is a small wine
estate. The village of Prémeaux-Prissey runs seamlessly
into Comblanchien which, in turn, borders the village of
Corgoloin. These three villages come within the Côte de
Nuits-Villages appellation. In the best vineyard in Corgoloin,
the walled Clos des Langres, there is a sign which marks the
boundary between the Côte de Beaune and the Côte de
Nuits. In the marvellous cellars of the Clos des Langres,
built by Cistercian monks, is a magnificent wine press from
the 18th century.

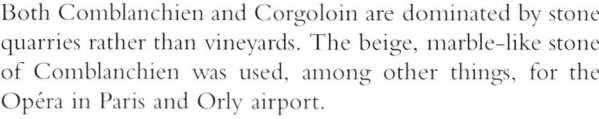

Both Comblanchien and Corgoloin are dominated by stone quarries rather than vineyards. The beige, marble-like stone of Comblanchien was used, among other things, for the Opéra in Paris and Orly airport.

LADOIX

Staying on the N74, you arrive after a few more kilometres, at the village of Ladoix (Ladoix-Serrigny) which has an attractive, small castle (it cannot be visited) and, near the exit to Aloxe-Corton, the chapel of Notre-Dame de la Chemin (11th- and 15th-century). Wines made here can be labelled under the appellations of Ladoix, Côte de Beaune-Villages; the better sited vineyards are sold generally as Aloxe-Corton Premier Cru. As the appellation of Ladoix itself is still relatively unknown, this village is a great source of excellent-quality, good-value Pinot Noir. A small amount of white wine is also produced, made either from Chardonnay or Pinot Blanc.

Domaine Daniel Rion & Fils
Modern equipped estate located along the *route nationale*. Clear tasting wines, with hints of oak, and aromas of red berry fruits. Nuits-Saint-Georges and Vosne-Romanée are excellently represented by several fine Premiers Crus.

PLACES OF INTEREST
After having been closed for years, the Clos des Langres in Corgoloin is now open to visitors. The estate is run by La Reine Pédauque from Aloxe-Corton and produces a good Côte de Nuits-Villages.

LADOIX-SERRIGNY

RECOMMENDED PRODUCERS
Capitain-Gagnerot
Reliable wines, with Corton-Charlemagne and Corton Les Renardes as its stars. The Ladoix La Micaude is also worth discovering.
Chevalier Père & Fils
Extremely hospitable winegrowing family (they live in Buisson) who produce fine white wines in particular, including Ladoix and Corton-Charlemagne. The most appealing of the reds are those from the commune of Ladoix itself.
Prince Florent de Mérode
The Prince is of Belgian origin, and his family has owned this property since 1700. He lives in a moated castle opposite his Corton vineyards. The wines from this estate are all strong Cortons of a high quality.
Domaine André Nudant & Fils
Rather large property with a good portfolio of white and red wines.

The Côte de Nuits

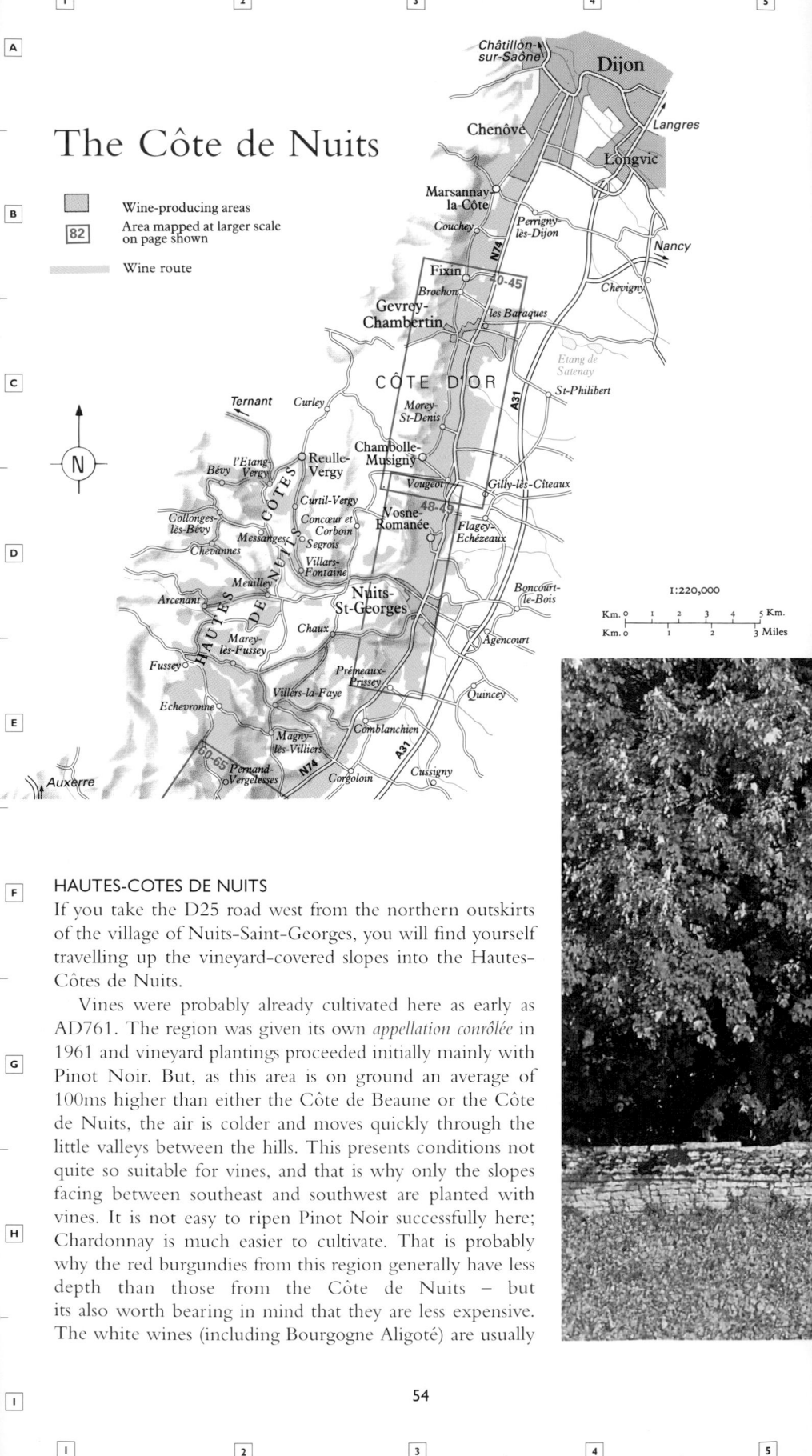

Wine-producing areas

82 Area mapped at larger scale on page shown

Wine route

Dijon

Châtillon-sur-Saône
Chenôve
Langres
Longvic
Marsannay-la-Côte
Couchey
Perrigny-lès-Dijon
Nancy
Fixin
Brochon
Gevrey-Chambertin
les Baraques
Chevigny
CÔTE D'OR
Etang de Satenay
St-Philibert
Ternant
Curley
Morey-St-Denis
Chambolle-Musigny
Reulle-Vergy
l'Etang-Vergy
Bévy
Gilly-lès-Cîteaux
Curtil-Vergy
Vougeot
Collonges-lès-Bévy
Concœur et Corboin
Vosne-Romanée
Flagey-Echézeaux
Messanges
Segrois
Chevannes
Villars-Fontaine
Meuilley
Boncourt-le-Bois
Arcenant
Nuits-St-Georges
Chaux
Marey-lès-Fussey
Agencourt
Fussey
Prémeaux-Prissey
Quincey
Echevronne
Villers-la-Faye
Magny-lès-Villiers
Comblanchien
Pernand-Vergelesses
Corgoloin
Cussigny
Auxerre

1:220,000

Km. 0   1   2   3   4   5 Km.
Km. 0   1   2   3 Miles

N74 40-45 48-45 60-65 A31 A31 N74

HAUTES-COTES DE NUITS

If you take the D25 road west from the northern outskirts of the village of Nuits-Saint-Georges, you will find yourself travelling up the vineyard-covered slopes into the Hautes-Côtes de Nuits.

Vines were probably already cultivated here as early as AD761. The region was given its own *appellation conrôlée* in 1961 and vineyard plantings proceeded initially mainly with Pinot Noir. But, as this area is on ground an average of 100ms higher than either the Côte de Beaune or the Côte de Nuits, the air is colder and moves quickly through the little valleys between the hills. This presents conditions not quite so suitable for vines, and that is why only the slopes facing between southeast and southwest are planted with vines. It is not easy to ripen Pinot Noir successfully here; Chardonnay is much easier to cultivate. That is probably why the red burgundies from this region generally have less depth than those from the Côte de Nuits – but its also worth bearing in mind that they are less expensive. The white wines (including Bourgogne Aligoté) are usually better than the reds in terms of quality, even though – as the predominating red grapevines indicate – more red wines are usually produced. Many growers also make Cassis or Framboise.

From the point of view of a tourist, Hautes-Côtes de Nuits is just as interesting as Côte de Nuits. Indeed, the landscape is, in many ways, far prettier up on these higher slopes. A few of the most picturesque villages are situated along the route picked out here.

Left *Many crops are grown in the Hautes-Côtes de Nuits, carrots and asparagus, as well as grapes.*
Below *A beautiful autumnal scene. Following this, when winter arrives, all the spring and summer growth is removed and only a couple of short canes will remain of the vine.*

HAUTES-COTES DE NUITS

HOTEL

Hôtel le Manassès
Curtil-Vergy
Tel: 03 80 61 43 81
Opened in 1991; 12 neat rooms
combining modern comfort with rustic
ambiance. Complementary winetasting.

RESTAURANTS

Auberge la Ruelée
Curtil-Vergy
Tel: 03 80 61 44 11
Rural inn, with lunch menus from about
FF69, other menus from FF145. Regional
cuisine. Small terrace.

By taking the D25 road from the direction of Nuits-Saint-Georges and then taking the D35 after the restaurant Le Sanglier, you pass the steep vineyard Les Genièvres and the tiny hamlet of Villars-Fontaine with its modest little castle. A beautiful road then leads up to the village of Curtil-Vergy – travelling this route you will pass the ruins of an early monastery.

Drive on northwards and you will come to Reulle-Vergy which has a regional museum to look at, an old bathing place and the church of Saint-Saturnin with its fine views looking down on to the village. Then follow the winding road to the next settlement, Ternant. When you go past this village in the direction of Rolle, two dolmen can be seen in the middle of the forest (and close to the road). Rolle also has a nice restaurant.

Go back to l'Etang-Vergy by way of the village of Ternant again. The overgrown walls of the former castle can be seen by driving towards Bévy and then looking back along the direction you came. Bévy itself is distinguished by its church tower, which has an unusual copper dome.

A beautiful road runs from Bévy to Collonges-lès-Bévy, with its 17th-century castle. After this comes Chevannes, which has a small, old church with a classic Burgundian multicoloured spire. Then proceed to Arcenant via Meuilly. Apart from wine, fruit liqueurs are produced here.

Continue south to Marey-lès-Fussey with its Romanesque church and the Maison des Hautes-Côtes restaurant, notable for its beautiful views. From Marey, you can either return to Nuits-Saint-Georges, or continue to Comblanchien or Corgoloin by way of Villars-la-Faye on the D115.

Ferme de Rolle
near Ternant
Hameau de Rolle
Tel: 03 80 61 40 10
Cosy restaurant situated in an old farm.
Regional cuisine. The façade is decorated with a red apple.
Maison des Hautes-Côtes
Marey-lès-Fussey
Tel: 03 80 62 91 29

Regional wines, with Burgundian dishes. Three menus, each at less than FF100. Various producers display their wines here.

RECOMMENDED PRODUCERS

Yves Chaley/Domaine du Val de Vergy (Curtil-Vergy)
Modern technology results in pure, delicious wines. Also a hotel.
Domaine Marcel et Bernard Fribourg (Villers-la-Faye)
Fruity white and good-quality red. Try the Bourgogne Aligoté and both red and white Hautes-Côtes de Nuits.
Domaine Bernard Hudelot-Verdel (Villars-Fontaine)
One of the pioneers of Hautes-Côtes. Charming white Hautes-Côtes de Nuits and an oaky red wine.
Jayer-Gilles (Magny-lès-Villers)
Excellent red wines are made here. Most of them – Echézeaux, Côte de Nuits-Villages, red Bourgogne, Hautes-Côtes de Nuits – are distinctly oaky.
Henri Naudin-Ferran (Magny-lès-Villers)
Fine white Hautes-Côtes de Nuits: Chardonnay/Pinot Blanc and subtle new oak. Good Bourgogne Aligoté and red Côte de Nuits-Villages.
Domaine Thévenot-Le-Brun & Fils (Marey-lès-Fussey)
Large properties making an unusually high proportion of white wine, including a Bourgogne Aligoté *perlant*.
Alain Verdet (Arcenant)
Fine organically produced wines, with a guarantee from the winemaker that 'If you have a headache from my wines I will give you your money back'.

Left *Rose bushes planted at the end of rows of vines are more frequently seen in the Médoc than here in Burgundy.*

Above *The Côte d'Or has many picturesque features to captivate the visitor, such as here in the village of Savigny-lès-Beaune.*

The Côte de Beaune

The Côte de Beaune begins seamlessly just south of Prémeaux. If you can spot any noticeable difference, it will be merely a variation in the colour of the soil. The Côte de Beaune generally has less iron in its soil and more chalk, and hence is less red in colour. This explains the lighter style of red wine produced and the extraordinary suitability of Chardonnay, which thrives in such conditions.

ALOXE-CORTON
From Ladoix take the N74 for 1km and then turn right into Aloxe-Corton. As you leave Ladoix, the flat-topped hill of Corton is on your right. The wooded summit rises to almost 390ms and its south- and east-facing slopes have more than 200ha of vines, nearly all Grands Crus.

History has it that King Charlemagne was crazy about the red wines of Aloxe, but often spilled them on his white beard. His mother, Berthe au Grand Pied (the queen with one foot larger than the other), complained so much that he commanded the vineyard be replanted with white grapes. A great wine was not the result: Aligoté was planted and only in the last century did Chardonnay replace it. With this a great white wine was born: full with a rich aroma of ripe fruit, oak, honey and cinnamon. In honour of Charlemagne it was called Corton-Charlemagne. Its vineyard, a Grand Cru, is situated on the southern and southwestern slope of the Corton hill, which dominates Aloxe-Corton with its wooded ridge. The other slopes yield red Corton, similarly formidable – firm wines with style and distinction.

Aloxe-Corton has a fine 15th-century castle, Château Corton-André, owned by *négociant* La Reine Pédauque. It has a multicoloured roof and is open to visitors. The delightful Hotel Clarion is nearby. On the village square there is a *caveau*, where wines can be tasted and bought.

Left A view of Pernand-Vergelesses, which produces both red and white wines, the whites being a little more approachable when young.

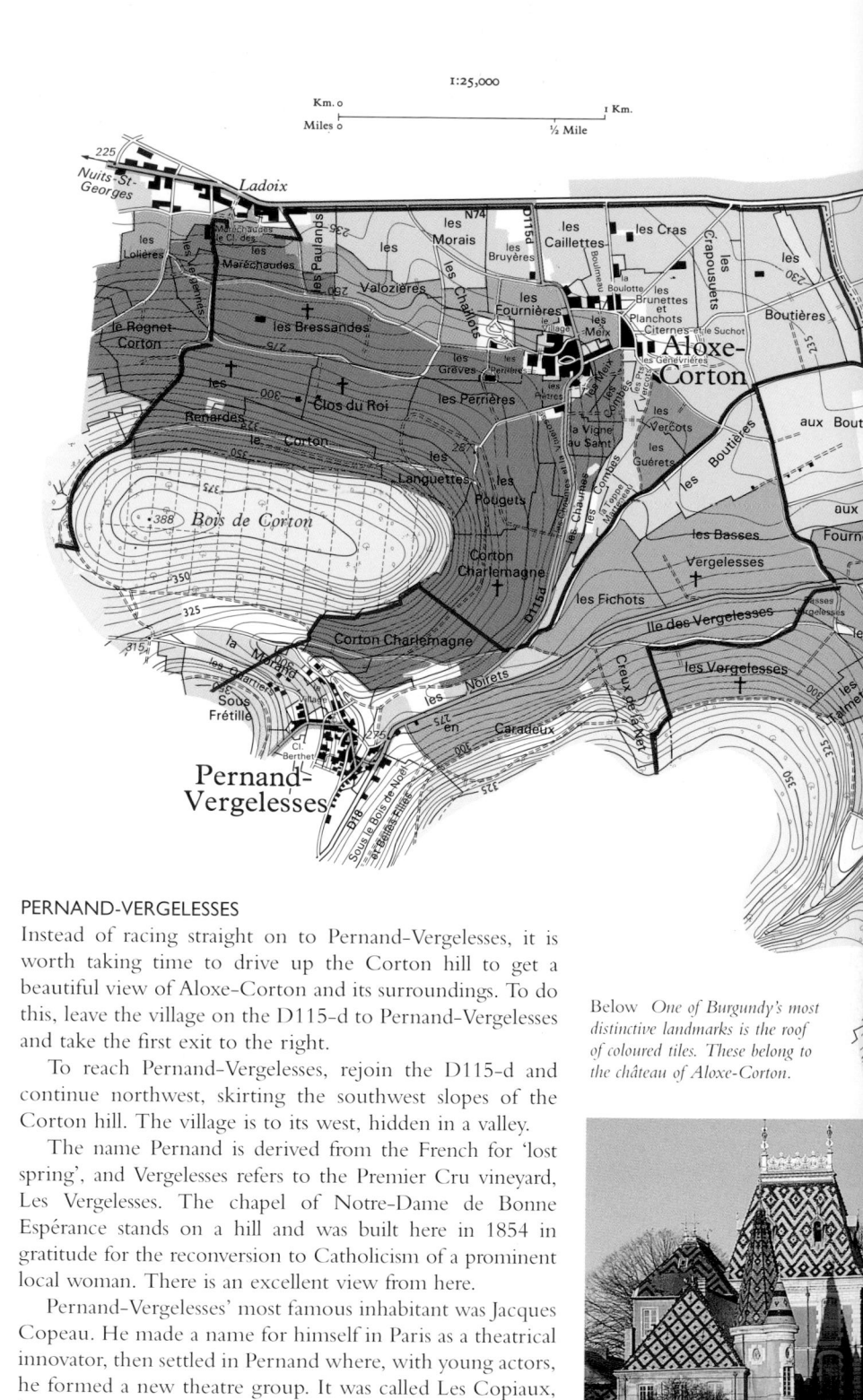

1:25,000

Km. 0   1 Km.

Miles 0   ½ Mile

225
Nuits-St-
Georges   *Ladoix*

les
Lolières

les
Maréchaudes

Valozières

le Rognet-
Corton

les Bressandes

Renardes

Corton

les Charlots

les
Morais

les

les
Bruyères

les
Fournières

les
Grèves

Clos du Roi

les Perrières

les

Languettes

les
Pougets

Corton
Charlemagne

388 *Bois de Corton*

350

325

315

la
Morache

Sous
Frétille

Cl.
Berthet

Pernand-
Vergelesses

Corton Charlemagne

les
Noirets

en

les Caillettes

les Cras

la
Boulotte

les
Brunettes
et
Planchots

les
Melx

Citernes

les Genevrières

la Vigne
au Saint

les
Guérets

les Vercots

Aloxe-
Corton

les
Crapousuets

les

Boutières

aux Bout

aux

les Fichots

les Basses

Vergelesses

Ile des Vergelesses

Fourne

les Vergelesses

Caradeux

PERNAND-VERGELESSES

Instead of racing straight on to Pernand-Vergelesses, it is worth taking time to drive up the Corton hill to get a beautiful view of Aloxe-Corton and its surroundings. To do this, leave the village on the D115-d to Pernand-Vergelesses and take the first exit to the right.

To reach Pernand-Vergelesses, rejoin the D115-d and continue northwest, skirting the southwest slopes of the Corton hill. The village is to its west, hidden in a valley.

The name Pernand is derived from the French for 'lost spring', and Vergelesses refers to the Premier Cru vineyard, Les Vergelesses. The chapel of Notre-Dame de Bonne Espérance stands on a hill and was built here in 1854 in gratitude for the reconversion to Catholicism of a prominent local woman. There is an excellent view from here.

Pernand-Vergelesses' most famous inhabitant was Jacques Copeau. He made a name for himself in Paris as a theatrical innovator, then settled in Pernand where, with young actors, he formed a new theatre group. It was called Les Copiaux, based on an idea of the local postman. Their performances were announced by trumpet flourishes, taking place in village squares or parks. Copeau (1879–1949) is buried in Pernand.

Below One of Burgundy's most distinctive landmarks is the roof of coloured tiles. These belong to the château of Aloxe-Corton.

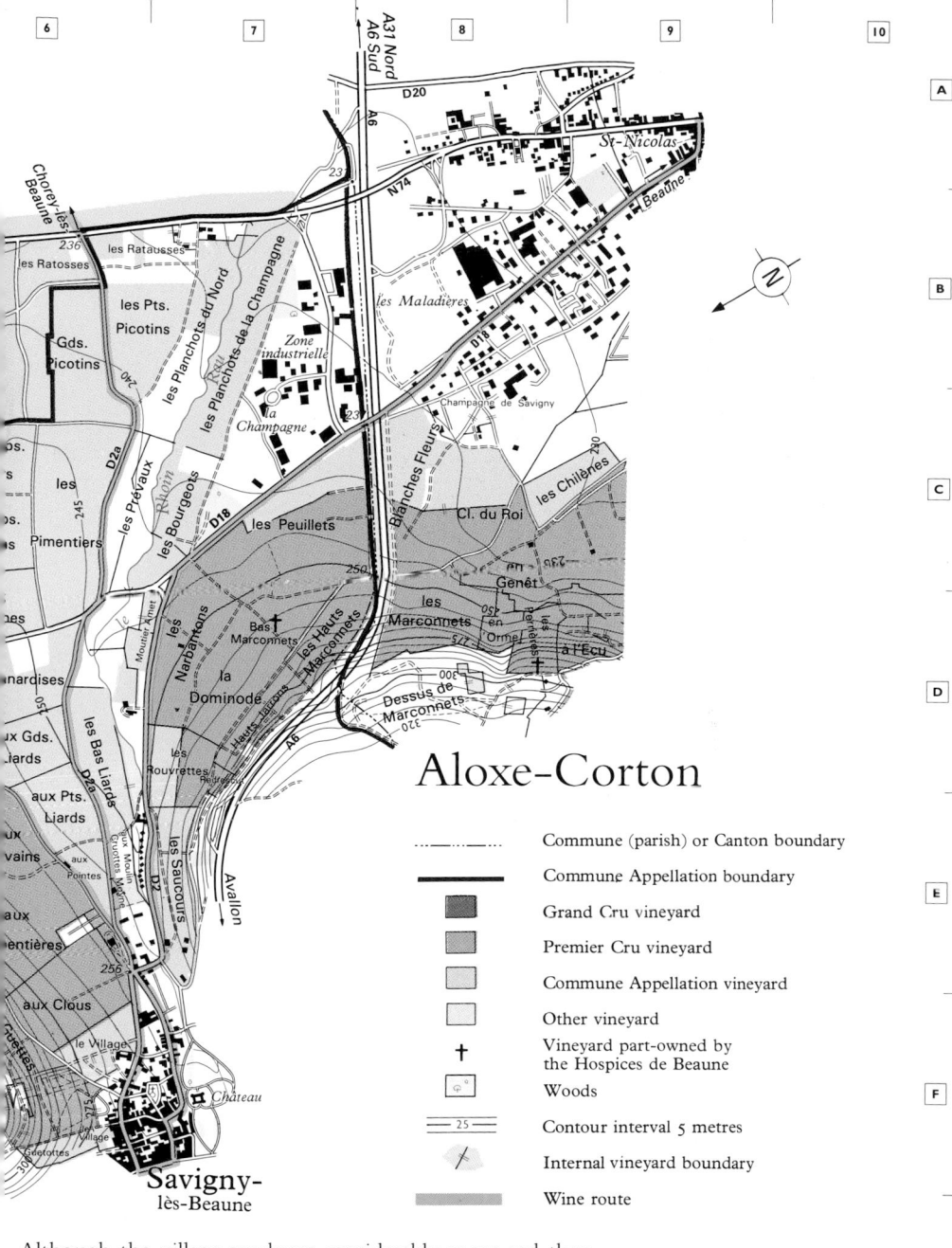

Aloxe-Corton

·······—··—··—	Commune (parish) or Canton boundary
▬▬▬▬	Commune Appellation boundary
■	Grand Cru vineyard
■	Premier Cru vineyard
▨	Commune Appellation vineyard
□	Other vineyard
†	Vineyard part-owned by the Hospices de Beaune
▨	Woods
═ 25 ═	Contour interval 5 metres
◿	Internal vineyard boundary
▬▬	Wine route

Although the village produces considerably more red than white wine, the white is generally more attractive. Red Pernand-Vergelesses in its youth tends to taste rather tight, and therefore benefits from a few years' bottle-age.

SAVIGNY-LES-BEAUNE

Leave Pernand-Vergelesses by retracing the route back to Aloxe-Corton on the D18. Instead of taking the left fork onto the D115-d back down to Aloxe, keep travelling straight on. After about 2kms turn right towards Savigny-lès-Beaune. This spectacular drive offers some fine views.

The history of Savigny goes back to the Gallic-Romanic period, but nowadays the village acts as a modern commuter suburb of Beaune. The old centre still retains its historic

Below *Paniers of grapes stacked up at harvesting time.*
Right and below right *Around Beaune there are many imposing buildings. These châteaux are in Aloxe-Corton and Savigny.*

ALOXE-CORTON

HOTEL
Villa Louise Clarion
Tel: 03 80 26 46 70
Owned and run by the Voarick family, ten rooms and one suite, from FF650.

RECOMMENDED PRODUCERS
Maurice Chapuis
Luxurious wines with depth and power.
Caves de la Reine Pédauque
Large firm. Best wines come from own sites and include Corton-Charlemagne.
Domaine Daniel Senard
Excellent wines. Rare white Aloxe-Corton.
Michel Voarick
Traditional, long-living wines of real class and quality.

PERNAND-VERGELESSES

RESTAURANT
Le Charlemagne
Tel: 03 80 21 51 45
Great-value regional dishes.

RECOMMENDED PRODUCERS
Domaine Bonneau du Martray
Thought to be the site of Emperor Charlemagne's vineyards. Now one of the largest and best-reputed local properties.
Domaine Dubrueil-Fontaine
Bernard Dubrueil makes delicate red Ile des Vergelesses and powerful Cortons.
Domaine Laleure-Piot
High-quality, fruity wines. Reds are best.

atmosphere, which you can sample in a visit to the church, with its 12th-century clock tower and octagonal spire. Inside is a 15th-century fresco depicting angels and saints.

It is only a few minutes' walk from the church to the castle, in the middle of a park on the south side of the village. The imposing building, flanked by round towers, is now a museum housing a collection of a few hundred motorcycles, racing cars and aeroplanes (including a Mirage III). Visitors enter by way of an annex, the so-called Petit Château, which dates from 1683 and was built in the form of an arch.

Wander through the village, particularly down the *rues* Chanoine Donin and Guy de Vaulchier, searching out the 15 or more wall inscriptions. They date from between the 17th and 19th centuries, and act as 'thoughts for the day', such as: *Il ne faut pas donner son appât au goujon quand on peut esperer prendre une carpe* (never give the bait to a gudgeon, when there's a chance you could catch a carp); and *Malgré les imposteurs, traîtres et jaloux, l'homme patient viendra à bout de tout* (despite impostors, scoundrels and the jealous, he who waits comes out on top). No-one knows who wrote these or why.

If you drive towards Beaune from the castle, you will see in a side street to the right the Manoir de Nicolay, a large Louis XIV-style mansion. Behind it is a marvellous garden. This is all part of the Chandon de Briailles wine estate.

Domaine Pavelot
Good whites and reds from the village.
Domaine Rapet Père & Fils
Well known for white Sous la Vierge,
Corton-Charlemagne and red Premier Cru.

SAVIGNY-LES-BEAUNE

HOTELS

Lud'Hôtel
Tel: 03 80 21 53 24
Peaceful hotel with rooms (from FF330).
Restaurant (Menu de Terroir FF100) and
swimming pool.
Le Hameau de Barboron
Tel: 03 80 21 58 35
Carefully and lovingly restored Cistercian
buildings in a magnificent wooded setting.
12 tasteful and comfortable rooms from
FF650.
Hostellerie du Vieux Moulin
Tel: 03 80 21 51 16
Exquisite hotel with 24 large rooms and
an excellent restaurant. Rooms from
FF420, menus from FF140.

RESTAURANT

La Cuverie
Tel: 03 80 21 50 03
Simple, rustic regional restaurant.

RECOMMENDED PRODUCERS

Simon Bize & Fils
Stylish, tasty wines and always a
smiling welcome.
Bonnot-Lamblot
Traditional methods. Good wines.
Capron-Manieux
Tiny quantities, but always high quality,
including both red and white Savignys.
Domaine de Chandon de Briailles
Flawless Savigny, Pernand-Vergelesses and
Aloxe-Corton wines.
Maison Doudet-Naudin
An old-fashioned _négociant_ firm now
making rich, supple, fruity reds.
Domaine Antonin Guyon
Pure, lively-tasting wines with an attractive
wood/vanilla aroma.

CHOREY-LES-BEAUNE

HOTEL

Château de Chorey
Tel: 03 80 22 06 05
The castle has six large, comfortable
rooms, which are let as _chambres d'hôtes_.
Prices from about FF760.

RESTAURANT

L'Ermitage-Corton
Tel: 03 80 22 05 28
Excellent cooking. Large wine list. Menus
from FF300. Also hotel.

RECOMMENDED PRODUCERS

Château de Chorey
Wines of great style and firm tannins.
Tollot-Beaut & Fils
Good, balanced reds and whites.

CHOREY-LES-BEAUNE

Chorey-lès-Beaune is on almost flat land. Although there
are no Grands Crus here, the lack of slopes is not necessarily
a handicap for making good wine, as proven by local estates.
The best have a rather sturdy structure and a soft fruitiness.

Château de Chorey is of most interest here. The main
building is 17th-century, the towers flanking it 13th. Around
it are a moat and park. Wine has been made here for centuries,
and on the beams in the _cuverie_ are etched a few striking
harvest dates: in 1893, it began as early as August 28th.

BEAUNE

Leave Savigny-lès-Beaune from the south side of the village, travelling in a westerly direction. At the four-way junction, turn right onto the D2 towards Beaune, with the slopes of the Montagne de Beaune on your right. The D2 joins the D18, which leads you straight into the town, crossing over the A6 on the way.

Beaune is the wine capital of Burgundy. Commercially, it is ideally placed near the junction of the A6 and the A31, but the attractiveness of the city itself undoubtedly plays a role, the ancient buildings giving Beaune huge historical importance.

The old centre is fantastically preserved and unusually rich in atmosphere. Beaune was probably founded in AD52 by Julius Caesar. Before they moved to Dijo the Dukes of Burgundy lived here at the beginning of the 13th century and their palace still stands today. In fact, because so many of the town's medieval buildings have been used for storing wine, they have been carefully preserved. Many of the former

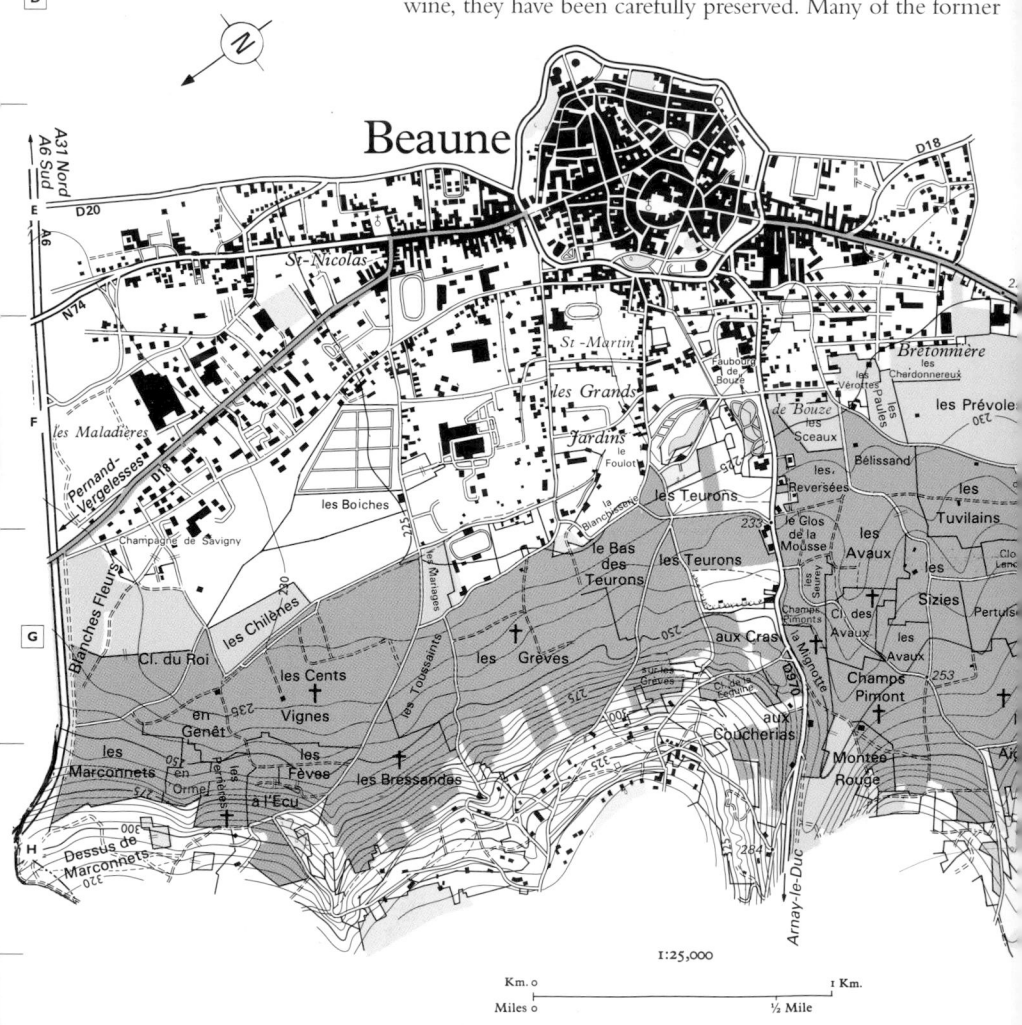

1:25,000

Km. o   1 Km.
Miles o   ½ Mile

Above   An example of the rich variety of architecture to be discovered in Burgundy, the beautifully decorative Hôtel Dieu is not only one of the most famous, but one of the most stunning of sights.

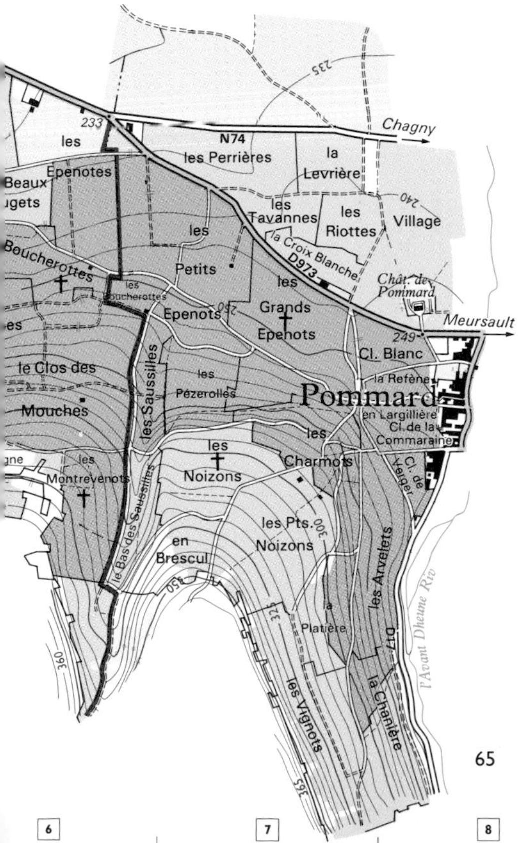

Map labels:
233
les
Beaux
ugets
Epenotes
N74
les Perrières
la
Levrière
235
Chagny
la Croix Blanche
les
Tavannes
les
Riottes
Village
240
Boucherottes
Petits
Boucherottes
les
Epenots
Grands
Epenots
Chât. de
Pommard
Meursault
249
Cl. Blanc
les
Pézerolles
te Clos des
Mouches
les Saussilles
Pommard
la Refène
en Largillière
Cl. de la
Commaraine
les
Charmots
les
Noizons
les
Montrevenots
le Bas des Saussilles
les Pts.
Noizons
en
Brescul
les Arvelets
l'Avant Dheune Rio
la
Platière
la Chanlère
les Vignots
25

Beaune

Commune (parish)
or Canton boundary

Commune Appellation boundary

Premier Cru vineyard

Commune Appellation vineyard

Other vineyard

† Vineyard part-owned by
the Hospices de Beaune

Woods

25   Contour interval 5 metres

Internal vineyard boundary

Wine route

Right and below Beaune is full of wonderful places to stock up on food and wine. There are cheese shops such as this and numerous wine shops.

BEAUNE

 HOTELS

Belle Epoque
15 rue Faubourg Bretonnière
Tel: 03 80 24 66 15
Stylish rooms. From FF400.

Bleu Marine
10-12 boulevard Maréchal-Foch
Tel: 03 80 24 01 01
Situated on the ring road. Bright, modern hotel. One of the pleasantest in town and close to everything. 40 rooms and 6 suites from FF490. The hotel also has a good restaurant called Le Clos du Cèdre.

Le Cep
27 Rue Maufoux
Tel: 03 80 22 35 48
Luxurious, stylish rooms from FF700 to FF1,250. Traditionally prepared dishes.

Le Parc
Levernois
Tel: 03 80 24 63 00
Rather rustic rooms (starting at about FF250). Peacefully situated, next to the Hostellerie de Levernois. No restaurant.

 RESTAURANTS

Le Bénaton
25 Faubourg Bretonnière
Tel: 03 80 22 00 26
Simply furnished, but with inventive dishes. Menus from FF110.

Le Bistro Bourguignon
8 Rue Monge
Tel: 03 80 22 23 24
Wine bar often offering burgundies by the glass. Inexpensive daily menu.

Chez Joël D
45 Rue Ma ufoux
Tel: 03 80 24 71 28
Specialities: oysters, seafood.

La Ciboulette
69 Rue Lorraine
Tel: 03 80 24 70 72
Pleasant place for good food, from fresh ingredients, for FF100 or less.

Ma Cuisine
Passage Sainte-Hélène
Tel: 03 80 22 30 22
Run by Pierre Escoffier and Julienne Parra. Absolutely vital to book in advance. The food is first-class and the wine list is enormous.

l'Ecusson
Place Malmédy
Tel: 03 80 24 03 82
Chic restaurant. One of Beaune's best. Original dishes – from about FF140.

Le Gourmandin
8 Place Carnot
Tel: 03 80 24 07 88
Inexpensive, regional dishes from FF85.

moats are now gardens and it is possible to walk around the ancient battlements.

The best and most pleasant way of getting to know Beaune is by taking a walk through the town. Begin in the central square, Place Carnot, where you can park. On the corner of Rue Carnot and the square is an excellent wine shop, Denis Perret. Leave the square, walking north along Rue Carnot, until you come to Place Monge, dominated by its 14th-century belfry with a remarkable wooden roof.

Now turn right into Rue des Tonneliers, which is lined with dignified 18th-century houses. At the end of the street turn left and then immediately right into Rue Rousseau-Deslandes. Number ten along here is one of the most remarkable buildings in Beaune: the Hôtel de Cîteaux, which was built at the end of the 12th century. Continue by turning right into the Rue de Lorraine. On the corner stands the Hospice de la Charité with its chapel and courtyard.

Follow the Rue de Lorraine and then turn right along a small side street to the Hôtel de Ville, a 17th-century former Ursuline convent which now also houses two museums, the Musée des Beaux-Arts and the Musée Marey which is devoted to Etienne-Jules Marey, who developed the earliest principles of photographic technique.

Now turn back towards Rue de Lorraine. At the end of the street on your right you will see the most beautiful of Beaune's town gates, the Porte Saint-Nicolas. Near this gate are the Chapelle de l'Oratoire, where art exhibitions are sometimes held, and the cellars of the firm La Reine Pédauque, which you can visit.

Continue the walk by turning left and following part of the old town walls. The round Bastion des Filles (or de l'Oratoire) on the corner of Boulevard Foch now serves as an above-ground wine cellar for Chanson Père & Fils. Now turn left back into the old town on Rue Paul Chanson, also called Rue du Collège. On the right is the entrance to Patriarche Père & Fils, whose cellars really do deserve a visit. There is a small charge, which goes to charity, and you can taste an extensive range of wines.

Now turn right, walking south along Rue Gandelot to the basilica of Notre-Dame. Despite much alteration and rebuilding, this church still has clear traces of Burgundian Romanesque architecture. From April to November, marvellous wall tapestries depicting the 'Life of the Virgin' are displayed.

It is only a minute's walk from here to the Musée du Vin de Bourgogne, one of France's most exciting museums, tucked away to the south of Notre-Dame. The museum, the 15th- and 16th-century former residence of the Dukes of Burgundy, houses a rich collection of objects and works of art connected with wine.

The Rue d'Enfer (with the offices of the firm Joseph Drouhin at number seven) leads to the Avenue de la République. Turn left and then take the first street on the right, which will bring you to a square with shops, including some selling wine. Also on this square is the hall where the Hospices de Beaune auction is held, the Office du Tourisme and, the climax of this walk, the Hôtel-Dieu.

Built in 1451, the Hôtel-Dieu was commissioned by Nicolas Rolin, chancellor under Philip the Good. He and

Attractive wine list, surprisingly not limited to the wines of Burgundy. Many wines are also served by the glass. Also a hotel with three comfortable rooms, from FF350.

Le Grand Blue
Place au Beurre
Tel: 03 80 24 70 70
Fresh-water and salt-water fish in very affordable *à la carte* menus.

Le Jardin des Remparts
10 Rue de l'Hôtel-Dieu
Tel: 03 80 24 79 41
Dishes are inventive and lightly cooked; sophisticated, contemporary creations. Menus from FF145.

Hostellerie de Levernois
Levernois
Tel: 03 80 24 73 58
Jean Crotet (formerly of La Côte d'Or in Nuits) has built a luxurious hotel complex ten minutes from Beaune. The cuisine is of a high quality and uses fresh regional ingredients. Weekday lunch costs about FF220, other menus about FF345. Very large wine list – including wines from outside Burgundy. 16 magnificently furnished rooms.

CAFE BRAS

Bernard Morillon
31 rue Maufoux
Tel: 03 80 24 12 06
Chic restaurant with excellent cuisine. The wine list is unfortunately rather predictable.

Les Tontons
22 rue Faubourg Madeleine
Tel: 03 80 24 19 64
Pleasant restaurant slightly away from the centre. In style and cuisine, it is halfway between bistro and restaurant. You will eat well, sometimes even very well, for very low prices. The friendly, pleasant atmosphere is an added bonus. Menus from FF98.

Hostellerie de la Paix
47 Faubourg Madeleine
Tel: 03 80 22 33 33
Two restaurants, the Rôtisserie (menus at about FF120) and Le Bouchon (FF100 or less), also a small hotel.

Relais de Saulx
6 rue Louis-Véry
Tel: 03 80 22 01 35
Small, stylish, busy restaurant with reliable,
rather conservative cuisine. Menus start
at about FF125.

RECOMMENDED PRODUCERS

Domaine Besançenot-Mathouillet
Medium-sized family estate owning
vineyards mainly in Beaune itself.
Some of the best Premiers Crus are
Cent Vignes, Clos du Roi and Theurons.
Albert Bichot
Modern, dynamic, successful exporter.
Most wines are reliable, but some are
excellent, eg Long-Depaquit in Chablis and
Clos Frantin in Vosne-Romanée.
Bouchard Père & Fils
Wines from own Grand and Premier Cru
vineyards. Distributor for a number of
other producers. After a fire in 1989, the
firm re-equipped with the latest technology.
All wines are of above-average quality.
J Calvet & Cie
Chiefly middle-ranking wines. Guided
tours are taken through its 15th-century
wine cellars.
Domaine Cauvard Père & Fils
Quality-conscious estate: good red and
white Bourgognes Les Monts Battois.
Champy Père & Cie
The oldest *négociant-éleveur* in Burgundy,
with price lists dating from 1720. A take-
over in 1991 meant transformation: old
winemaking equipment was thrown out,
carefully selected wines bought in. Beaune-
Avaux is one of best reds.
Chanson Père & Fils
Lighter-style reds, especially Beaune Clos
des Fèves. Wines are aged in a 15th-
century castle with walls several feet thick.

Above *The delights to discover in a
Beaune charcuterie.*
Above right *The intricately
patterned roof of the Hôtel-Dieu.*

his wife, Guigone de Salins, decided to build a home for the
sick and poor. The building was in use as an old people's
home until as recently as 1971; now it is mainly used as a
museum. It must have been quite an experience for the
patients, because their accommodation had the air of a palace
rather than that of a hospital. The sick-room borders on a
magnificent paved courtyard from whence a wooden
veranda and gallery may be seen, as well as a superb
multicoloured roof of glazed tiles. There is a hall for the sick
with 28 places for beds, an enormous kitchen, a dispensary
and a second courtyard boasting statues of Nicolas Rolin
and his wife. There is also an exhibition of tapestries and
furniture as well as the magnificent alterpiece by Rogier
van der Weyden, *The Last Judgement* (1443), which was
specially commissioned by the Hospices de Beaune and is
one of the transcendental masterpieces of Flemish art. This
building alone justifies a visit to Beaune.

In the course of the centuries, various benefactors have left no fewer than 60ha of wine land to the Hôtel-Dieu. The wines from this land are sold at an annual auction to benefit the collective hospitals of Beaune, the Hospices de Beaune. This takes place on the third Sunday of November, and is the world's largest charity auction. The selling of wines is the highlight of Les Trois Glorieuses, the three days of celebration throughout the whole of Burgundy, at which time in Beaune and other wine villages there are tasting sessions and receptions.

From the Hôtel-Dieu, it is only a minute's walk back to the Place Carnot.

Wine can be bought everywhere in Beaune, which offers wine stores on every street. Beaune is also one of the largest wine communes of the Côte d'Or. The majority of the wine produced here is red. They seldom have striking individual characteristics, but are supple when young and can be left to mature for ten years or more. Centuries ago, Erasmus van Rotterdam sighed that he wished to live in France, 'not to lead armies, but to drink the wines of Beaune'.

It is also possible to look at Beaune from above. Two different companies organise trips by hot-air balloon over the vineyards and villages of the Côte. A firm called Beaune Autrement offers guided walks round the town's ramparts and courtyards, as well as a tour of first-growth vineyards and a visit to the American Camp where, in 1918, thousands of American soldiers camped on their way home from the war. Details of all these can be found in the Office du Tourisme.

Joseph Drouhin
Among the Burgundian elite. Wines of unreproachable quality, charming fruitiness, style and fine complexity.

Camille Giroud
Craftsman-like firm with especially good reds. Some of the best are Les Cras, Teurons, Pommard Clos des Eveneaux and Cortons.

Louis Jadot
American-owned big name since 1985, with strict quality policy, character, power and style.

Jaffelin
Range of wines – Les Villages de Jaffelin – which are well priced from the lesser-known communes.

Louis Latour
Family firm of high standing. Red wines are best from the company's own estate (eg Château Corton Grancey), but the white wines are generally of a higher quality.

Patriarche Père & Fils
Négociant firm whose cellars are certainly worth a visit. Range includes generous, sturdy-tasting, quality burgundies.

Domaine des Pierres Blanches
Modest estate with white and red Cote de Beaune of excellent quality.

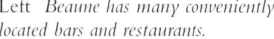

PLACES OF INTEREST

There is an 18-hole golf course at Levernois, and in Meursanges balloon trips can be booked at Château de Laborde. During the season, a sound and light show takes place in the courtyard of the Hôtel-Dieu. Find information at the Office du Tourisme or hotels. On Saturday, there is a market in the town centre.

RELATED TO WINE

Across from Hôtel-Dieu, Patriarche Père & Fils and the Parisian publisher Flammarion have set up a unique documentation centre, the Athenaeum de la Vigne et du Vin. Exhibitions take place there, and the library has approximately 100,000 books about wine, Burgundy and gastronomy.

Left Beaune has many conveniently located bars and restaurants.

POMMARD

Pommard lies just 3.5kms south of Beaune: leave on the
N74 heading south and when the road splits, take the right
fork (the D973) into the centre of Pommard.

The village is easily recognised by its spireless church.
Vines almost completely cover the hills behind and to the south,
although this has not always been the case — a fact belied by
the name of one of Pommard's Premiers Crus, Les Epenots,
named after the pine-tree wood which used to be there.

Pommard's good reputation for wine spans centuries. It
was praised by Henry IV, Louis XV and Victor Hugo, while
the 16th-century poet Ronsard wrote how wondrous it was
'...that in such a small place such a great wine could be born'.
A true Pommard has intense colour and power, and must age
a long time before its initial toughness changes into velvety
smoothness. Unfortunately, not all satisfy this description;
many are of uninspiring, average quality. However, Château
de Pommard (open to visitors), with its walled 20-ha
vineyard, proves that Pommard of village level can impress.

A busy road runs straight through the village. To the side
of it is the surprisingly spacious church square, the heart of

Left *Monthélie produces a red wine which is closer in style to that of its neighbour, Volnay. A tiny amount of white is also produced.*

Pommard

·····—·—···	Commune (parish) or Canton boundary
——	Commune Appellation boundary
▨	Premier Cru vineyard
▢	Commune Appellation vineyard
▢	Other vineyard
✝	Vineyard part-owned by the Hospices de Beaune
▢	Woods
═25═	Contour interval 5 metres
/	Internal vineyard boundary
▨▨▨	Wine route

1:25,000

Km. 0 .... 1 Km.

Miles 0 .... ½ Mile

POMMARD

RESTAURANT

Café du Pont
Tel: 03 80 22 03 41
Gastronomic delights such as *coq à la lie de vin* and *estouffade de boeuf bourguignon* are served for FF100 or less. Pommards start from about FF140.

RECOMMENDED PRODUCERS

Comte Armand/Domaine du Clos des Epeneaux
A top estate, easy to find near the church. The wines are intensely concentrated and need years of cellaring.

Domaine Michel Gaunoux
A 'working museum', offering wines from recent years, and housing stock from the past decades. Concentrated Pommards, excellent with age.

Jean-Marc Boillot
Excellent wines, including Premier Cru Montrevots.

Domaine de Mme Bernard de Coursel
Cellar beneath a fine house on the square. Good Pommards: Grand Clos des Epenots and Rugiens.

Domaine Michel Ganoux
High-quality, concentrated Pommards.

Domaine Lejeune
Perfect Pommards, foot-trodden in truly traditional manner, with fruit, charm and enough backbone to develop in bottle.

Domaine Mussy
Traditional estate, with distinctive wines showing power and complexity.

Domaine Parent
Reliable, expertly made wines. Legend has it that Thomas Jefferson was guided by a Parent on his Burgundy visit in 1787 and bought his wine for the White House.

Château de Pommard
Beautifully renovated property. The wines are sublime – and expensive.

PLACES OF INTEREST

A low, white, stone cross – the *croix de Pommard* – southeast of the village marks the spot of a once fordable point in the Dheune River. It took on special meaning in the expression *'Tu n'est pas encore à la croix de Pommard'.* ('You are not at the end of your problems yet.')

VOLNAY

RESTAURANTS

Le Cellier Volnaysien
Place de l'Eglise
Tel: 03 80 21 61 04
Near to the church. One of the dining rooms is an arched cellar. Authentic regional dishes. Various wines, served by the glass. Menus from FF100.

Auberge des Vignes
Tel: 03 80 22 24 48
Pleasant rustic restaurant with affordable, well-prepared regional dishes and attractive wines.

the village. There are wood carvings to be seen in the church itself, which dates from the 18th century. Some of the streets in Pommard are only four metres wide, a reminder of the days of the stagecoach. There is an interesting wine shop called Les Domaines de Pommard, situated opposite the post office, which stocks wines from more than 20 producers.

VOLNAY

Leaving Pommard travelling south on the D973, take the fork off to the right and up-hill through the Premier Cru vineyards surrounding Volnay. The vineyards of Les Brouillards and Les Angles are on the left, Frémiets on the right.

Volnay nestles against a steep slope and looks down on Pommard. To the north it is marked by a tasting centre and a giant bottle. There is also a 16th-century chapel – all that remains of a castle built by the first duke of Burgundy. Most of the houses date from the 17th and 18th centuries.

Volnay's Romanesque church is actually 14th-century and has recently been completely restored, thanks to donations from the inhabitants. By following a path leading upwards behind the church (there is a signpost *panorama* pointing the way), you will find a delightful vantage point. On clear days you can even see Mont Blanc from here.

Volnay's red wine has enjoyed fame for centuries. Records show that as early as the 6th century it was served in Italy, and in 1328 at the crowning of Philippe de Valois in Reims. After the conquest of Burgundy in 1477, Louis XI confiscated the entire harvest. Louis XIV and XV were also enthusiasts.

These are among the Côte de Beaune's finest red wines. They are striking for their elegance, soft taste, perfect balance and delicate bouquet. The best come from Premiers Crus Caillerets, Champans, Clos de la Bousse d'Or, Clos des Chênes and Clos des Ducs. Wines from Premier Cru vineyard Clos des Santenots bear the name Volnay but, strictly speaking, this vineyard is in the commune of Meursault.

MONTHELIE

Leaving Volnay on the D973, turn right (south) and you will pass on your left the Grand Cru vineyards of Champans and Cailleret Dessus. After a while, the road splits. Take the right fork, follow the hillside round and you will reach Monthelie.

Two multicoloured spires dominate the skyline: the highest is 12th-century Romanesque, the other belongs to Château de Monthélie. Monthélie boasts buildings from the 16th, 17th and 18th centuries, most inhabited by winegrowers.

In 1855, a Dr Lavalle wrote that Monthélie wines were worth only three-quarters Volnay's. What he meant was they resemble Volnays, with similar grace, but were rustic and somewhat softer – qualities the price does indeed tend to reflect.

PLACES OF INTEREST

Alain Hess is a *maître fromager* and has an excellent cheese shop in Beaune (Au Tast' Fromage, 23 rue Carnot). Try his Le délice de Pommard – perfect with Volnay.

RECOMMENDED PRODUCERS

Domaine du Marquis d'Angerville
Very fine and often velvety Volnays, such as Champans and Clos des Ducs.
Domaine Yvon Clerget
One of Europe's oldest family estates (1268). Volnays are elegant and firm.
Bernard Glantenay
Delicious Volnays: charming, supple and fruity. Dependable wines at good prices.
Domaine Michel Lafarge
Top wines of colour, roundness, distinction.
Hubert de Montille
Great traditionally-made wines, stern when young, softening after 6 to 10 years.
Domaine de la Pousse d'Or
Cellars beneath a stately mansion. Sublime, refined and balanced Volnays.

MONTHELIE

RECOMMENDED PRODUCERS

Denis Boussey
Consistently good, especially Premier Cru Champs Fulliots.
Château de Monthélie
Wine to withstand any criticism: Firm Premier Cru, with grace and hints of vanilla.

POINTS OF INTEREST

The name is pronounced 'Mont'lie'. Its many owners have included the monastery of Cluny, and a pharmacist from Beaune who bought it in its entirety in 1730.

The heritage of this part of the Côte de Beaune is steeped in wine:
Far left *The gateway of the Château les Communs in Pommard.*
Left *Château de Pommard's cellar with its intricate wrought-iron door.*
Above *Example of a stone plaque incorporating a bunch of grapes in the design (Pommard).*

AUXEY-DURESSES

RESTAURANT
La Crémaillière
Tel: 03 80 21 22 60
In a chic interior you can enjoy regional specialities and local wines. There is usually a menu offered at under FF100; the next price is almost twice as much. The quality of the food is good and usually a few inexpensive wines are available which are not on the wine list.

RECOMMENDED PRODUCERS
Gérard Creusefond
Strong, dependable red wines.
Jean-Pierre Diconne
Rustic reds and sometimes excellent whites. Quality can vary greatly from bottle to bottle so choose carefully.
Domaine André et Bernard Labry
Situated in Melin, with magnificent, pure Auxey-Duresses; regrettably there are no Premiers Crus.
Jean et Vincent Lafouge
Vincent now works with his father, after attending the Lycée Viticole in Beaune. Long-established domaine producing good wine.
Henri Latour
Modern equipment makes fruity, expressive wines, including red Auxey-Duresses and Bourgogne Hautes-Côtes de Beaune.
Leroy
A small, almost legendary name in the wine trade which specialises in well-matured wines. Their cellars (situated on the banks of the little Watteau River, not far from the church) contain priceless, mostly old, wines. Quality is top priority here, but prices are extremely high.
Michel Prunier
Superior wines from a small estate with modern equipment. Try the red Auxey-Duresses Clos du Val (which needs quite a few years' bottle-age) and the exquisite white Auxey-Duresses.
Roy Frères
With nearly 11ha, this is one of the largest properties in the district. Not all the wines are consistently successful, but the red Auxey-Duresses is reliable.
Dominique et Vincent Roy
A domaine covering 11ha. A good name, and recent vintages of the Clos du Val are especially recommended.

AUXEY-DURESSES

Leave Monthélie and head towards the D973. Turn right onto this road, travelling west towards Auxey-Duresses. Auxey-le-Petit and Melin also make up part of this commune.

The most important place in Auxey-Duresses is the church, whose clock tower has been declared a monument. Inside there is a triptych with depictions from the life of the Holy Virgin. The weather-beaten grey chapel of Auxey-le-Petit is also worth a visit. On the plateau of Mont Mélian, below Auxey-Duresses, lie the remains of a prehistoric settlement.

Due to its difficult name, sometimes rather reserved taste and modest production, red Auxey-Duresses is mostly sold simply as Côte de Beaune-Villages. The whites have more charm and quality, but less than half as much is made. The reds come from the west- and southwest-facing vineyards adjoining Volnay, while the whites come predominantly from the other side of the valley, closer to Meursault.

Right *The appreciation of wine in Burgundy can be surprisingly straightforward, even for the region's finest wines.*

SAINT-ROMAIN

A narrow, winding road leads from Auxey-Duresses to Saint-Romain, which has a high and low part: Saint-Romain-le-Haut situated a few dozen metres above Saint-Romain-le-Bas.

The upper village attracts quite a few visitors on Sunday afternoons as a local society has set out a nice walking track around the remains of the castle. The ruins themselves are not particularly impressive, but the views are wonderful.

A well-known barrel-maker, François Frères, lives here. He supplies the Domaine de la Romanée-Conti, the Hospices de Beaune, Domaine Leflaive and wineries in California and Oregon. If you look down the hill from le-Haut, you can see his oak staves stored in piles to weather. Also in the higher village is a 15th-century church with a Romanesque tower, a sloping nave and a sculpted pulpit dating from 1619. Archaeological finds from the surrounding caves prove people have lived near Saint-Romain since prehistoric times.

SAINT-ROMAIN

RESTAURANT
Hôtel-Restaurant Les Roches
Tel: 03 80 21 21 63
The service in this country hotel is friendly and the menus (starting at about FF100) consist of regional dishes (*coq au vin, poulet de Bresse aux morilles et à la crème*). There are a few simple rooms available.

RECOMMENDED PRODUCERS

Domaine d'Auvenay
One of the properties owned by Lalou Bize-Leroy. A small wine estate with excellent wines from all corners of the Côte d'Or. High prices.
Domaine Henri et Gilles Buisson
Gilles now runs this average-sized wine estate with more than 12ha, not only in Saint-Romain, but also in six other communes of the Côte de Beaune. Wines are of good average quality.
Domaine Germain Père & Fils
Son Patrick now runs the business. Improving every year. All white wines are now vinified in wood. Interesting estate.
Bernard Fèvre
Small property: reliable red Saint-Romain.
Alain Gras
Situated in Saint-Romian-le-Haut, produces whites and reds, with freshness and charm.
Guyot Père & Fils
Small, biodynamic wine estate. Thierry Guyot and his son-in-law Alain Lehais produce fine, slow-maturing wines.
Taupenot Père & Fils
Locally this is the fifth-largest estate. Very decent red and soft, fresh white Saint-Romain and Auxey-Duresses. The cellars store over 100,000 bottles from the last ten vintages.
Domaine René Thévenin-Monthelie & Fils
Delicious wines of great charm: white and red Saint-Romain, red Monthélie, red Beaune.

PLACES OF INTEREST

From Saint-Romain there are several attractive routes to La Rochepot. One of them passes the attractive village of Orches, built against the vertical rock face and known for its rosé.

MEURSAULT

HOTELS

Les Arts
Tel: 03 80 21 20 28
Spartan rooms, creaking floors, loud water pipes: a simple country hotel for guests who sleep soundly. Prices from about FF120. You can also eat well and inexpensively here.

Les Charmes
Tel: 03 80 21 63 53
Two styles of rooms here: light and modern or classic – all tastefully furnished. Friendly reception. Swimming pool. Prices at about FF430.

Les Magnolias
Tel: 03 80 21 23 23
Beautiful hotel in renovated, 18th-century building opposite Domaine Prieur. 12 rooms (starting at FF420).

Le Mont Mélian
Tel: 03 80 21 64 90
In the centre of Meursault. 12 light, rustic rooms with bathrooms. Free bicycles and maps of cycling routes. Prices about FF275.

RESTAURANTS

Hôtel du Centre
Tel: 03 80 21 20 75
Affordable, regional dishes. Menus begin under FF100. Also a few rooms available.

Relais de la Diligence
Tel: 03 80 21 21 32
A large restaurant, a few km from the village centre. Offers a variety of menus from around FF80, including dishes such as *aiguillette de boeuf à la moutarde ancienne.*

Above *Meursault produces highly distinctive white wines. Surprisingly, none of its vineyards has been recognised as a Grand Cru – despite the often unsurpassable level of quality from the top Premiers Crus.*
Left *Traditional wicker paniers once used to be used for the harvest. Buckets or plastic paniers are now de rigueur, being kinder to the grapes.*

Right *The ancient art of cooperage remains a highly respected craft. This cooper, based in Saint-Romain, has illustrious clients from all over the world.*

The town hall houses a small exhibition of them. This was practically a forgotten wine village until Roland Thévenin became mayor. His promotional activities included exhibiting wines at the exchange in Dijon in 1962 under the theme 'Mon Village'. For a long time this was used on labels, folders and signposts. You still see it on a few road signs.

The red wines of Saint-Romain belong to the lighter types of burgundy and commonly have a fruity, cherry-like taste and agreeable suppleness. Again, the white is not especially full, but it certainly has plenty of fresh, juicy fruit and is in general somewhat higher in quality than the red.

MEURSAULT

To reach Meursault, you need to retrace your steps through Auxey-Duresses on the D973. Then, where the road forks, take the right turn (the D17E) into Meursault.

Anyone visiting Meursault can see immediately that it's a wine village by the signs the winegrowers hang on the front of their houses. Nearly every building along the long street that leads out of the village towards Puligny is decorated in this way. This is typical of Meursault – it is one of the most energetic villages of the Côte d'Or, holding many wine events, including the Paulée de Meursault on the third Monday in November: a six-course afternoon meal in the *cuverie* of Château de Meursault. There is a similar festival and tasting session, the Banée de Meursault, in September.

White wines are in the majority here – there are ten times as many as reds – and it is these that have given Meursault international fame. They have a fine, almost buttery taste, hints of ripe, sun-drenched fruits, nuts and toasted bread, and the acidity to remain fresh for decades. Meursault has no Grand Cru vineyards; the best wines come from six Premier Cru sites: Les Perrières, Les Genevrières, Les Poruzots, Les Charmes (the largest), La Gouttes d'Or and Les Bouchères.

The Château de Meursault is the main feature here. It has a wine-theme art exhibition, and offers plenty of opportunities to taste its marvellous wines. There is another castle in the the village. It has a fine multicoloured roof and today functions as the town hall. It looks out over the 14th-century church Saint-Nicolas, with its striking, Gothic spire.

RECOMMENDED PRODUCERS

Robert Ampeau et Fils
Leading estate, with stylish wines of intense fruit and elegant balance: Meursault, Puligny-Montrachet, Beaune, Pommard and Savigny-lès-Beaune.

Raymond Ballot-Millot & Fils
Fairly large estate with some 20 high quality wines, including 5 Meursaults (brilliant Premiers Crus), 2 white Chassagne-Montrachets, 3 Pommards.

Pierre Boillot
Excellent white Charmes and red Volnay.

A Buisson-Battault
Owns land in 4 Premiers Crus: excellent wines, very good Meursault.

Domaine des Comtes Lafon
Painstakingly nurtured wines: both the white (6 Meursaults and a Montrachet) and reds (3 Volnays) are near-perfect.

François Jobard
Aristocratic wines, leanly refined in youth, maturing very slowly. Buy here only if you have a cellar to store them in for years.

Château de Meursault
Wines made at the castle: excellent quality; even ordinary burgundies are delightful. Well worth a visit.

Michelot-Buisson
Classic Meursaults. Various family members have their own labels.

Raymond Millot & Fils
Attractive Meursaults, full of nuances. Also a good Puligny-Montrachet.

Domaine Jean Monnier et Fils
Beautiful, rather firm Meursaults with a slightly nutty taste, and a hint of toast in the aftertaste.

Domaine René Monnier
Extensive estate with excellent red and white wines. The whites need bottle-age to lose some of their acidity.

Pierre Morey
Great wines with wonderful bouquet and complexity: Bâtard-Montrachet, Meursault-Perrières, Meursault-Tessons, Meursault.

Domaine Jacques Prieur
Many Côte d'Or gems: Chambertin, Chambertin-Clos de Bèze, Musigny, Clos de Vougeot, Volnay Santenots, Meursaults-Perrières, Puligny-Montrachet Les Combettes, Chevalier-Montrachet, Montrachet.

Ropiteau Frères
Négociant with tasting cellars in Meursault itself and offices beside the *route nationale*.

PLACES OF INTEREST

The hamlet of l'Hôpital de Meursault (along the *route nationale*) is organised well for visitors, with tasting rooms and hospitable restaurants. Its name derives from a leper colony founded in 1180 whose portal, though now half buried, can still be seen. There is also a weekly market on Fridays.

Chagny

Croix
Nudant
le
Buisson
Certaut
D113b

Meursault

les Pelles -
Dessous

le Limozin

les Charmes
Dessous

les Charmes
Dessous

les
Charmes

les
Levrons

la
Rousselle

les Charmes
Dessous

les Referts

les
Perrières

les Porusot
Dessous

les
Crotots

les
Genevrières
Dessous

les Charmes - Dessus

les
Combettes

Cl. de
Mazeray

Terres

le Porusot

les
Porusot
Dessus

les
Genevrières
Dessus

Cl. des
Perrières

les
Perrières
Dessous

les
Perrières
Dessous

Champ

Canet

les
Gouttes
d'Or

les Bouchères

les Chaumes
de Narvaux

aux Perrières

les
Perrières
Dessus

les
Chalumeaux

la Trut

les Gds.
Charrons

Chaumes des Narvaux

les Narveaux
Dessous

Sous le dos
d'Âne

Chaumes des
Casse-Têtes

les Narvaux
Dessus

les
Casse-Têtes

les Gorges
de Narvaux

les Chaumes

la Pièce
sous le Bois

Blagny

le
Jesson

les Tillets

les Clous
Dessus

les Ravelles

le Bois de Blagny

la
Jeunelotte

les Clous
Dessous

Montagne du Chatelet
de Montmellian

les
Vireuils
Dessous

les
Vireuls
Dessus

N

PULIGNY-MONTRACHET

Drive south out of Meursault on the D113-b and, after about 2kms, passing Premier Cru vineyards Les Charmes Dessous and Les Charmes Dessus, you will arrive in Puligny.

Without prior knowledge, no one would suspect that Puligny-Montrachet produces some of the world's greatest and most expensive white wines because the village itself has no allure. Its ordinary streets come out onto two squares and the only notable building is Château de Puligny-Montrachet (visitors are welcome and wine can be tasted). The village church is worth a brief visit for its marvellous choir stalls.

But despite its rather plain appearance, no trip can be complete without visiting this village. The true greatness of Puligny-Montrachet is not found above ground, but in the soil, which is perfectly suited to Chardonnay grapes. Natural factors result in a truly brilliant white wine: aromatic, full of peach and apricot flavours and great complexity. Alexandre Dumas (1802–70) believed that the top wine, Le Montrachet, should be drunk 'on your knees and with bared head'; another compared the bouquet to singing in a Gothic cathedral; in fact nobody disputes its place today as potentially the greatest white wine of Burgundy. It should never be drunk before it has aged at least eight years in bottle.

The Le Montrachet vineyard is marked by small gates, and is surrounded by the village's three other Grand Cru

Below Chassagne-Montrachet and the similarly unassuming-looking Puligny-Montrachet produce some of the world's most glamorous wines.

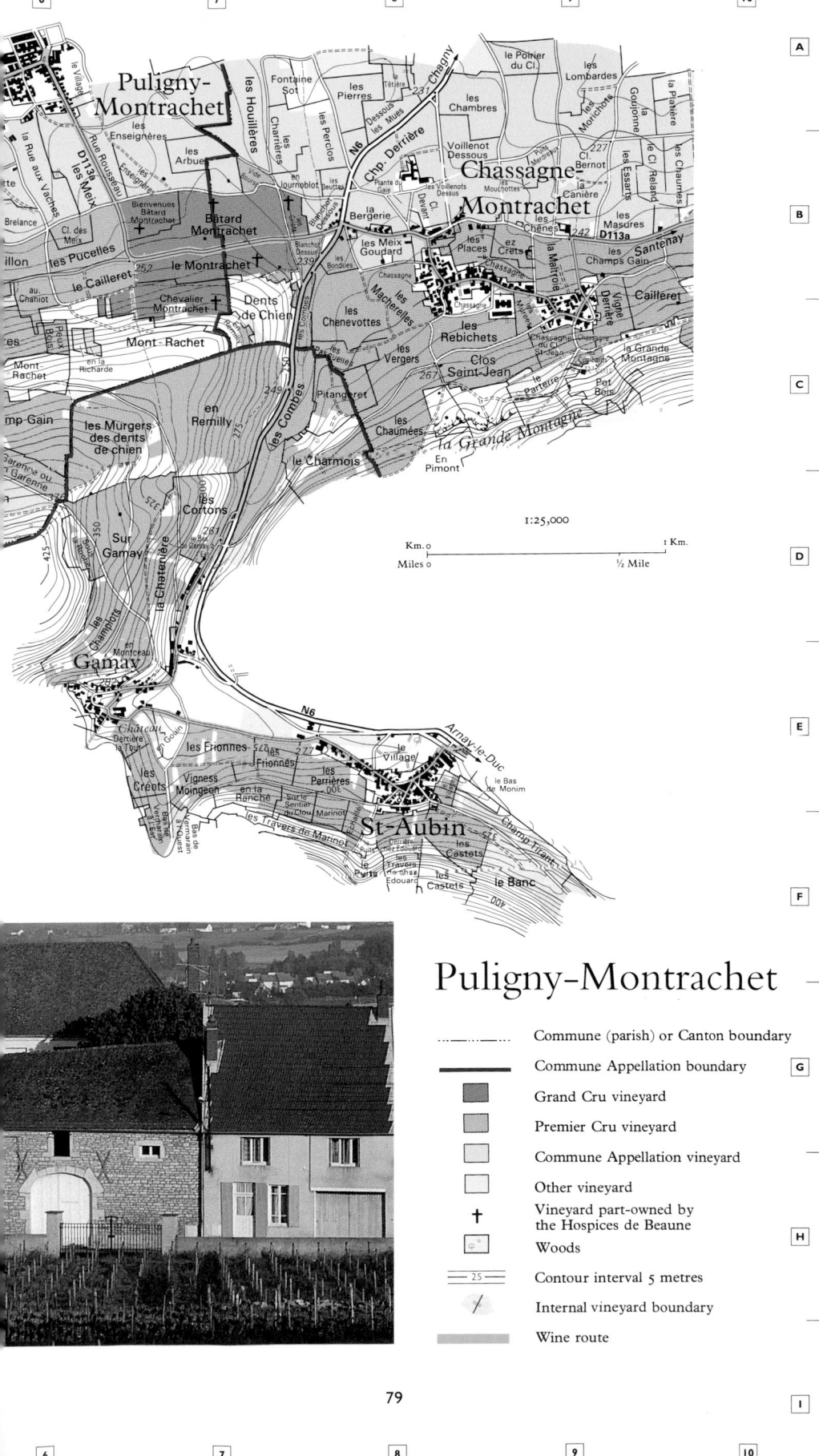

A

le Poirier
du Cl.
les
Lombardes

Puligny-
Montrachet
les
Enseignères
Fontaine
Sot
les
Pierres
Tétières
les
Chaumes
la Pièrre
la Goujonne
les
Monchots
Cl.
Reland
les
Essarts

les
Houillères
les
Charrières
les Perclos
les Mues
Dessous
Chp. Derrière
les
Chambres
Voillenot
Dessous
Cl.
Bernot
227

les
Arbues
en
Journoblot
les Beuttes
Plante de
Gain
Chassagne-
Montrachet
la
Canière

D113a
Rue Rousseau
Enseignères
Bienvenues
Bâtard
Montrachet
Bâtard
Montrachet
Blanchot
Dessous
la
Bergerie
les Voillenots
Dessus
Mouchottes
les
Chênes
242 D113a
les
Masdres
Santenay

B

les Pucelles
252
le Montrachet
les
Bondues
les Meix
Goudard
Chassagne
les
Places
ez
Crets
la Maltroie
Champs Gain
Cailleret

le Cailleret
Chevalier
Montrachet
Dents
de Chien
les
Chenevottes
les
Macherelles
Chassagne
Vigne
Derrière

Mont-Rachet
en la
Richarde
les
Rebichets
Chassagne
du Cl.
St-Jean
la Grande
Montagne

Mont
Rachet
les
Vergers
Clos
Saint-Jean
267
le
Partière
Pot
Bois

C

mp-Gain
les Murgers
des dents
de chien
en
Remilly
275
les
Combes
les
Chaumées
la Grande Montagne

Pitangeret
le Charmois
En
Pimont

les
Cortons
287

Sur
Gamay
la Chatenière
1:25,000

Km. 0   1 Km.
Miles 0   ½ Mile

D

425
les Champlots
en
Montceau
Gamay

Château
Derrière
la Tour
Golin
les Frionnes
les
Frionnes
le
Village
Arnav-le-Duc

E

les
Crêts
Vignes
Moingeon
en la
Ranché
sur le
Sentier
du Clou
Marinot
les
Perrières
le Bas
de Monim

Bas de
Vermarain
à l'Ouest
les Travers de Marinot
St-Aubin
Champ Tirant

les
Castets

le
Puits
les
Travers
de chez
Edouard
les
Castets
le Banc

F

Puligny–Montrachet

G

H

I

PULIGNY-MONTRACHET

RESTAURANTS

Le Montrachet
Tel: 03 80 21 30 06
Regional and inventive modern dishes from about FF200. Also a marvellous collection of burgundies and often terrific Aligoté. 30 rooms too, with old rustic furniture, from about FF525.

La Table d'Olivier Leflaive
Tel: 03 80 21 37 65
The dynamic Olivier Leflaive has a lunchtime restaurant on the Place du Monument. Specialises in regional dishes and you can also taste many wines. Two formulas: the first with 7 wines (FF190) and the second with 12 wines (FF250). Open from 1 March to 1 December.

RECOMMENDED PRODUCERS

Louis Carillon & Fils
Established 1632, with cellars in a house of stones from the old château. It is said that during the revolution the *curé* of Puligny hid here: his makeshift confessional and his escape route still remain. Expertly run, with excellent Puligny-Montrachet Premiers Crus.

Chartron et Trébuchet
A *négociant* founded in 1984, which has strict quality controls for its excellent Grand Cru vineyard sites.

Domaine Leflaive
The most respected Puligny estate, with white wines of rich complexity, style and sensuality. The range includes Montrachets, marvellous Premiers Crus, an excellent commune wine and an attractive red Blagny. Also uses biodynamic methods.

Olivier Leflaive Frères
Small, successful *négociant* founded due to demand for Leflaive wines becoming greater than supply. Buying grapes in from other growers, vinifying and maturing.

Domaine Etienne Sauzet
Sublime whites with depth and distinction: among the very best of the village.

sites: Chevalier-, Bâtard- and Bienvenues-Bâtard-Montrachet. The first of these produces wines famous for their finesse and elegance; the second for richer, fatter wines; the third for less weighty but still amazingly complex wines.

Nestling above Puligny-Montrachet is the hamlet of Blagny. The walk there is very pleasant, with a fine view of Puligny as well as Meursault on arrival. Blagny is also surrounded by Premier Cru vineyards, yielding slightly more austere wines.

CHASSAGNE-MONTRACHET

The peace of present-day Chassagne-Montrachet belies its bloody history. In the 15th century, John of Chalon, Prince of Orange, decided to oppose Louis XI. As a result, the king proclaimed that the prince must hang and that all his possessions should be burnt. After a series of skirmishes, John retreated to the château of Chassagne, then had to flee for safety, abandoning Chassagne unprotected. The king's soldiers began to plunder and murder, and the village and its château went up in flames. The inhabitants thus received the nickname 'the crushed'. Here and there, among the narrow, winding streets, you can still find an old well or a part of a wall from the vanished castle.

The village of Chassagne added the name of its most famous vineyard to its own on the same day as neighbouring Puligny did the same. Thus, on November 27, 1879, Chassagne became Chassagne-Montrachet. It also owns part

Far left The neat lines of a vineyard in Puligny-Montrachet. Left Old buildings, such as this, evoke the timelessness of the area.

CHASSAGNE-MONTRACHET

HOTEL

Chambres d'Hôtes du Domaine Bouzereau-Gruère
Tel: 03 80 21 96 96
This winegrowing estate, situated in Meursault, has a caveau near the bascule. You can also taste and buy wine here. On the first floor are 3 charming, comfortable rooms which are let as chambres d'hôtes. FF250 for 2 people, including breakfast.

RESTAURANT

Le Chassagne
Tel: 03 80 21 94 94
Food is light and creative, with beautiful regional dishes. Menus from FF110. Attractive wine list.

RECOMMENDED PRODUCERS

Domaine Guy Amiot-Bonfils
Try the white Chassagne les Caillerets and les Vergers, the white Puligny les Demoiselles, the red Chassagne les Clos St-Jean and majestic Montrachet.

of Bâtard-Montrachet and all of the tiny Grand Cru, Criots-Bâtard-Montrachet.

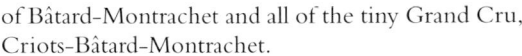

Besides these Grands Crus, which produce brilliant, richly concentrated, complex white wines, the wines from the Premiers Crus of this commune can also offer impressive depth and distinction.

In contrast to Puligny, Chassagne produces more red than white wine, and, if they do not reach the exalted level of the whites, Chassagne reds can be richly coloured, smooth-drinking wines of quality.

SAINT-AUBIN AND GAMAY

Follow the D113-b west out of Puligny-Montrachet, turn south (past the Grands Crus vines of Bâtard- and Le Montrachet) to the N6. Head right for Saint-Aubin.

Saint-Aubin's central feature is its church, with its striking, grey-stoned clock tower, and there is also a castle (built in 1850) now used as a cellar for maturing wines.

White Saint-Aubins have an agreeable hazelnut aroma and soft freshness with, occasionally, some finesse. They are a good-quality alternative to more expensive burgundies. Reds tend to be firm, with a touch of rustic earthiness.

If you keep going through the village you will reach the hamlet of Gamay, dominated by the weather-beaten, grey château of the Seigneur Du May, who, legend says, brought the Gamay grape back from the crusades.

Blain-Gagnard
Small estate with distinguished Caillerets, Morgeot, Criots-Bâtard-Montrachet, Bâtard-Montrachet and Montrachet.
Jean-Noël Gagnard
A prime source for great white burgundies.
Marc Morey
Pure white burgundies with elegant firmness. Red Caillerets is also delicious.
Michel Niellon
Sublime, but rare Grands Crus and splendid Les Vergers.
Paul Pillot
Sumptuously appealing, fruity white Premiers Crus.

SANTENAY

There are two roads that lead south out of Chassagne-
Montrachet, and you can take either to reach Santenay. You
will pass the Premier Cru vineyards of Chassagne-Montrachet
– Les Fairendes and Les Petits Clos on the right and Morgeot
on the left – and then the Premier Cru vineyards belonging
to Santenay: Les Gravières and Passetemps on the right, and
on the hillside behind, La Comme and Beauregard.

Just like Chassagne-Montrachet, Santenay is made up of
a higher and lower village part, although these two are much
further away from each other. The first to be approached is
Santenay-le-Bas, which is the largest section of the village.

Before it was famous for its wine, Santenay was better
known for its water; medicinal spring waters were found
here in Roman times and are still used today. In fact, the
village was formerly called Santenay-lès-Bains. It is said that
the water has healing qualities, helping rheumatism, among
others things. Because of this, it has the status of a health
resort and, under an idiosyncratic French law, it is therefore
allowed a casino! Thus Santenay has the only gambling
palace in the whole of the Côte d'Or.

Right *Dezize-lès-Maranges,*
although in the Côte de Beaune,
is not in the Côte d'Or, but in the
département of Saône-et-Loire.

Santenay

·····—·····—	Commune (parish) or Canton boundary
▬▬▬▬	Commune Appellation boundary
▨	Premier Cru vineyard
▢	Commune Appellation vineyard
▢	Other vineyard
▢	Woods
═ 25 ═	Contour interval 5 metres
╱	Internal vineyard boundary
▬▬▬	Wine route

Domaine Ramonet
Top Chassagne estate: fantastic whites, from local to Montrachet, and exceptional red Clos de la Boudriotte and Clos Saint-Jean.

ST AUBIN

RECOMMENDED PRODUCERS
Jean-Claude Bachelet
In Gamay, this small producer makes showpiece Bienvenues-Bâtard-Montrachet.
Raoul Clerget
Distinctive white Saint-Aubin Le Charmois and white and red Saint-Aubin Les Frionnes.
Marc Colin
Gamay grower with delicious white Premiers Crus from St-Aubin and Chassagne-Montrachet, also Le Montrachet.

SANTENAY

RESTAURANTS
L'Ouillette
Tel: 03 80 20 62 34
An established name in Santenay. People from the village and its surroundings come to enjoy regional dishes such as fillet of perch in Aligoté sauce, *coq au vin* and *entrecôte grillée*. Menus from about FF80.
Le Terroir
Tel: 03 80 20 63 47
Next to L'Ouillette, on the village square. Pleasant interior, good service and dishes somewhat less conventional than its

neighbour's. Thus, there is always a fresh fish of the day, and sometimes pasta. Menu prices start at about FF85, on weekday lunchtimes.

RECOMMENDED PRODUCERS
Adrien Belland
Medium-sized domaine producing robust, reliable reds. Successful Santenay, and Grands Crus such as Corton and Chambertin.
Domaine Roger Belland
With 23ha, this is one of the most important local producers. Roger has taken over from his father Joseph Belland.

In Santenay-le-Bas you can visit two interesting castles. Château Philippe le Hardi derives its name from the first duke of Burgundy (Philip the Bold) and has a massive, 14th-century tower. It houses a wine museum, and wine is made in its ultra-modern *cuverie*. Not far from the large village square is the Château du Passe-Temps. Its cellars go down as deep as ten metres and are the largest of the Côte d'Or.

Santenay-le-Haut is just 1km away and there is a pleasant walk through gently sloping vineyards to reach it. Close by is the hamlet of Saint-Jean.

Directly behind Saint-Jean rise the steep cliffs which surround the entire commune on the west side. In fact, the underlying geology of this part of the Côte is complex, with faults breaking up the smooth sequence of the strata. Consequently the soil in Santenay is very varied, enabling it to produce many different styles of wine, mostly red. A local saying states that the best vineyards of the commune lie 'east of the belfry', and it is there that most of the Premiers Crus are found – Les Gravières, La Comme and Clos de Tavanne. Les Gravières, with its heavy, stony soil is the best known, while Clos de Tavanne has a name for solid, reserved wines.

La Comme, further up the slope, has lighter soil and produces a correspondingly lighter style of wine.

Red Santenay is a rather reserved burgundy style with firm structure, modest finesse and complexity. Some of the wines can be excellent and mature into fine bottles.

MARANGES

As you travel up from Santenay to the Hautes-Côtes, you will pass through at least two of the three villages which make up the appellation of Maranges. Created in 1989, this appellation sits just outside the *département* of Côte d'Or, but still belongs to the wine district of the same name. The villages are (north to south) Dezize-lès-Maranges, Sampigny lès Maranges and Cheilly-lès-Maranges.

The small village of Dezize is clustered around a crossroads and its pretty Romanesque church lies close by. The road from here winds downwards to Sampigny-lès-Maranges which nestles in a small, wooded valley, fringed by dramatic rock formations – more and more of them as you travel south. Cheilly-lès-Maranges, stretching out across the low hills, is surrounded by vineyards and lush pastures. The hamlet of Mercey, a few kilometres away, also belongs to this commune.

The best Maranges wines, mainly red, are strong-flavoured with good colour and fruit (they were once used to beef up lighter Côte de Beaune-Villages blends). They can be of good quality and are generally reasonably priced.

although the latter's name is still mentioned on certain labels.

Michel Clair
Respected, sturdily-structured wines.

Vincent Girardin
Medium-sized, dynamically-run estate. Showpiece wine is the exclusive Clos de la Confrérie. Santenay Premier Cru Maladière is also highly praiseworthy. Plus glorious whites, eg the Chassagne-Morgeot, and the luscious Savigny-lès-Beaune-Les Vermots with complex wood flavours.

Jessiaume Père & Fils
Traditional wines, powerful and rich in tannin.

Domaine Lequin-Rousset
Award-winning reds, offering good balance between fruit and tannin.

Prosper Maufoux
Expertly managed wine establishment on the village square, owned, since 1994, by an American importer, Robert Fairchild. Generally, whites are of better quality than reds. Clos des Gravières is delicious.

Jean Moreau/Domaine de la Buissière
One of the best producers of Santenay. Well-rounded reds with colour, tannin, fruit and suppleness – try the Santenay-Clos des Mouches.

Mestre Père & Fils
Large property with distinctive red wines from various Santenay Premiers Crus as well as wines from other communes.

Domaine Prieur-Brunet
Juicy, supple reds and fine white Premiers Crus from Meursault. The cellars (with a small wine museum) are also worth a visit.

Lucien Muzard et Fils
Large wine estate run by Claude en Hervé Muzard.

MARANGES

RECOMMENDED PRODUCERS

Domaine Bachelet & Ses Fils (Dezize)
Large estate – the largest owner of Maranges Premiers Crus. 20 different wines, from the Côte de Beaune and the Côte de Nuits. Usually good, fruity reds.

La Cave de Cheilly (Cheilly)
This estate produces engaging wines, including a Maranges Premier Cru.

Maurice Charleux (Dezize)
Traditional estate. Fresh, red wines.

Domaine du Château de Mercey (Cheilly)
A respected estate with fresh whites (Aligoté, Hautes-Côtes de Beaune and Mercurey) and smooth, refined reds (Hautes-Côtes de Beaune, Mercurey and Santenay). Part-owned by Antonin Rodet in Mercurey, who is currently experimenting to improve the wines.

Domaine Fernand Chevrot (Cheilly)
Situated in a large farm above the village. Fine source of modestly-priced, attractive red and white wines, including Cheilly-lès-Maranges and Santenay-Clos Rousseau. It has a fine 18th-century cellar, and you are sure to experience a friendly welcome.

Yvon et Chantal Contat-Grangé (Dezize)
This couple come from Annecy in Haute Savoie. They started renting their vines in

Far left A traditional vertical press. Horizontal pneumatic presses are used nowadays and tend to be more gentle on the grapes.

Left and above Images of Santenay and Maranges, communes producing a range of generally reasonably priced wines.

1980 and now have a modern business with fine red and white Maranges.

René Martin (Cheilly)
Although situated in Cheilly, Martin makes a flavoursome red wine from Sampigny.

HAUTES-COTES DE BEAUNE

RESTAURANTS

Chez Denise
Evelle
Tel: 03 80 21 70 38
Denise Lagelée cooks in a homely way; tasty regional dishes in an unpretentious, cosy ambiance. All this can be had for less than FF100 a menu. An address to cherish.

Hôtel Sainte-Marie
Nolay
Tel: 03 80 21 73 19
Country dishes, friendly service. Also hotel, but can be noisy.

Below A view of La Rochepot, the main town of the Hautes-Côtes. It is worth visiting if only to see its magnificent castle.

HAUTES-COTES DE BEAUNE

The vineyards of the Hautes-Côtes de Beaune lie on the hillside slopes above the Côte d'Or just south of Beaune. Here, instead of the well-regimented lines of immaculately pruned vines, you see the rather spindly, more untidy Aligoté and Gamay grape varieties which are more suited to the less hospitable soil and climate here. The grapes ripen quicker in the Hautes-Côtes de Beaune than in the Hautes-Côtes de Nuits, and the resulting wines are somewhat sturdier.

To visit the charming villages of the Hautes-Côtes takes only half a day, although there are many delightful picnic spots if you can afford a more leisurely pace. From Santenay you can follow the signs up to small villages such as Dezize-lès-Maranges and then to the top of the Montagne des Trois Croix where there are stunning views of the Côte d'Or and Chalonnais. From here the road continues through the villages of Sampigny-lès-Maranges and Change, then on towards Nolay. This is the quieter, less commercial side of Burgundy. Extremely rural, time seems to matter less here and prices for the wines are much more reasonable than further down

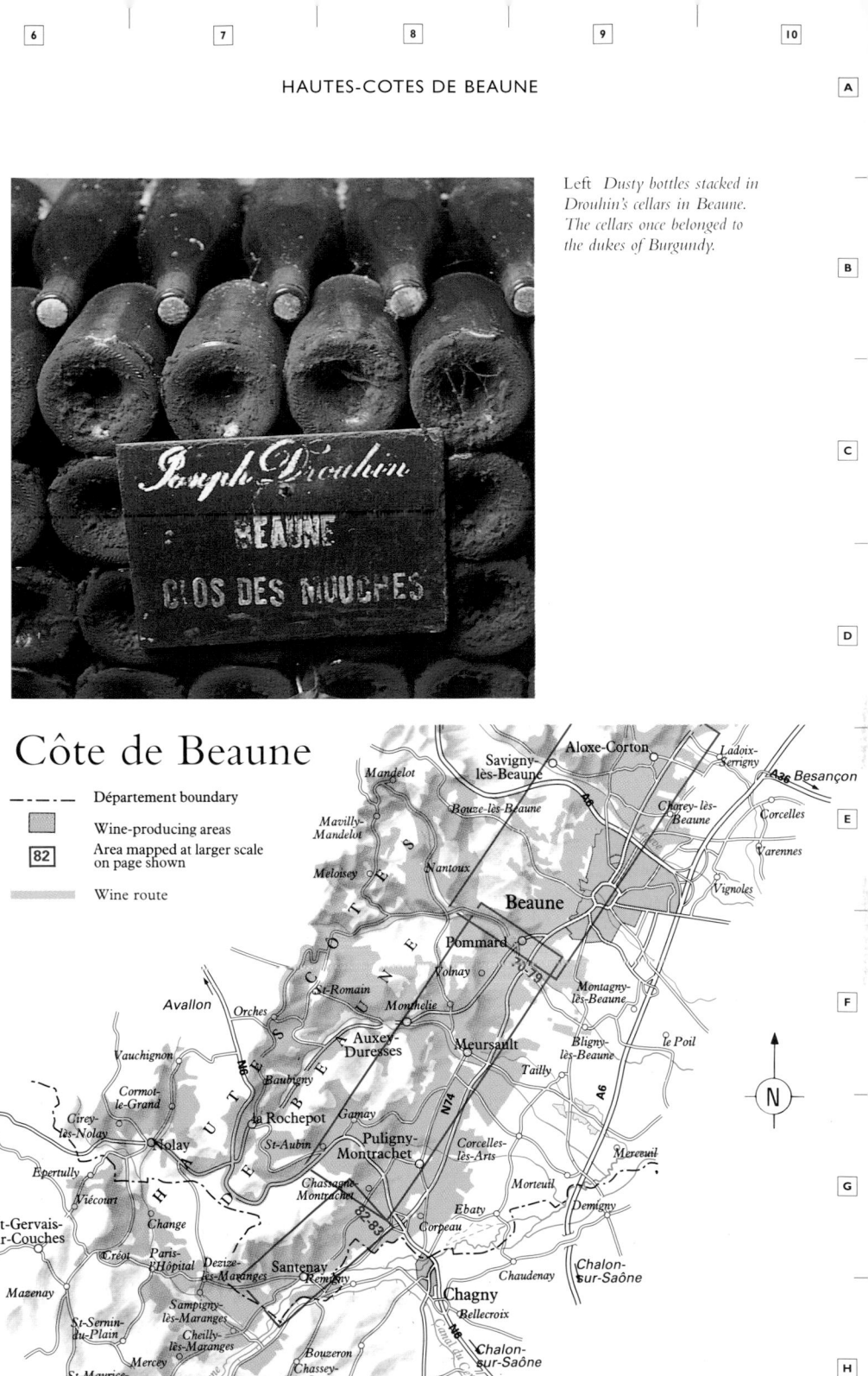

Left *Dusty bottles stacked in Drouhin's cellars in Beaune. The cellars once belonged to the dukes of Burgundy.*

Côte de Beaune

— · — · — Département boundary

Wine-producing areas

82 Area mapped at larger scale on page shown

Wine route

1:220,000

Left *Views of La Rochepot: the Café de France in the town centre and picking blackcurrants near the château, for the production of Crème de Cassis.*

La Bouzerotte
Bouze-lès-Beaune
Tel: 03 80 26 01 37
Surprisingly fun little restaurant which serves excellent food – regional and sophisticated at the same time. Lunch menu FF90, other menus from FF110. Good wine list. An address to remember.

Le Burgonde
Nolay
Tel: 03 80 21 71 25
Pleasant bistro, set in an old shop. Striking orange-pink façade in the high street. Menus from FF100. The wine list only includes burgundy.

Auberge du Vieux Pressoir
Évelle
Tel: 03 80 21 82 16
Delicious fine cooking (*cuisine de terroir*) in a tiny little village between La Rochepot and Saint-Romain. Menu de la Colline FF100.

RECOMMENDED PRODUCERS

Domaine François Charles & Fils (Nantoux)
Good Hautes-Côtes, but also a Beaune Les Epenottes and a Volnay Les Fremiets.

Guillemard Dupont & Ses Fils (Meloisey)
Wines of above-average quality, some whites bottled *sur lie*.

Domaine Fouquerand Père & Fils (La Rochepot)
At the foot of the local castle: good red and white Hautes-Côtes de Beaune, as well as Volnays and a Santenay-Comme.

Domaine Lucien Jacob (Echevronne)
Large, sound estate with red Hautes-Côtes de Beaune, Savigny-lès-Beaune, Savigny-Vergelesses.

Domaine Joliot (Nantoux)
Mainly reds, but white Aligoté has merit. Blackcurrant Hautes-Côtes de Beaune, plus Beaune Boucherottes and Pommard.

Mazilly Père & Fils (Meloisey)
Mazilly is a dynamic figure; he makes three kinds of red and a lovely Beaune Les Vignes Franches.

Parigot Père & Fils (Meloisey)
Range of excellent wines: Bourgogne Aligoté, Meursault les Vireuilles-Dessous, red Hautes-Côtes de Beaune, Beaune Grèves and Pommard.

PLACES OF INTEREST

In various villages of the Hautes-Côtes de Beaune and in Saint-Romain there are well-signed walking routes.

the hillside. Change is a pretty village with its oak-beamed market hall being particularly appealing. Nolay is also charming: half-timbered houses, a church with a striking stone spire and a 14th-century market hall (Place Monge). Nearby is the statue of Lazare Carnot, 'the organiser of the conquest' during the French Revolution. Not far from the village is the spectacular Gorge du Bout du Monde, at the end of the ravine Falaises de Cormot. Here, dramatic sheer cliffs look down over a stream running along the valley floor and a spectacular 30-metre waterfall. To get there, take the road from Nolay which runs north to Vauchignon and the ravine.

From Nolay, the D973 continues to La Rochepot, dominated by the magnificent Château de la Rochepot. Built in the 15th century, this was almost totally destroyed during the revolution, and was fully restored in the original style by the French president, Sadi Carnot, last century. It has six pepper-pot towers, a Chinese room and a Gothic chapel. Near the entrance, a local farmer offers his wines to be tasted.

The route now continues to Orches, a village set against a stunning backdrop of dramatic rock formations. From the top of the cliff here, if the weather is good, you can look down on the village of Saint-Romain, the valley leading down to Meursault, the plain of the Saône, the Jura Mountains and, if it is a very clear day, Mont Blanc. Here also, above the village, is a small well with a few Gallo-Roman gravestones nearby. Grape growers at Orches make a quite pleasant, delicate rosé wine as well as Poire William distilled from fruit grown in the local orchards.

Now take the narrow road to the winegrowers' village of Meloisey, with its monumental church tower. Follow the road to Mavilly-Mandelot and Mandelot with its 16th-century castle. Finally, head towards Pommard, with a stop in Nantoux, known for its good wines and its 15th-century church.

The Côte Chalonnaise

Just south of Santenay, the Côte d'Or comes to an end, but Burgundy by no means finishes here. Continue on to the next belt of vines, the Côte Chalonnaise, which takes its name from the town of Chalon to the east. Its northern anchor-point is the lovely town of Chagny.

Even though the Côte Chalonnaise is a direct continuation of the Côte d'Or, the landscape is entirely different. Vineyards mingle here with many other crops, there are fields filled with goats and white Charolais cattle, interspersed with woods. Vineyards are found throughout this charming, leafy and sleepy region.

The wines from the Chalonnais are less famous than those of the Côte d'Or. This is because most of the wine produced in this district has historically been sold as straight Bourgogne without any other regional reference. But the Chalonnais now has five appellations of its own. Four of these are connected to communes or groups of communes. They are, from north to south, Bouzeron, Rully, Mercurey (by far the largest), Givry and Montagny.

A good place to start discovering Chalonnaise wines is the Maison des Vins de la Côte Chalonnaise in the city of Chalon-sur-Saône. Although Chalon is not actually within the wine district, the Maison des Vins holds wines from all over the region, and you can both taste and buy wine here. The best white wines from the Chalonnaise are made with Chardonnay and the reds with Pinot Noir, although Aligoté thrives well on this terrain; much of it is used to make Bourgogne Côte Chalonnaise. This appellation was created as recently as 1989 and can be used on the labels of red and white burgundies from the 44 specified communes dotted around the main villages – if they attain the high quality standards demanded by the tasting panel. The quality of Bourgogne Côte Chalonnaise is such that it is rapidly gaining a good reputation.

Winemakers in the Chalonnais, particularly around the village of Rully, also produce some excellent Crémants de Bourgogne, as well as Bourgogne Passe-Tout-Grains – a red wine made from a mixture of Pinot Noir and Gamay.

Left *These vines in Montagny, at the southernmost end of the Côte Chalonnaise, produce white wines of good body and refreshing acidity.*

Above *A country lane running alongside vineyards. Beautiful rural sights like this become more frequent as you travel further south.*

NORTHERN CHALONNAIS

Leaving Santenay and travelling in an easterly direction, you will reach the largest city in northern Chalonnais – Chagny. This is really an industrial town and so much so that only once a year is the emphasis on wine. That is during the wine exchange which takes place in the middle of August.

Chagny does, however, have some attractive old buildings well worth visiting in the centre of town. These include, on the corner of the Rue de la République and Rue de la Boutière, a stunning large house dating from the Middle Ages. Additionally, behind the town hall there is a peaceful garden with old wells and some ruins, while in a chapel of the sober Cistercian church, a copy of the cave of Lourdes has been made.

Below *This old house surrounded by colourful plants is typical of the region's sleepy, timeless character.*

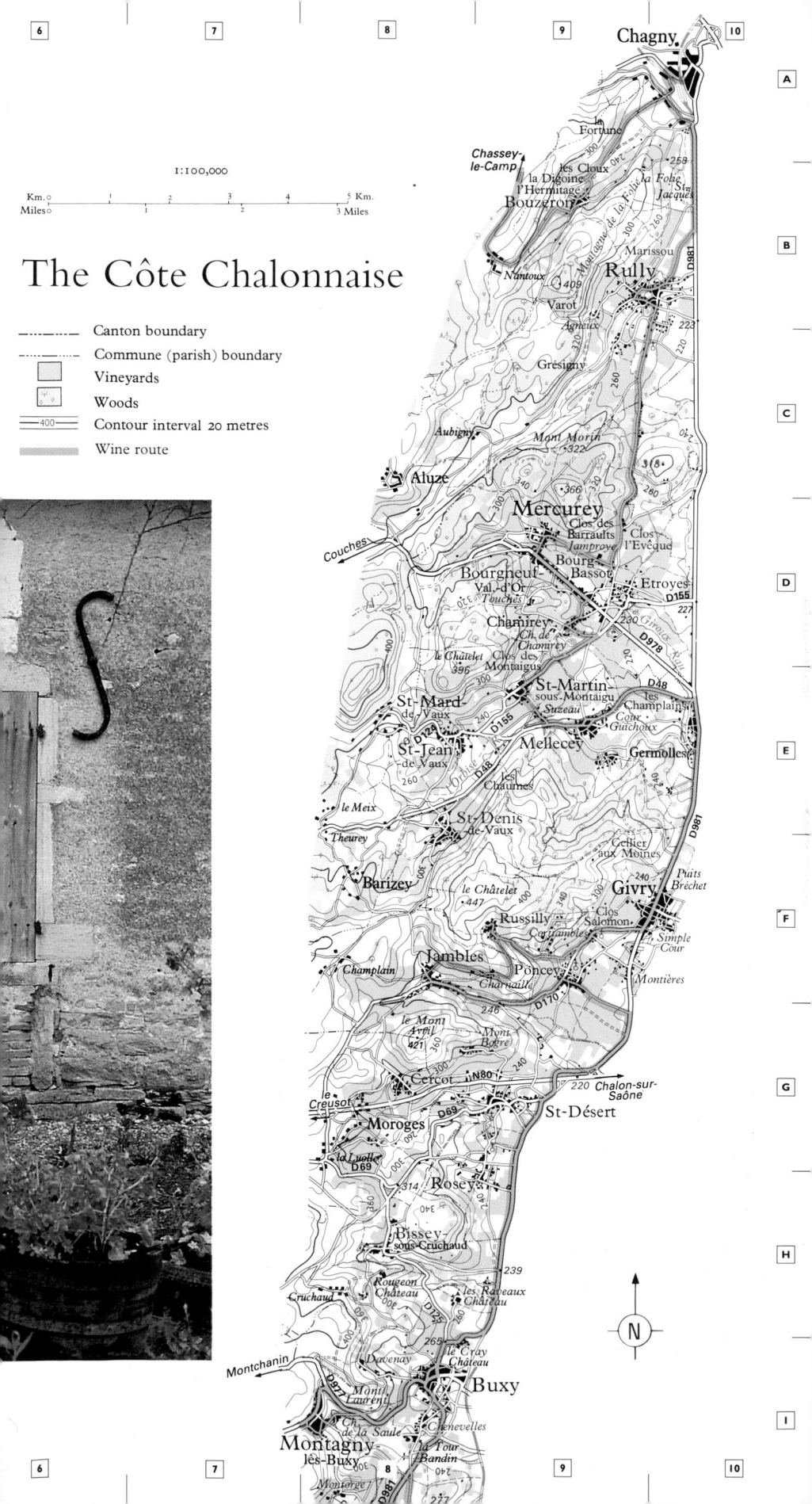

BOUZERON

HOTELS

Auberge du Camp Romain
Chassey-le-Camp
Tel: 03 85 87 09 91
Peaceful hotel with views across the valley.
Simply, but comfortably furnished. The
restaurant cuisine is rather traditional
(starting at about FF125 for a menu).
Rooms start at approximately FF300.
Swimming pool.
Hostellerie du Château de Bellecroix
Chagny
Tel: 03 85 87 13 86
Luxurious accommodation in an ivy-
bedecked castle. Rooms start at about
FF600 – try to book one in one of the
towers. Excellent restaurant with menus
starting at around FF200. Swimming pool.

RESTAURANTS

Lameloise
Chagny
Tel: 03 85 87 08 85
Michelin-starred restaurant, fantastic
cooking and sublime wine. Menus start at
FF400. Also a hotel. Prices from FF750.
Relais Gaulois
Nantoux
Tel: 03 85 87 33 00
Country inn on a hill. Regional dishes with
menus starting at under FF100.

RECOMMENDED PRODUCERS

Chanzy Frères Domaine de l'Hermitage (Bouzeron)
This estate, founded in 1974, is among the
best in the Chalonnais. The whites from
the Clos de la Fortune are admirable.
A et P de Villaine (Bouzeron)
Aubert de Villaine of Domaine de la
Romanée-Conti runs this well-respected
property in Bouzeron with his wife
Pamela. Exquisite wines, including the
local Aligoté and white Les Clous.
Domaine de La P'tiote Cave (Chassey-le-Camp)
In spite of the fact that it is a small
domaine, Jean-Paul Mugnier produces
nearly 15 different wines, among which
are Rully and Bourgogne Aligoté.
GAEC des Vignerons (Remigny, Le Bourg)
The sons-in-law Guy Fontaine and Jacky
Vion cultivate 14ha and make a wide
range of wines, from Bourgogne Aligoté,
Bourgogne Chardonnay and Bourgogne
Passetoutgrains to Rully, Crémant de
Bourgogne, Santenay, Chassagne-
Montrachet and Bâtard-Montrachet.

PLACES OF INTEREST

By taking, slightly to the south of Aluze,
the D978 west, you reach the Couchois,
a group of wine communes producing
red and white burgundy as well as other
generic wines. Included among these
villages are Couches, Dracy-lès-Couches
and Saint-Maurice-lès-Couches. The first
two villages have impressive castles.

*Above and right Images of
Rully – a sprawling village which
produces equal quantities of red and
white wine. The wines can offer
good value for money and are often
of a reasonable quality.*

*Left A large proportion of Crémant
de Bourgogne is produced in Rully,
although the base wine generally
comes from other wine communes in
the region.*

BOUZERON

From Chagny, the narrow D219 runs southwest to the
hamlet of Bouzeron. This is the home of a superior Bourgogne
Aligoté, of such good quality that, since 1979, it has been
allowed to be sold with the name of the village on the label.

For a touch of archaeology and some marvellous views,
take the winding road over the hilltops to Chassey-le-Camp,
via Nantoux. You will see the village long before you reach
it as it sits low down in the valley. On the west side are the
remains of a large Neolithic settlement (3200–2000BC)
which were discovered in the 18th century. The spot can be
reached on foot from the village and, although the long
walk does not offer many archaeological surprises, there is a
marvellous panorama to be seen.

RULLY

From Bouzeron, return to the D981 and head
south. All along the right side of the road are
the Rully vineyards. A signpost indicates the
right turn into the village.

The oldest part of the village stands on a hill,
with most of the houses at its foot. This is
because, after the plague of 1347, the
inhabitants fled the old village and built a new
community on lower ground. There are a number
of stately mansions, and the atmospheric triangular
Place Sainte-Marie has a park where you can sit and relax.

From the centre of Rully, it is only a short stroll up the
hillside to the west to Agneux where there are some
interesting caves. The route is clearly shown by signposts.

The most important local building is Château de Rully,
splendidly preserved on top of a hill and dominating the
surrounding landscape. It has a square tower which dates
from the 13th century. In front is a vineyard and behind it
an English-style park which can be visited at weekends.

Winegrowing around Rully has revived since the 1970s,
and in general the white wines – which are aromatic, fresh

RULLY

RESTAURANT

Le Vendangerot
Tel: 03 85 87 20 09
Situated on the Place Sainte-Marie, this
has a rather chic and at the same time
rustic dining room. There is always a
choice of various menus, with regional
dishes traditionally prepared. The most
inexpensive menu costs less than FF100.
It is also a simple hotel with large rooms
from about FF200.

RECOMMENDED PRODUCERS

Jean-Claude Brelière
Passionate winegrower who produces a
fresh, pure white Rully and a constantly
improving red. Welcomes visitors from
England, the US, Spain and Germany in
their own tongue.
Michel Briday
A typically Burgundian atmosphere of
disorderly scruffiness reigns here but, with
careful searching, there are some delicious
white wines.
André Delorme
The elongated cellar complex of this
dynamic business is situated behind the
local church. The main wine is sparkling,
under the estate's own label as well as for
a number of growers who do not have
the know-how and equipment to make
their own Crémant de Bourgogne.
Délorme's own sparkling wine is excellent.
The same family runs the large Domaine
de la Renarde, whose wines include a
first-class Rully and an equally attractive,
minerally Montagny.
Domaine de la Folie
Between Chagny and Rully there is a hill
on which the Bouton family has created
the 'estate of foolishness'. Has a Provençal
feel, being surrounded by pine and oak
trees. The wines – mainly white and red
Rullys – can be good.
Raymond Dureuil-Janthial
A reliable estate producing full-bodied
white wines and firm reds.
Henri et Paul Jacqueson
A spotless winery, run with skill and
passion and producing successful red
wines from Rully and Mercurey. The
white wine can also be good.

Right and far right Mercurey has produced wine for centuries. One of its most famous fans was Gabrielle d'Estrées, although her lover, Henri IV, preferred Givry.

Domaine du Prieuré
This property belongs to a former Parisian restaurateur, Armand Monassier. Good reputation for its fruity white Rullys, its firm reds and the Crémant de Bourgogne.
Château de Rully
The Antonin Rodet firm has recently been working to turn this estate into one of the best and most highly valued in the appellation. Here you can enjoy fine wines, both white and red Rully, the latter characterised by wood and vanilla.

MERCUREY

RESTAURANTS
Hostellerie du Val d'Or
Tel: 03 85 45 13 70
A large inn offering 13 spacious and comfortable rooms. In the rustic dining room you can enjoy tasty dishes based on regional ingredients (*le feuilleté de grenouilles aux champignons*). There is an impressive wine list. Menus start at about FF150 (weekdays).
Le Guide de Marloux
Tel: 03 85 45 13 03
This simple inn, serving traditional food, is situated at the intersection of the roads from Mercurey to Chalon and Rully to Givry. Corinne Lagarreiro provides a friendly service while her husband busies himself in the kitchen, with excellent results. Menus from FF90.
Le Petit Blanc
Tel: 03 85 45 15 43
On the road from Mercurey to Couches, an attractive restaurant, some 4km outside Mercurey. The Prost family offers its guests *la cuisine d'autrefois*. The food is excellent, with menus from FF70.

RECOMMENDED PRODUCERS
Domaine Bordeaux-Montrieux
Supple, juicy red Mercureys. Owner is the director of the Domaine Thénard in Givry.
Luc Brintet et Frédéric Charles
Average-sized estate which produces pleasant-tasting Mercureys. The best ripen in new casks.
Michel Juillot
This is one of the largest local, private estates, with arched cellars under an 18th-century building on the main street. The red wines taste rather firm and supple, while the white is sometimes worth a try.

and fruity – have more depth than the reds and are usually excellent value for money. There are also a number of sparkling wine producers here; their Crémant de Bourgogne appellation is worth looking out for as these are often the richest *crémants* in Burgundy. Most of the still base wines used for Crémant de Bourgogne in Rully do not come from the local vineyards but from other Chalonnais communes.

MERCUREY

Leaving Rully heading south, you travel up, over and down a small hill, before turning right into the village of Mercurey.

This is the best-known village in the Chalonnais, where 95 per cent of the vintage consists of red wine. That it has, thanks to wine, known periods of prosperity is shown by the large winegrowers' houses, most of which were built in the 18th and 19th centuries. In fact, a number of Côte d'Or firms and estates have considerable holdings here and in the surrounding hamlets, including Philippe-le-Hardi (Santenay), Faiveley (Nuits-Saint-Georges) and Bouchard Aîné (Beaune). The Maison du Mercurey of the collective wine producers

Jean Maréchal
It is a pleasure to buy here – you can park easily opposite the cellar and the tasting is directed by Monsieur Maréchal, who calmly talks about his wines' best points, passing quickly over any shortcomings, but is always a pleasure to listen to. Many of his wines need patient cellaring, although some may be enjoyed when young, and the prices are very reasonable.

Domaine de la Monette
Sturdy red Mercurey.

Antonin Rodet
A company in which the Champagne firm Laurent Perrier has a controlling interest. The quality of the burgundies rose steadily in the 1980s. From its own land come the red and white Mercurey from Château de Chamirey (a hamlet near Mercurey).

PLACE OF INTEREST

By driving from Mercurey to Givry, you pass Germolles, on the south side of which is an interesting castle whose oldest part dates from the 12th century. It was formerly owned by Philip the Bold and can be visited.

is located in Château de Garnerot, while Château de Chamirey (in the hamlet of the same name) is the property of Antonin Rodet, along with the wine tavern.

Mercurey has well over 2,000 inhabitants and consists mainly of one long street, which is dominated by striking copper lanterns. A side street, near the Hostellerie du Val d'Or, runs upwards to Mercurey-le-Haut, where there is an 11th-century Romanesque church. On the other side of Mercurey stands the attractive church of Touches. It was built between the 12th and 15th centuries and has a monumental clock tower positioned in the middle of the nave. From Touches there is a lovely view of Mercurey.

Mercurey's red wines are usually sturdy and tasty, with concentrated fruit and firm tannins, if lacking in finesse. They have good potential for ageing rather than youthful charm. White Mercurey nowadays has more freshness and character than previously.

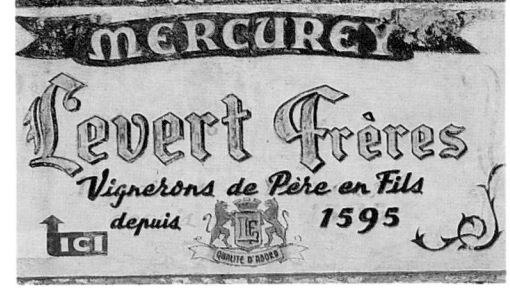

GIVRY

GIVRY

HOTEL

Le Dracy
Dracy-le-Fort
Tel: 03 85 87 81 81
This modern operation is situated next to
a large orthopaedic centre. It has about
40 comfortable rooms (prices from about
FF300). There is also a restaurant, La
Garenne, where you can eat decently with
menus from about FF100.

RESTAURANTS

Auberge de la Billebaude
Tel: 03 85 44 34 25
This bistro, near the church, offers regional
and mainstream dishes at low prices.

From Mercurey, there is a choice of routes to Givry, the
third of the Chalonnais appellations. The long, more scenic,
route leads out of Mercurey heading east on the D978. After
about 1.5kms, turn right into the village of Chamirey. At
the crossroads in the centre of this hamlet, turn left and then
hard right onto the D155, heading south towards Saint-Jean
de Vaux. This route leads through the hamlets of St-Martin-
sous-Montaigu, Saint-Jean de Vaux, Saint-Denis de Vaux
and Jambles. At Jambles, you turn left onto the D170,
heading east and then northeast, passing through Poncey
and entering Givry from the south. You will have travelled
about 15kms.

The shorter, more direct route from Mercurey to Givry is only 7kms. Leaving Mercurey the same way, heading east on the D978, continue on this road until the T-junction where it joins the D981. Turn right onto this road, passing by the hamlet of Germolles on the right on your way to Givry, entering Givry from the north.

It has been said that Henry IV's mistress Gabrielle d'Estrées liked to drink Mercurey, but Henry himself preferred Givry, a story the winegrowers of Givry subscribe to and commemorate on many of their labels. Of all the wine communes in the Chalonnais, Givry is the richest in history, because its wine was already renowned in the 6th century and the Middle Ages. Around 1780, the village functioned as the wine centre for the entire region, and the enormous cellars of present-day Domaine Thénard bear witness to this.

Nowadays, there is not much of this illustrious past to be seen. This does not mean that Givry is not worth a visit, as the village does have some striking buildings. These include the Halle Ronde, along the main street, a round building with a spiral staircase (1830). Nearby is the town hall, which was completed in 1771 and built around a gateway, the Porte de l'Horloge, with its small clock tower. Passing through the gateway, you come to a large, rectangular square which is dominated on the north side by a post office that looks more like a castle, with angels and grapes decorating a carved façade. From a distance you can see the large, octagonal church (designed by Emile Gauthey, who also designed the town hall), which is crowned by domes. The village is also dotted with several attractive fountains.

Like Mercurey, the district of Givry produces mainly red wines. These are strong, rounded, richly fruity and supple, with cherry-like aromas. The white wines are fresh, but at the same time firm and can be deliciously aromatic.

Usually also a fish menu and you can order *fondue vigneronne*. Menus from FF70. Cabaret on Saturday evenings.

Hostellerie de la Halle
Tel: 03 85 44 32 45
Typical country restaurant, where the cooking is unpretentious but tasty (*rôtis, grillades, lapin aux deux moutardes*, etc). Magnificent cheese platter. The menus begin under FF100. It is also a simple hotel.

RECOMMENDED PRODUCERS

René Bourgeon (Jambles)
Active, small winegrower whose wines have received international awards.
Domaine Chofflet-Valdenaire (Russilly)
The Chofflet family has made wine here since 1710. The red Givry is very reliable, as is the white.
Propriété Desvignes (Poncey)
Average-sized estate, of which the white Givry is quite aromatic and the red Givry Clos du Vernoy has sufficient power and structure to benefit from some bottle-age.
Lumpp Frères
Exemplary Givrys.
Domaine Ragot (Poncey)
The white Givry here is generally more interesting than the red. Small, arched lasting cellar.
Clos Salomon
This estate, which goes back to the 14th century, produces only one wine: red Givry. It has a good colour, reasonable tannin and a pleasant dose of fruit.

Left Grand architecture and vines in Givry.
Below Jambon persillé is perfect with Givry, due to the wine's delightful elegance and vibrant cherry (almost cranberry) fruitiness.

Domaine Thénard
The family has owned its Givrys since 1760. The wines ferment and mature here in the magnificent 18th-century cellars. The estate also has land in the Côte d'Or and offers a high-quality range of wines, including Le Montrachet, Grands Echézeaux and Corton Clos du Roi as well as the Givrys.

Jean-Marc et Vincent Joblot
The Joblot brothers are among the best producers in Givry. Their reds are dark coloured, bursting with fruit and wood, and are magnificently complex. Their whites are rich but refreshing with a bouquet of burnt new wood. They are superbly concentrated wines.

CHALON-SUR-SAONE

HOTELS

Saint-Georges
71100 Chalon-sur-Saône
Tel: 03 85 48 27 05
Comfortable hotel with a Michelin-starred restaurant. Rooms start at around FF400 and the menus range from FF150 to FF390.

Saint-Régis
71100 Chalon-sur-Saône
Tel: 03 85 46 22 81
Centrally located, well-equipped, with a restaurant. Prices for rooms start around FF400. Restaurant closed Sundays. Menus from FF110.

CHALON-SUR-SAONE

From Givry it is only about 5kms to Chalon-sur-Saône, the town from which the Chalonnais receives its name. Take the D981 heading south out of Givry and turn onto the N80, heading east to Chalon-sur-Saône.

With approximately 55,000 inhabitants, this city is the second largest in Burgundy, after Dijon and before Mâcon. Because of its location along the Saône River, it has been a centre for trade as far back as recorded history takes us. Its annual fairs were known throughout the whole of Europe. This is still the case for the Foire aux Sauvagines, a game market which takes place at the end of February.

The suburbs of Chalon are uninteresting, but the old centre has unquestionable charm. It fans out from behind the river quay and has many half-timbered houses. Along the quay itself there is, on a small square, the statue of Chalon's most famous son: Nicéphore Niépce (1765–1833) who made history by inventing photography. Near the statue is the Musée Niépce, which is one of the most important photographic museums in the world, exhibiting the history of photography in a fascinating and well laid-out way. The collection includes Niépce's equipment (and that of his pupil Daguerre, who was able to shorten the lighting process) and the world's very first photographs. There is also a design for a jet engine, another invention of Niépce's, as well as an exhibition of modern equipment and contemporary photographs.

Above *A display of fresh vegetables in the local market.*
Right *Chalon, only 5kms from Givry, is a charming and historical town, which makes an ideal detour.*

From the museum, you can walk into the centre of the town and the town hall square (Place de l'Hôtel de Ville). Here you will find the church of Saint-Pierre, a Gothic-style building which was completed in the 18th century. Also on the square is the Musée Denon, which was founded in 1819 in a former monastery. It has many exhibits from prehistoric times, including finds from the excavation near Chassey-le-Camp, (*see* Northern Chalonnais, page 92). There are also finds from the Middle Ages and later periods. Besides paintings, the collection also contains marvellous pieces of furniture, nautical instruments and Egyptian art. The founder of the museum, Dominique Denon (1747–1825), took part in Napoleon's Egyptian campaign and became a celebrated Egyptologist.

Between the Place de l'Hôtel de Ville and the Place Saint-Vincent there is an attractive shopping street which runs parallel to the quay. The Place Saint-Vincent is surrounded by half-timbered houses, one of which is the 15th-century Maison aux Trois Greniers with its stunning balustrades. The church of Saint-Vincent, built and rebuilt between the 12th and 19th centuries, displays a multitude of sometimes unharmonious architectural styles, but is still worth visiting. To one side is a three-galleried cloister.

From here it is a short walk to the Promenade Sainte-Marie where you will find the chalet-like Maison des Vins de la Côte Chalonnaise. This is a promotion centre for wines from the Chalonnais. Wines of every appellation,

Above *The cloisters of the Eglise Saint Vincent, in Chalon, built and rebuilt between the 12th and 19th centuries.*

St-Jean
Chalon-sur-Saône
Tel: 03 85 48 45 65
Reasonably priced hotel overlooking the river, with simply furnished rooms from around FF230.

RESTAURANTS
Le Bourgogne
Chalon-sur-Saône
Tel: 03 85 48 89 18
Beautifully situated in a 17th-century house. Menus start at about FF90. The restaurant is closed for three weeks in July.
L'Isle Bleue
Chalon-sur-Saône
Tel: 03 85 48 39 83
Reasonably priced seafood restaurant, from around FF80. Closed August 2 to 22.
Le Bistrot
Chalon-sur-Saône
Tel: 03 85 93 22 01
Situated near the river; good value, with menus from around FF85. Closed August and on Saturday lunchtimes and Sundays.
Le Florilège
1 rue du Pont
Chalon-sur-Saône
Tel: 03 85 48 81 01
Excellent: inventive dishes and good prices. Small wine list. Menus from FF75 to FF280.
Le Verre Galant
6 place Saint-Vincent
Chalon-sur-Saône
Tel: 03 85 93 09 87
Pleasant restaurant with creative dishes; good prices, from FF69. Wine by the glass.
Moulin de Martorey
Chalon-sur-Saône
Tel: 03 85 48 12 98
South of Chalon, this is one of the most

Right *View of Givry, with vines in foreground.*
Below *A wall painting in Buxy, location of one of Burgundy's largest and most influential cooperatives.*

exciting restaurants in Burgundy. Inventive dishes, cooked in a simple manner. Menus from FF135. The wine list is excellent.

MONTAGNY

HOTELS

Château Sassangy
Sassangy
Tel: 03 85 96 12 40
This 18th-century castle, which has recently been entirely renovated, has six rooms available following the *chambre d'hôte* formula (bed and breakfast). Traquility, stylish comfort and hospitality are the key words here. Prices start at about FF550 and you can also have dinner here. Sassangy is just west of Buxy. Closed November to March.

Le Relais du Montagny
Buxy
Tel: 03 85 92 19 90
Opened in 1990, situated close to the local cooperative. Its 30 rooms are neat and functionally furnished, if a little on the small side. There is a swimming pool. It is owned by the proprietors of Girardot restaurant. Prices from FF300.

Manoir des Chailloux
Jully-lès-Buxy
Tel: 03 85 92 13 62
In the rural village of Jully-lès-Buxy, south of Buxy, Mme Flèche lets two pretty rooms in her little château which is set in a park, surrounded by a tall fence. There is also a swimming pool. Prices from FF380 and FF480, breakfast included. Closed from November to April.

RESTAURANTS

Girardot
Buxy
Tel: 03 85 92 04 04
Regional dishes are offered in a simple ambience. Menus from about FF100. When the weather is fine you can eat outside.

selected by a jury of local experts, can be bought here. You may also taste the wines and there is a simple restaurant, La Feuillette, where regional and grilled dishes are served at reasonable prices.

Otherwise, simply wander along the river. Groups of men play the implicitly French *jeu de boules* near here and there is a bridge which crosses the river to the Île Saint-Laurent. On the west side of this small island, next to an enormous lime tree, is the hexagonal Tour du Doyenné. It is sometimes open to visitors, and if you are feeling energetic you can climb to the top and admire the beautiful view of the city. This tower formerly stood next to the church of Saint-Vincent but, in 1926, with the help of a rich American, it was moved stone by stone to its present location.

Golf-lovers can also enjoy themselves in Chalon-sur-Saône, because on the east bank, in a loop of the river, the city has set out a fine, 18-hole golf course.

MONTAGNY

To reach Montagny from Chalon, retrace the route back along the N80 in a westerly direction. Look out for the turn-off onto the D981 and take the southbound route for Buxy and Montagny. If you go north on the D981 you will end up back in Givry.

The D981 follows the contour of the hills into the village of Buxy. That the wines of Montagny, the southernmost district of the Chalonnais, were formerly sold as Côte de Buxy is completely understandable, because apart from Montagny-lès-Buxy and Buxy, the nearby villages of Jully-lès-Buxy and Saint-Vallerin also fall within the Montagny appellation. Buxy is by far the largest commune of the four. In the 12th century, the village was fortified, two towers being the only remaining evidence of this. Near the Tour Rouge there is a large, humourous wall painting, depicting, with tongue in cheek, the wines from the surroundings. Some of the surrounding houses, or parts of them, date back as far as the Middle Ages. The only wine cooperative of the district is also found in Buxy.

Just as the name suggests, Montagny-lès-Buxy is largely situated on a hill. The streets are narrow and the vineyards run from the village centre downwards into a broad U-shaped valley. Jully-lès-Buxy, just like Montagny, offers a panoramic view over the area, while Saint-Vallerin has a Romanesque church. Slightly to the south of this wine village is the hamlet of La Tour, where the remains of an enormous medieval building can be seen.

The wines of Montagny are exclusively white, made from the Chardonnay grape, and are characterised by sturdy, juicy flavours with a light nuttiness. Although they may lack the liveliness and individuality of white Rullys, these wines can offer some of the best value for money for white wines in the whole of Burgundy. It used to be the case that all Montagny of 11.5 per cent or stronger could be sold as Premier Cru, regardless of the vineyard site. That curious rule has now been reversed, and the best vineyards have been formally identified as Premiers Crus – all 53 of them. The best-known are Montcuchot and Les Coères.

RECOMMENDED PRODUCERS

Pierre Bernollin (Jully-lès-Buxy)
Good Montagny wines here as well as Crémant de Bourgogne.

Cave des Vignerons de Buxy (Buxy)
Cooperative with a modern cellar – one of Burgundy's showpieces. New equipment is invented and tested here, and many New World winemakers have visited. The red Bourgogne Pinot Noir is well worth tasting, as is the Montagny.

Bernard Michel (Saint-Vallerin)
Small producer of, among others, Montagny Les Coères.

Château de la Saule
Castle situated at the foot of the village of Montagny and the property of Alain Roy-Thévenin. His Montagny (ordinary and Premier Cru) is delicious and one of the most beautiful of the entire appellation.

Veuve Steinmaier & Fils (Montagny)
Various types of Montagny, the best being the buttery Montcuchot.

Jean Vachet (Saint-Vallerin)
Expanding his estate since 1959, this serious winegrower now produces some excellent wines. One of the best is the pure, generous Montagny Les Coères.

Below The charming village of Jully-lès-Buxy, like many in Burgundy, is situated on a hill overlooking its vines.

The Mâconnais

Retrace the route back into Buxy in order to rejoin the D981 heading south. Travelling along this road you will cross an imperceptible boundary between the Côte Chalonnaise and the Mâconnais. When you see signposts for the village of Saint-Gengoux-le-National, you will know you have arrived in the Mâconnais.

Although there are no clearly defined signs to show you have passed from one wine region into another, some clues exist. The landscape remains agricultural; crops other than grapes are grown and Charolais cattle graze on lush meadows. As you continue south, a small ridge rises, followed by broad wooded hills. Then come the first hints of the Mediterranean south: houses with Provençal red-tiled roofs and open-galleried façades.

Even more than the Chalonnais, the Mâconnais is a district of peaceful villages, whose silhouettes are often determined by a Romanesque church. Romanesque architecture in Burgundy probably first flowered in Cluny, where the Bénédictine monks had their headquarters. The region is named after the city of Mâcon, situated on the River Saône. There is strong historical evidence that the Romans made wine here, but it was the monks at Cluny in the 11th and 12th centuries who really made viticulture flourish. The wines they made enjoyed local fame, but it was not until the 17th century that they found wider recognition. The story has it that a local grower, Claude Brosse, loaded two casks of his wine onto a cart and travelled for 33 days, braving bad roads and highwaymen, until he arrived at the court of Versailles. King Louis XIV is said to have been very impressed by the man and his wine, declaring it to be of a better quality than the Loire wines he had been drinking. And so Mâcon wines made their name.

Left Cluny demands a visit, not just for its beauty, but for its place in the history of the wines of Burgundy.

Above The impressive Solutré rock dominates its surrounding landscape.

The Mâconnais

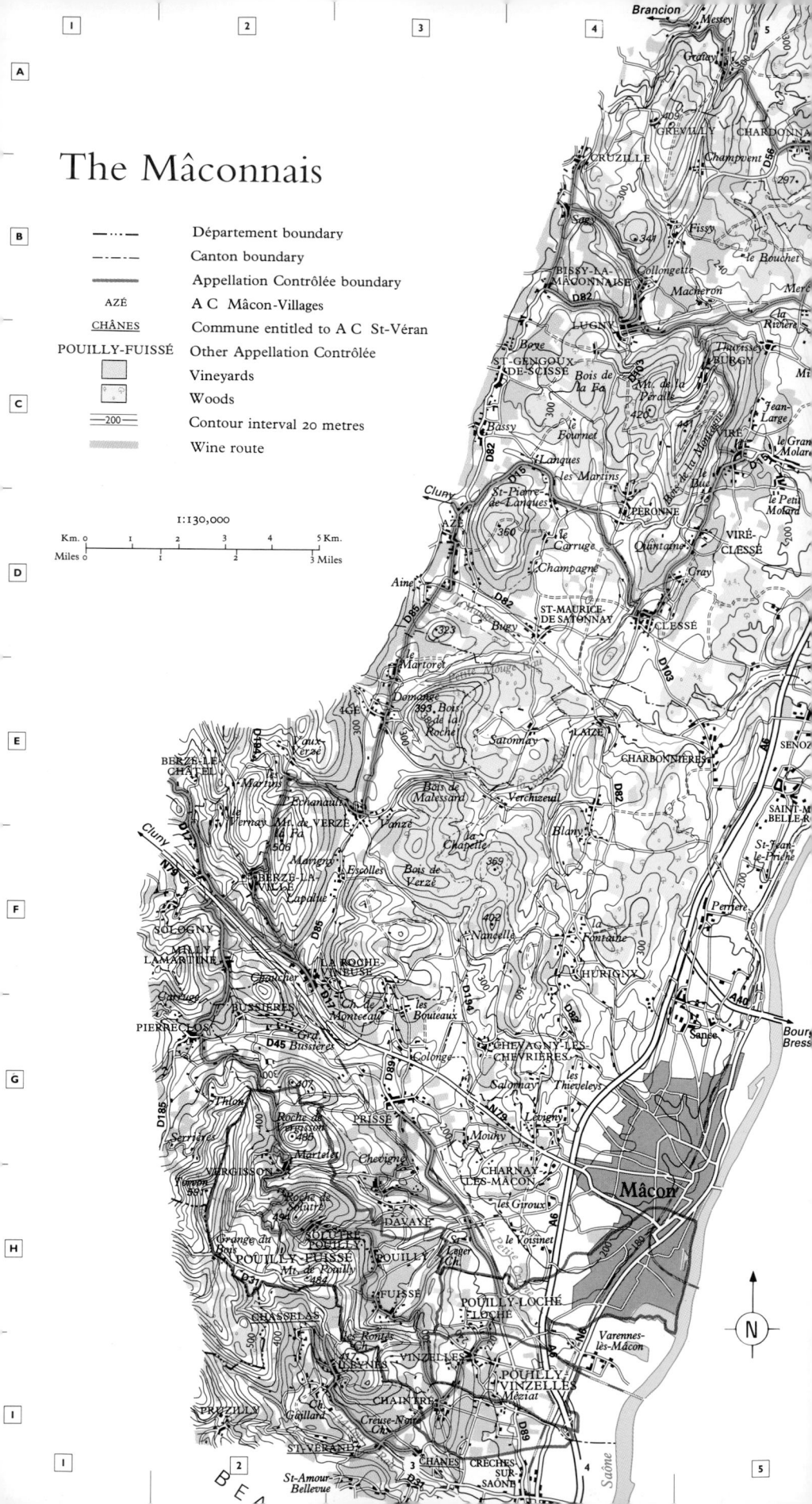

The weather here already begins to take on a Mediterranean character, which means that the grapes ripen a little earlier than in the rest of Burgundy and consequently the harvest is usually a week or two earlier. About 90 per cent of the region's wine comes from cooperatives, and, while in the past it has been the reds that have dominated, it is now the white wines which are more important, in terms of both quantity and quality. Chardonnay grapes are grown in roughly two-thirds of the vineyards.

The biggest appellation is Mâcon-Villages, or Mâcon followed by a village name. Other white wines can be labelled as Mâcon and Mâcon Supérieur (one per cent more alcohol). These last two are also appellations for red wines, with most labelled under the Supérieur category. The grape used for red wines in the region is Gamay, and some Pinot Noir is also grown and used in blends.

The best, most famous and most expensive wines are produced in the extreme south of the region and are exclusively white – Pouilly-Fuissé, Pouilly-Vinzelles, Pouilly-Loché and Saint-Véran.

NORTHERN MACONNAIS

The mountain chain of the Mâconnais runs parallel with the A6 Autoroute du Soleil from the town of Tournus in the north of the region to Mâcon further south. The city of Mâcon lies just a few kilometres outside the appellation to the east. The northern Mâconnais is one of the most delightful parts of Burgundy to explore, as the beautiful countryside offers many wonderful views from the hilltops over the surrounding hills and valleys, and it also produces some excellent (mainly white) wines.

Below *A row of houses in the medieval hamlet of Brançion.*

Right *The immense, lavish interior decoration on the walls and ceiling of the Château de Cormatin.*

Below *A view of the magnificent Romanesque church of Brançion.*

NORTHERN MACONNAIS

HOTELS

Auberge du Château
Cruzille
Tel: 03 85 33 28 02
Simple: six rooms, from FF150, with a restaurant where you can eat for under FF100. Open Easter through October.

Château de Fleurville
Fleurville
Tel: 03 85 33 12 17
Castle hotel with park. 15 rooms (starting at around FF430); good restaurant (menus from about FF165). Swimming pool.

Château d'Igé
Igé
Tel: 03 85 33 33 99
Luxurious accommodation in a beautiful medieval castle. 13 large, finely furnished rooms and apartments (starting at around FF500). The cuisine is high quality with a classic touch. Menus start at about FF200.

La Montagne de Brançion
Brançion
Tel: 03 85 51 12 40
High on a hill in the vicinity of Brançion. Beautiful view from all 20 rooms (starting at about FF450). They have been furnished with taste and offer adequate comfort. Good restaurant. Light, sophisticated cuisine. Menus from FF180. Outdoor pool.

The following touring route takes in all the major Mâconnais wine villages, as well as following some of the most picturesque roads through the region. From Buxy in the Chalonnais, follow the D981 travelling south towards the village of Cormatin. This village marks the beginning of the tour of the northern Mâconnais.

Before you start the tour proper, you might like to take the opportunity of stopping in Cormatin to visit its 17th-century castle with six charmingly furnished rooms. To start the wine tour, leave Cormatin driving in an easterly direction on the D14 to Brançion, a medieval hamlet situated on a steep slope beside a fortress that was once one of the most important fortifications of southern Burgundy. Cars are forbidden in the village, which has 14th-century market halls as well as a Romanesque church with some amazing frescos. From Brançion, continue east on the D14 to Ozenay. Turn right here onto the D463 travelling south, then left onto the D163. At the next T-junction, turn left onto the D56, which then brings you into the village of Chardonnay.

Up to this point vineyards have scarcely been seen; this changes near Chardonnay. No-one is absolutely certain, but it is thought that this ancient hamlet may possibly have given its name to the famous white grape variety.

Relais Lamartine
Bussières
Tel: 03 85 36 64 71
Peacefully situated hotel with eight rooms,
from about FF380. Outside dining when
weather permits. Menus from about FF100.
Hostellerie de Greuze
Tournus
Tel: 03 85 51 13 52
Magnificent hotel with 21 comfortable
rooms. Prices from FF635. One of the
best restaurants in Burgundy. Superbly
prepared dishes. Menus from FF275.
Excellent wine list.

RESTAURANTS

Le Relais de Mâconnais
La Croix Blanche
Tel: 03 85 36 60 72
The superb cuisine attracts many guests,
with menus starting at about FF140. Varied
menu, with a regional accent Also a hotel
with 10 rooms. Prices from FF350.
Relais de Montmartre
Viré
Tel: 03 85 33 10 72
Smart inn on village square. Stylish interior,
regional cuisine. Menus begin under FF100.
Saint-Pierre
Lugny
Tel: 03 85 33 20 27
Simple, with winetasting room. Regional
dishes and local wines. Panoramic view.

SPECIAL INTEREST

Goat's cheese is served everywhere in the
Mâconnais, in all possible variations.

UCHIZY

The route continues east on the D163
to Uchizy, a wine village with a
strikingly large church with frescoes
and a five-storey tower. Now take the
D120 travelling southwest, through
Mercey, turning right onto the D103
shortly afterwards and into Burgy, with
its 11th-century church and panoramic
view over the valley. The road continues
southwards to Viré. At the higher part
of this village there is a church with a
pointed tower, and in the lower area,
you will find the wine cooperative, the
Château des Cinq Tours (a 16th-
century wine estate) and the village
square with its statue of Bacchus.

The road goes to Clessé, via
Quintaine. Since the 1998 harvest, the
wines of Clessé, Viré, Montbellet and
Quintaine have been given the new appellation of Viré-
Clessé. The stainless-steel tanks of the wine cooperative
contrast with the little 11th-century church and its
octagonal tower. At Clessé, turn right heading west towards

*Above An enchanting tree-covered
walk in the gardens of the 17th-
century Château de Cormatin. There
are also delightfully furnished rooms*

RECOMMENDED PRODUCERS

Auvigue-Burrier-Revel (Charnay-lès-Mâcon)
Small *négociant* firm, specialising in white Mâconnais, especially Saint-Véran and Pouilly-Fuissé. It sells the wines of several estates, also buying in grapes for vinification. The wines are the opposite of big, open Chardonnays from the New World. They are lean, discreet and usually need cellaring.

Domaine André Bonhomme (Viré)
Well-respected winemaker; tasty Mâcon-Viré usually matured in barrels for six months.

Château des Cinq Tours (Viré)
Beautiful Mâcon-Viré.

Collin et Bourisset (Crèches-sur-Saône)
Nice table wines, particularly the two Moulin-à-Vents in the range.

Coopérative de Chardonnay (Chardonnay)
Above-average quality expectations. Award-winning Mâcon/Chardonnay.

Domaine de Chervin (Burgy)
Good white Mâcon and Mâcon-Burgy.

Coopérative Charnay-lès-Mâcon (Charnay-lès-Mâcon)
Saint-Véran is the speciality, but the Mâcon-Villages has just as much class.

Saint-Maurice de Satonnay on the D403b, turning left there to head south to the village of Satonnay. At the T-junction after Satonnay, turn right onto the D434 through the beautiful Bois de Malessard and into Verzé. According to legend the water from the village fountain here posseses healing powers.

From Verzé, take the road down the valley to La Roche Vineuse, with its 12th-century bell tower and views over the Charolais countryside. In the hamlet of Eau-Vive, just outside La Roche Vineuse, there is an open-air museum, Au Bout du Monde, with houses from various cultures, including African.

From here turn right onto the N79 and drive westward to Berzé-la-Ville with its Romanesque church and – just outside the village – La Chapelle aux Moines. This 11th-century chapel is famous for its rich Byzantine wall paintings. There is also another beautiful view from a point near the chapel.

From Berzé-la-Ville, take the road heading north to Le Cloux and then take the D194 which follows the contours of the Mont de Verzé, winding slowly round to the east and back to Verzé. From here, take the D85 northwards to the village of Igé. On the north side of Igé stands the 11th-century chapel of Domange. During weekends and on holidays you can visit the Musée de la Vigne, including a winetasting room that is situated in the chapel. Continue

north on the D85 to Azé where, in the season, you can visit the prehistoric caves and archaeological museum. The village also has a Romanesque church and an old market hall.

Travelling north from Azé, you pass through Saint-Gengoux-de-Scisse and on to Bissy-la-Mâconnaise where, in the massive Romanesque church tower, there are interesting wooden statuettes of the saints. Then, driving east on the D82, you arrive in Lugny. On a hill above this village is the most important wine cooperative of the Mâconnais, with a tasting and sales room. On the south side of Lugny's main street is a large 16th-century church and two round towers which are all that remain of a 16th-century castle.

After Lugny, carry on along the D56 but take the left fork at Collongette, driving along the narrow valley floor (the road runs parallel with a stream) until you

Coopérative Clessé (Clessé)
Juicy white Mâcon-Clessé, which is bottled by the cooperative itself.
Coopérative Igé
Reliable, clean-tasting wines. White Château London and Mâcon-Igé are worth tasting.
Coopérative Lugny (Lugny)
Largest cooperative in Burgundy, producing 4,000,000 bottles a year. Good Crémant de Bourgogne (Eugène Blanc), white Mâcon-Lugny, red Mâcon and Mâcon Supérieur and Bourgogne Passe-Tout-Grains.
Coopérative Mancey (Mancey)
Try the white Mâcon (Supérieur).
Coopérative Viré (Viré)
Reliable white Mâcon-Viré. The Crémant de Bourgogne produced here is also tasty.
Domaine Goyard (Viré)
Excellent white Mâcon-Viré.
Henri Lafarge (Bray)
Pleasant wines: rather full, lightly nutty white Mâcon as well as red Mâcon-Bray and the basic Bourgogne.
Domaine Manciat-Poncet (Lévigny)
Wines fermented in stainless steel (Mâcon-Charnay) and small oak casks (Pouilly-Fuissé). Both are excellent.
Domaine de Montbellet (Lugny)
Deliciously fresh white Mâcon-Villages, often with spicy hints.
Domaine de Roally (Viré)
Aromatic, complex Mâcon-Viré. Top quality but small production.
Domaine Philibert et Gérald Talmard (Uchizy)
The brothers Paul and Philibert Talmard have divided the original domain, each producing excellent fresh, lively wines.
Jean Thévenet (Quintaine)
Outstanding domaine. White Mâcon-Clessé of impeccable quality, usually with fruity aroma.
Trénel Fils (Charnay-lès-Mâcon)
The white as well as the red wines are rich in fruit. Especially fine are the Mâcon-Villages, Saint-Véran, Pouilly-Fuissé, crus from Beaujolais and red Mâcon.
Domaine de l'Arfentière (Uchizy)
Raphaël and Gérard Sallet produce a harmonious, fresh Mâcon-Uchizy.
Domaine d'Azenay (Azé)
Georges Blanc, a great chef in Vonnas, has his own vineyards in the Mâconnais where he produces a good Mâcon-Azé.
Domaine de la Bongran (Quintaine)
Jean Thévenet has a great reputation. He uses biological working methods, keeps the yield low, and harvests late. His wines have magnificent nuances and are sometimes botrytised.

Left Detail of the old stone clocktower at Uchizy, one of more than 40 villages entitled to sell its wines under the name 'Mâcon' and its own name.
Far and above left The château at Brançion, once one of the most important fortifications in southern Burgundy, and surrounding landscape.

Pierrette et Marc Guillemot-Michel (Quintaine)
Marc Guillemot uses biodynamic working methods. The wine matured in the *cuverie* and cellar is allowed to develop freely. Excellent wines, with clean taste; lively and full of fruit.

Hubert Laferrère/Domaine Saint-Denis (Lugny)
Small domain with attractive wines.

Domaine de la Sarazinière (Bussières)
Excellent source of red Mâcon. Philippe Trébignaud is a conscientious producer.

WINE FESTIVALS

During the second half of May, one of France's largest wine fairs takes place annually in Mâcon. And in Créches-sur-Saône, along the N6, the Cellier-Expo is situated, where information about the wine area and a wine route is given. Also during the Palm Sunday weekend, Lugny has a wine fair.

reach the hamlet of Sagy. Turn right here and on into Cruzille. Just before this village, on the left side of the road, the Musée des Outils d'Autrefois exhibits about 3,500 tools from the past. Cruzille also has a well-preserved 14th-century castle, which now houses a medical institute.

CLUNY

No tour of the northern Mâconnais is complete without visiting the fascinating town of Cluny. The following route makes for a pretty and relaxed drive. You must retrace the route back to the village of Azé, turning right there onto the D15 to Cluny. This marvellous road runs past the charming village of Donzy-le-Pertuis (with its 11th-century church) and through the beautiful forests of Cluny.

Cluny itself is steeped in history. The Bénédictine monastery founded there in the 10th century became the largest and most powerful in Europe. The ruins of the abbey church, and the model of it in its heyday, do much to show how impressive the complex must have been.

From Cluny, drive south on the D980 to Berzé-le-Châtel. This hill village is dominated by a massive castle with 13 towers (12th to 15th century) which was once the seat of the first barony of the Mâconnais. Follow the same road south to the pretty, sleepy village of Milly-Lamartine, where the poet and politician Alphonse de Lamartine (*see* Mâcon, page 114) spent his youth. A bust of the famous poet can be found here, as well as a charming Romanesque church. It is not far from here to Pierreclos, with its 14th-century castle, which is now a museum; for those who enjoy walking, there is a Lamartine walking route around these last two villages. The village of Pierreclos also has some of the finest vineyards in the Mâcon appellation.

This completes the tour of the northern Mâconnais. From here the journey can be continued in a southerly direction to Vergisson and the district of Pouilly-Fuissé.

Above *A directional sign for the Caveau Dégustation by a roadside.*
Right *View of the landscape and chapel at Berzé le Châtel.*
Far right *The elegant interior of the Abbey of Cluny, a sight that should not be missed when visiting the area.*

MACON

HOTELS
Mercure-Bord de Saône
26 Rue Coubertin
Tel: 03 85 38 28 06
One of Mâcon's two best hotels. 64
comfortable and well-equiped rooms
with pleasant views, from about FF540.
Also restaurant, Le St-Vincent, from
about FF130.

Bellevue
416 Quai Lamartine
Tel: 03 85 21 04 04
Wonderful location overlooking the river
in the centre of Mâcon. 24 comfortable
rooms priced from FF470. Also restaurant,
from FF140.

Nord
313 Quai Jean Jaurès
Tel: 03 85 38 08 68
Medium-sized hotel on the River Saône.
Fairly comfortable rooms priced from
about FF190. Closed November to March.

La Huchette
Replonges
Tel: 03 85 31 03 55
Pretty hotel, set in a park, with 12
comfortable rooms – not far from the
Bourg-en-Bresse/Geneva *autoroute*.
Friendly and peaceful. Swimming pool.

Right *The entrance to a
boulangerie-patisserie in the
fascinating old city of Mâcon.*

*Burgundy is full of shops selling
wonderful delicacies such as:*
Above *Artichokes.*
Top *A selection of luxurious
patisserie.*

MACON

Mâcon is situated, just like Chalon-sur-Saône, on the River Saône, east of the main Mâconnais wine region. To reach it, drive east on the N79. The town has about 40,000 inhabitants, and dates back to Roman times when it was an important garrison settlement full of workshops making spears and arrows for both soldiers and hunters. Winegrowing was already practised around Mâcon at that time; the poet Ausonius mentions it in his writing.

Mâcon's places of interest are mainly found in the old centre, along the Saône. The poet and politician Alphonse de Lamartine (1790–1869) was born in Mâcon, and there are constant reminders of this fact as you wander through the town. A street, a quay and a promenade have been named after him, and in the Hôtel Senecé (rue Sigorne) a museum has been devoted to him. What is more, you can see

a life-size Lamartine surrounded by other personages in an enormous mosaic on the side of a wall (corner of Rue Gambetta and Rue Edouard-Herriot).

On the quay, close to the statue of the famous citizen, is the Hôtel Montrevel, an imposing, palatial building from the 18th century which today is used as the town hall. Directly behind lies a lively shopping street and the strikingly designed Office du Tourisme. Here you can ask for entrance to the chapel of the Résidence Soufflot, previously a hospital, which is situated nearby. The chapel is built in an unusual oval form, and in the small tower to the right of the gateway is a small hatch through which unwanted babies could be discretely handed over to the hospital in days gone by.

Across from the Office du Tourisme is the neo-Romanesque church of Saint-Pierre with its elegant, pointed towers. By following the shopping street in a northerly direction, you arrive at the Place aux Herbes, with the Maison de Bois on a corner. This is the oldest building of Mâcon – and the city's most famous. On the wooden façade of the building are numerous small sculptures of people and animals in various unusual settings. After walking to the end of the shopping street you reach the Vieux Saint-Vincent. This was a cathedral which has been repeatedly destroyed over the centuries; all that remains now are two, unequal octagonal towers. Continuing west you will find the Musée des Ursulines, which houses a collection of historic objects and works of art. The oldest date from the prehistoric age and were found near Solutré (*see* Pouilly-Fuissé, page 116). The glass windows and ceramics are also interesting to see.

Prices from FF450. Plus excellent restaurant, traditional with a personal touch, from FF160.

Hôtel du Beaujolais
Saint-Laurent-sur-Saône
Tel. 03 85 38 42 06
Simple hotel on the left bank of the river. Spacious rooms at reasonable prices. The rooms at the front have a wonderful view over Mâcon

RESTAURANTS

Mâcon has a good and varied selection of restaurants. The finest, though, are situated in some of the neighbouring villages. The following are just a small selection:

Le Saint-Laurent
1 quai Bouchacourt
Tel: 03 85 39 29 19
Bistro-style restaurant with great views over the river, outside seating is available. Great value, menus from around FF150.

Pierre
7 rue Dufour
Tel: 03 85 38 14 23
Located in the old town, just behind the Bellevue hotel, this restaurant offers menus from around FF100.

L'Amandier
74 rue Dufour
Tel: 03 85 39 82 00
Popular among local winegrowers. Menus from around FF100.

Le Poisson d'Or
Allée Parc
Tel: 03 85 38 00 88
Beautifully located restaurant in a shaded spot on the river bank. Good food, friendly service, some English spoken. Menus from about FF100.

Rocher de Cancale
393 quai Jean Jaurès
Tel: 03 85 38 07 50
Excellent place to eat, on the quay on the river. Great value, from FF98.

Left *View of the riverside buildings overlooking the Saône River in the centre of Mâcon. See the listings for a selection of hotels and restaurants located nearby.*

POUILLY-FUISSE

HOTEL
La Vigne Blanche
Fuissé
Tel: 03 85 35 60 50
Simple rooms (from about FF200). In the unpretentious restaurant you can eat Burgundian dishes such as frog's legs and *coq au vin*; a few regional wines are served by the glass. Menus begin under FF100.

RESTAURANTS
Au Pouilly-Fuissé
Fuissé
Tel: 03 85 35 60 68
The best restaurant of the district. In the light interior you can enjoy tasty regional dishes such as *mousseline de brochet à la crème de cèpes, poulet rôti à la fleur de thym* or *andouillette braisée à la moutarde*. The weekday menu is often less than FF100. The ordinary menus begin at about FF115.
Bourgogne
Cluny
Tel: 03 85 59 00 58
Dining room overlooks the abbey. Welcoming restaurant with good traditional cuisine, from FF200 (lunch menu from FF160). Also a hotel with 12 rooms. Prices from FF470.
Le Potin Gourmand
Cluny
Tel: 03 85 59 02 06
Pretty restaurant serving very reasonably priced food. With terrace. Menus from FF78. There are also three elegant, comfortable rooms. Prices between FF250 and FF350.

Above *Sign on the side of a house in Fuissé advertising one of the town's many wine producers.*
Above right *A stage of the cheesemaking process, which can sometimes be as lengthy and painstaking as winemaking.*

Not far from the museum is the neoclassical cathedral of Saint-Vincent. It was built by the Parisian Guy de Gisors, commissioned by Napoleon, which is why it was initially called Saint-Napoléon. After the departure of the emperor, the building was renamed Saint-Louis (in homage to Louis XVIII), but when Napoleon returned from Elba, the neutral name of Saint-Vincent was chosen to avoid any further confusion. The Hôtel-Dieu, which is situated nearby, was built in the 18th century and is dominated by a large, elliptical dome. On the ground floor there is a chemist where you can see a fine collection of pots from the time of Louis XV.

Slightly to the north of Mâcon's old centre, in an area of parkland, lies the Maison Mâconnaise des Vins (484 Avenue de Lattre-de-Tassigny). Here you can taste and buy wines from the Mâconnais and northern Beaujolais, and enjoy a meal in the restaurant.

POULLY-FUISSE
There is no doubt that Pouilly-Fuissé is the most famous wine from the Mâconnais – and also the most expensive. The appellation lies directly to the west of the city of Mâcon and can be recognised from a distance by two steeply rising rocks, which seem to cut through a stormy sea of green grapevines like the petrified bows of ships. These are the cliffs of Vergisson (to the north) and Solutré (to the south). From Mâcon, travel west on the N79 and, after about 5 or 6kms, turn left onto the D45 to Pierreclos.

At Pierreclos (Mâcon and Mâcon-Villages appellations), turn left onto the D177, arriving in the village of Vergisson after about 2kms. This is a small village with sloping streets and a steep cliff towering high above the pointed church spire. Parts of the cliff are ochre and pink in colour, and a cave has been found nearby with the remains of a Neanderthal man. In the hamlet of Chancerons, on the south side of Vergisson, is a three-metre-high menhir.

From Vergisson there runs a narrow, winding road through wooded slopes to Solutré. The cliff above this

Left *The dramatic, towering presence of the Solutré rock above an expanse of vines. The majority of these grapes are used for the production of Pouilly-Fuissé.*

village is even more impressive than that of Vergisson. Legend has it that the Gallic leader Vercingetorix lit a fire on the rock in order to assemble the tribes before the struggle for independence. This is remembered on Saint-John's day (Midsummer's day) each year with a large bonfire on the same spot.

In 1866, the remains of a prehistoric hunting camp were found at the foot of the rock, including the fossilized bones of thousands of horses believed to have been driven off the top of the cliff to their deaths by hunters, between 35,000 and 10,000BC. Excavations have resulted in one of Europe's richest collections of prehistoric objects, some of which can be seen in the Musée Départemental de Préhistoire in Solutré. Apart from hunting tools, the museum, which was opened in 1987, has statuettes, including a small sculpture of a mammoth.

Solutré itself is a charming village. In the Caveau Pouilly-Fuissé you can taste the local wine (for a fee) and buy bottles of it. Diagonally opposite stand the church (Romanesque, 12th-century) and La Boutique, a store for wine, wine-related articles, jewellery, ceramics and other items.

The area is also a good place for walking – keen and energetic walkers can climb to the top of the Solutré cliff,

RECOMMENDED PRODUCERS

Château de Beauregard (Fuissé)
Important estate, producing distinguished wines, fermented in wooden casks.

Cave des Grands Crus Blancs (Vinzelles)
Cooperative dominating the district, accounting for about 80 per cent of the production of both Pouilly-Vinzelles and Pouilly-Loché.

Louis Curveux (Fuissé)
Excellent wines.

Château Fuissé (Fuissé)
For years the appellation's prime standard-bearer. Superb Pouilly-Fuissé Vieilles Vignes. Other quality wines worth tasting here are the Saint-Véran and Morgon Charmes.

Roger Duboeuf & Fils (Chaintré)
Roger is the elder brother of Georges Duboeuf. Visitors can taste delicious wines, including white Beaujolais and Pouilly-Fuissé, in the 16th-century tasting room.

Domaine Guffens-Heynen (Vergisson)
Belgian owner Jean-Marie Guffens has a striking personality and great dynamism. High-quality wines: Pouilly-Fuissé and white and red Mâcon-Pierreclos.

Verget (Sologny)
Jean-Marie Guffens' commercial establishment. Very good Mâcon wines, Chablis and other Bourgognes.

ST VERAN

 RESTAURANTS

Au Fin Bec
Leynes
Tel: 03 85 35 11 77
Appetizing aromas waft from this restaurant where the owner is the cook. The cuisine is regional. A couple of different menus for less than FF100.

Relais Beaujolais-Mâconnais
Leynes
Tel: 03 85 35 11 29
Simple, regional dishes and indeed, regional wines. The menus begin under FF100.

Le Tire Bouchon
Saint-Vérand
Tel: 03 85 37 15 33
A winegrowing family owns this restaurant, situated at the foot of the village. *Coq au Béaujolais-Villages, entrecôte charolaise* and similar dishes. Menus from less than FF100.

RECOMMENDED PRODUCERS

Domaine de la Croix Senaillet (Davayé)
The Saint-Véran here is usually fresh, firm and fruity. The red Mâcon is distinguished by its fruit too.

where the exertion is rewarded with a wonderful view. There is also a walking route starting from the hamlet of La Grange du Bois, situated on a hill just outside Solutré. The view is fabulous and as a treat afterwards you can eat, mainly *grillades,* in the rustic Auberge de la Grange du Bois (tel: 85 37 80 78).

By driving from Solutré to Fuissé, you pass through the hamlet of Pouilly. In the higher part of the village, from where there is a fine view of the surrounding countryside, there is a 15th-century chapel and a castle, flanked by towers.

About 1km down the road is Fuissé, from which Pouilly-Fuissé takes the second part of its name. The village sits in a natural 'amphitheatre', the slopes of which spread out from it, planted with its now world-famous grapevines. The important role wine has played in Fuissé's history is demonstrated by the allegorical depiction of the struggle against phylloxera above the entrance to its church.

From Fuissé, take the winding D172 west and turn left onto the D31. This road takes you through the village of Leynes. At the crossroads about 1km outside Leynes, turn left to the village of Chaintré. On a wall near the church is a colourful wall painting and a large bottle with the names of winegrowers reminding you once more that this is a wine village.

While a good Pouilly-Fuissé is a rich white wine which gives impressions of fruit, flowers, nuts and also often of vanilla and oak, there are two other local wines which have a slightly lighter structure, but which cost much less. These are Pouilly-Vinzelles and Pouilly-Loché. Unfortunately, both of them are hard to find.

The origin of Pouilly-Vinzelles is the village of Vinzelles. To reach it, continue north from Chaintré. Pouilly-Loché originates from the village of Loché, which is another kilometre further north, and is now celebrated for its TGV station. The local castle, the Château de Loché (13th to 18th century), has made its own wine since 1989, but the quality is variable. It can be visited, but by appointment only.

SAINT-VERAN

The appellation of Saint-Véran was created in 1971 out of land in eight communes dotted haphazardly around the district: Chânes, Chasselas, Davayé, Leynes, Prissé, Saint-Amour, Saint-Vérand and Solutré. Formerly, these villages produced Mâcon-Villages or white Beaujolais. As a wine, the (always white) Saint-Véran is usually somewhat leaner and less rich than Pouilly-Fuissé. There are exceptions though: a superior Saint-Véran, more usually from the communes of Prissé or Davayé, can often offer better quality than an average Pouilly-Fuissé.

The northernmost municipality is Prissé, situated on the D89 travelling north from Loché. There are two castles in this village, Manoir de la Cerve and Château de Monceau, neither of which is open to the public. The poet Bauderon lived in the first and Lamartine in the second.

About 2kms to the south of Prissé is the neighbouring village of Davayé where there is more to see, including, on a hillside nearby, a Romanesque church and an old communal bath. There are also several castles and a well-known school for winegrowing.

To the south of Chaintré is the village of Saint-Vérand. The village was formerly called Saint-Véran-des-Vignes, but the name was changed to avoid confusion with Saint-Véran in Beaujolais. Dating from the Middle Ages, this attractive hill village has a carefully restored, small church with a beautiful fresco inside. At the village of Leynes you will find one of the very few 16th-century churches in Burgundy. It is situated near the village square.

Finally, you will come to the village of Chasselas, which gave its name to both a table and a wine grape (though no longer cultivated in this part of France). It is worth stopping off to see the small Romanesque church in the centre of the village and the large, attractive castle on the outskirts.

Henri-Lucius Grégoire (Davayé)
Modest property with some good Saint-Vérans and a Crémant de Bourgogne.
Jean-Jacques Martin (Chânes)
Some delicious wines are produced here, fermented in stainless steel. Try the white Burgundy, Saint-Véran and a sublime Pouilly-Vincelles.
Domaine des Pérelles (Chânes)
This estate is run by André Larochette and produces, among others, a successful Saint-Véran.
Cooperative Prissé (Prissé)
Modern, well-equipped business. Excellent white wines. Try the Saint-Véran, Mâcon-Villages and Bourgogne Aligoté.
Domaine des Pierres Rouges (Chasselas)
This estate enjoys a good name thanks to its soft, fresh Saint-Véran.
Domaine des Valanges (Davayé)
Delicious, well-balanced Saint-Véran.
Domaine des Deux Roches (Davayé)
Large estate producing excellent Saint-Véran Les Terres Noires, a Vieilles Vignes, a Mâcon-Villages/Davayé) and a red Mâcon.

PLACES OF INTEREST

On a hill behind the old church of Davayé stands the angular building complex of the Lycée Viticole de Davayé. Young winegrowers are educated here. It makes wine from its own vineyards, including a Saint-Véran.

Far left (bottom) *The Solutré Rock, and surrounding hills.*
Top *A street sign advertises the Maconnais' most famous wine.*
Main picture and above *The charming village of Solutré.*

Beaujolais

With more than one half of the total vineyards under its appellation, Beaujolais is by far the largest of the five Burgundian districts. It is also one of the most beautiful. It is made up of a long sequence of granite hills, the spurs of a chain of wooded mountains that vary in height from 700 to 1,000ms. These hills act as a shield against westerly winds so that the region enjoys a mild climate. Narrow, winding roads criss-cross the district past green hills, through quiet valleys and idyllic villages. In a timeless, romantic way the Beaujolais symbolizes the best of the French countryside. With good reason, author Gabriel Chevallier chose Vaux-en-Beaujolais as the model for his novel *Clochemerle*, the comic story of rural life (translated into many languages).

Wine grapes reign supreme here, in particular Gamay, or, to give it its full title, Gamay Noir à Jus Blanc, which thrives in the sandy, stony or schistous soils of the district. Helped by the climate, these soils give the wines a rounded quality and depth of flavour that is seldom achieved elsewhere with this grape variety. There is also a certain amount of white Beaujolais made, based on Chardonnay.

The best and most powerful wines of Beaujolais are the ten *crus*. These come from villages or groups of villages in the northern part of the area. These are, from north to south, Saint-Amour (part of which actually lies within the Mâconnais), Juliénas, Chénas, Moulin-à-Vent, Fleurie, Chiroubles, Morgon, Régnié, Brouilly and Côte de Brouilly.

Ordinary Beaujolais is mainly grown in the southern part of the district, with the slightly better quality, fuller Beaujolais-Villages wines produced in and around 39 villages, most of which are situated in the north of the region.

But the world has come to know Beaujolais, not through its best wines but through its simplest – Beaujolais Primeur or Beaujolais Nouveau. This is sold from the third Thursday

Left *Beaujolais offers Burgundy's most beautiful landscape.*

Above *Traditional sign made from the end of a barrel.*

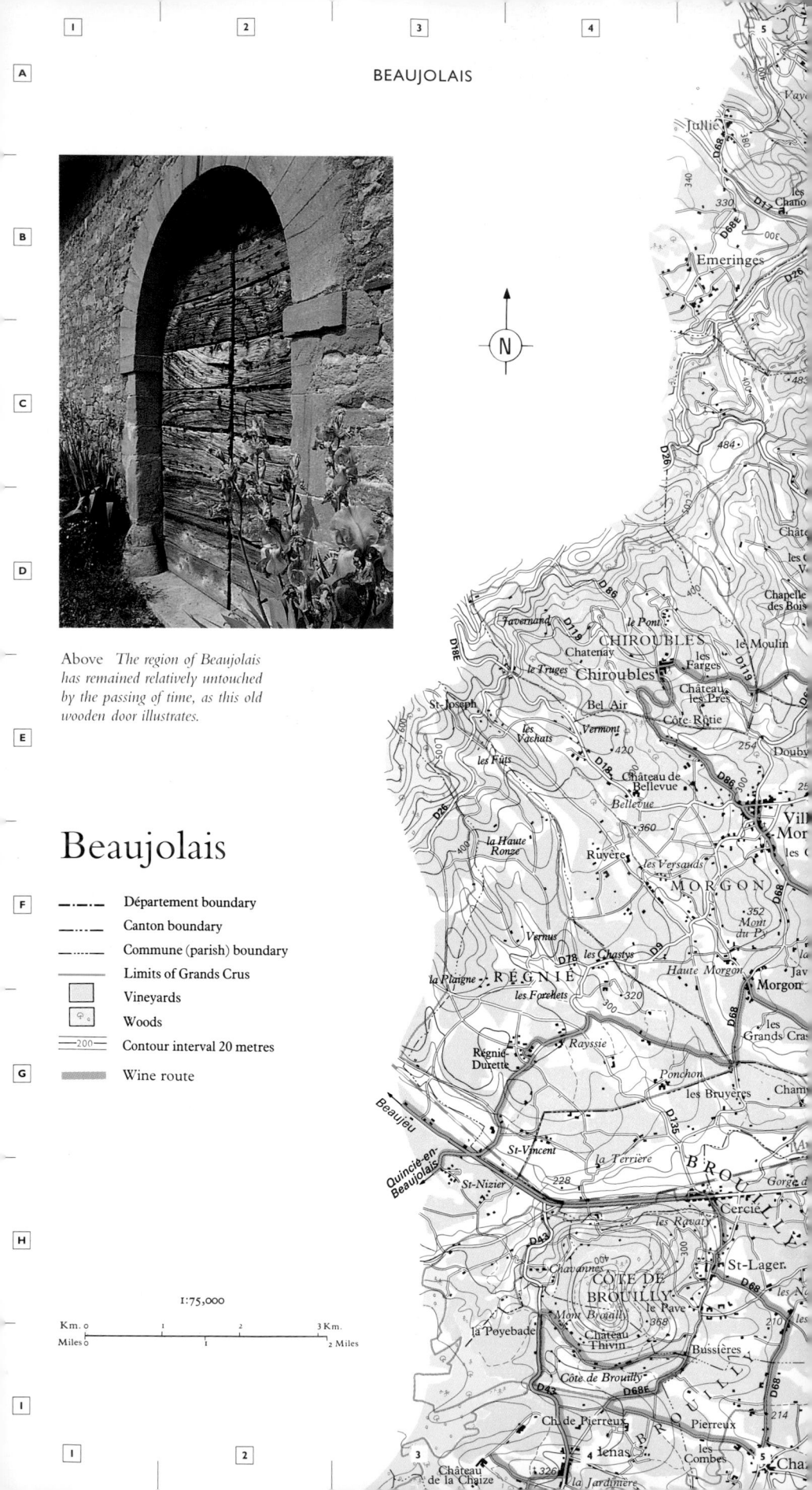

Above *The region of Beaujolais has remained relatively untouched by the passing of time, as this old wooden door illustrates.*

Beaujolais

—·—·—	Département boundary
—··—··—	Canton boundary
—·····—	Commune (parish) boundary
——	Limits of Grands Crus
▢	Vineyards
▢	Woods
—200—	Contour interval 20 metres
▬▬	Wine route

1:75,000

Km. 0   1   2   3 Km.
Miles 0   1   2 Miles

Map labels: Jullié, les Chano, Emeringes, Château, les V, Chapelle des Bois, Favernand, le Pont, CHIROUBLES, le Moulin, Chatenay, les Farges, le Truges, Chiroubles, Château les Prés, St-Joseph, Bel Air, Côte-Rôtie, les Vachats, Vermont, Douby, les Fûts, Château de Bellevue, Bellevue, la Haute Ronze, Ruyère, les Versauds, MORGON, Mont du Py, Vernus, les Chastys, Haute Morgon, Morgon, la Plaigne, RÉGNIÉ, les Forchets, les Grands Cras, Rayssie, Régnié-Durette, Ponchon, les Bruyères, Cham, Beaujeu, St-Vincent, la Terrière, BROUILLY, Quincié-en-Beaujolais, St-Nizier, Cercié, les Ravat, Chavannes, CÔTE DE BROUILLY, St-Lager, Mont Brouilly, le Pavé, la Poyebade, Château Thivin, Bussières, Côte de Brouilly, Ch. de Pierreux, Pierreux, Iénas, les Combes, Château de la Chaize, la Jardinière

in November and is made to be drunk immediately. Commercially Beaujolais Nouveau has been a tremendous success with the result that it now represents about half of all Beaujolais production. But for true wine-lovers, finding really excellent examples of what can be achieved with the Gamay grape is the main aim and, if you look carefully, some are superb.

Fruit is characteristic of all good Beaujolais red wines, and the best offer juicy flavours of red fruits (strawberries, raspberries, cherries). They are often best served slightly chilled: about 16°C is ideal.

SAINT-AMOUR

The most northern *cru* in Beaujolais, Saint-Amour derives its name from the commune of Saint-Amour-Bellevue, which is made up of several hamlets. From Chânes in the southern Mâconnais, travel southeast, crossing over the D31 to join the D186. The first hamlet you come to is the hilltop village of Le Bourg Neuf. From here, the road (D186) runs through vineyards to Plâtre-Durand, a hamlet consisting mainly of a large square with two restaurants and a winetasting room, the Caveau du Cru Saint-Amour, which is open most of the year. A statue of a Roman legionary, near the reception hall of Saint-Amour-Bellevue, is witness to the legend that a soldier called Amor(e) or Amator, settled here at the end of the third century, having been converted to Catholicism, and was canonized because he was killed for his religion.

Further west along the same road is the hamlet of La Ville. On the hill above it is the Château de Saint-Amour, a 19th-century building built on the foundations of a 16th-century castle. Its wines are sold mainly through a *négociant*. Saint-Amour wines are fairly reserved but have fruit, charm and supple structure. Like all the *crus*, Saint-Amour wines must contain at least 10.5 per cent alcohol, 11 per cent if the name of the vineyard appears on the label.

JULIENAS

At Plâtre-Durand, you must turn right onto the D486. After about 3kms you arrive at the village of Juliénas.

The fact that this is a wine village is immediately clear to visitors who park their cars on the Place du Marché, because not only is there a shop selling wine-cellar equipment (as well as wine-related items for the home), but there is also a shop owned by winegrower Pierre Perrachon (from Chénas) and a strikingly designed restaurant called Le Coq au Vin. Should there still be doubts, then a walk in the direction of the church will dispel them, because across from the currently used church is the old church – which, since 1954, has been

ST-AMOUR

RESTAURANTS

Auberge du Paradis
Tel: 03 85 37 10 26
Village inn, suitable for large groups, with menus under FF100.

Chez Jean-Pierre
Tel: 03 85 37 41 26
Diagonally opposite its competitor. The restaurant is slightly smaller and the prices a little higher.

RECOMMENDED PRODUCERS

Domaine de la Cave Lamartine
Saint-Amours full of fruit, including white.

Domaine des Ducs
Family firm with charming wines. Saint-Amour is award-winning; among the best.

André Poitevin
Possibly the oldest cellar in Saint-Amour, dating from 1399. Intensely fruity and well-structured wines.

Domaine de Savy
Excellent reds and whites, eg Saint-Véran, Pouilly-Fuissé.

Georges Trichard
Talented grower with wines in top Paris restaurants.

JULIENAS

HOTEL

Hôtel des Vignes
Tel: 04 74 04 43 70
Two-star hotel, 25 good rooms. Prices from FF230. No restaurant.

RESTAURANTS

Le Coq au Vin
Tel: 04 74 04 41 98
Stylish place to eat, with excellent cuisine. Menus from FF100.

Above *A chais in Saint-Amour.*
Above right *The commune of Juliénas produces structured wines which can age, although most should be drunk after 2 to 3 years.*
Right *Local crafts on sale in Saint-Amour.*
Far right *Domaine des Chers – one of the best estates in Juliénas.*

used as a winetasting room. The interior of this Cellier de la Vieille Eglise is decorated with bacchanalian depictions and attracts many visitors, especially at weekends.

The origins of this wine village apparently go back to Roman times. Perhaps the name Juliénas is derived from Julius Caesar – but this is also said to be the case for neighbouring Jullié (whose vineyards belong to Juliénas, too).

One of the oldest local buildings is the Château de Juliénas, situated just outside the village centre on the D137. It has impressive 18th-century cellars which cover 200 square metres. Slightly further along the same road is the Maison de la Dîme, a tollhouse from the 16th century. Juliénas also has an important wine cooperative, the headquarters of which are housed in the 17th-century Château du Bois de la Salle, where visitors can taste the wines.

CHENAS

Coming out of Juliénas travelling south, turn right onto the D17. At the tiny hamlet of Le Fief, follow the road right round to the left, almost in a U-turn, onto the D68, which skirts the steep sides of a hill on your right. At the hamlet of Les Deschamps, the D68 turns right and leads into Chénas.

Chénas is the smallest of the Beaujolais *crus*. Confusingly, most of the vineyards in Chénas are labelled as Moulin-à-Vent, while the neighbouring village of La Chapelle-de-Guinchay produces twice as much Chénas wines as Chénas itself.

The name Chénas comes from *chêne*, oak, because there used to be a large forest of oak trees here. The trees, however, were cut down centuries ago. Now the village consists of a few houses in the midst of hilly vineyards. The Château de Chénas, not so attractive from the outside, has impressive, arched cellars used by the local cooperative.

As a wine Chénas is closely akin to its neighbour Moulin-à-Vent: substance and strength are its characteristics, and it benefits from a few years' ageing. Locally, Chénas is described as 'a bouquet of flowers in a basket of velvet'.

MOULIN-A-VENT

If, instead of following the D68 round to the right, you continue straight on at the crossroads just south of the village of Chénas, shortly afterwards you will arrive in the Moulin-à-Vent district.

The building which gave its name to the cru Moulin-à-Vent is an old 18th-century windmill which was closed down in 1850, since grain was no longer cultivated in Beaujolais; today it is a sea of vineyards. In the winter of 1910, the region was hit hard by bad weather and wild storms which destroyed the windmill's sails. Since then the mill has stood in ruins in the Beaujolais landscape. Nevertheless, it was and is still seen as a beacon in this sea of vines. It has been declared a monument *historique* and stands on a hill between the villages of Romanèche-Thorins (in whose boundaries it is situated) and Chénas. In the summer of 1999, it was finally given new sails, meaning the Moulin-à-Vent labels have to be redesigned. The monument is surrounded by an official tasting room and a few wine-producing estates.

The appellation Moulin-à-Vent encompasses Romanèche-Thorins as well as approximately three-quarters of Chénas. The wine is among the best of Beaujolais, thanks to its dark colour, robust, generous, soft, fruity flavours and a sufficient level of tannin to allow it to mature for a few years.

The Musée Guillon in Romanèche-Thorins is worth a visit. It houses a collection of about 100 models of wooden towers, made by the French guild of carpenters. On the square there is a bust of Benoît Raclet (1780–1844) who, in the first half of the last century, discovered a remedy for the *pyrale*, a small worm that destroys vine leaves. He is honoured annually during the Fête Raclet, which takes place on the last Saturday of October. His house is now a museum.

Chez la Rose
Tel: 04 74 04 41 20
Menus start under FF100 and include mainly regional dishes. Also a simple hotel with 10 rooms, from FF220.

RECOMMENDED PRODUCERS

Domaine des Chers
Fruity Juliénas with potential to mature well.
Château de Juliénas
Must visit to see the magnificent cellars.
Domaine Jean-Pierre Margerand
Good Juliénas which ages well.
Jean-Marc Monnet
Excellent Juliénas: soft blackcurrant and red-fruit flavours.
Michel Tête
Top estate: good Cuvée Prestige Domaine du Clos du Fief.

CHENAS

RESTAURANT

Robin/Relais des Grands Crus
Tel: 03 85 36 72 67
One of the best restaurants in Beaujolais. The *salade Beaujolaise and poulet de Bresse rôti au four* are worth a detour. Menus start at about FF200.

RECOMMENDED PRODUCERS

Château Bonnet (La Chapelle-de-Guinchay)
Château and park and firm, fruity Chénas.
Domaine des Brureaux
Chénas needing three years' ageing plus.
Domaine Champagnon
Outstanding: dark, meaty, juicy Chénas

Above *Famous mill, giving its name to the appellation Moulin-à-Vent. New sails since summer 1999.*
Right *Tradition and modern technology combined at Georges Duboeuf, in Romanèche-Thorins.*

MOULIN-A-VENT

 HOTEL

Les Maritonnes
Tel: 03 85 35 51 70
Stylish rooms from FF400. Swimming pool. Restaurant is good, menus from FF200.

 RESTAURANT

La Maison Blanche
Tel: 03 85 35 50 53
Cosy restaurant on the N6, where you can eat well for reasonable prices. Menus begin under FF100. Also a few hotel rooms.

RECOMMENDED PRODUCERS
Domaine de la Bruyère
Masterful, concentrated Moulin-à-Vent.
Georges Duboeuf
Since 1964, Duboeuf has worked his way up from paid bottler to biggest Beaujolais *négociant*. Now often called 'pope', 'king' or 'emperor' of this region. Fruity wines.
Château des Jacques
Perfectly maintained estate with strong Moulin-à-Vent; superior white Beaujolais.
Jacky Janodet
Wines to lay down.

FLEURIE

Fleurie lies directly west of Romanèche-Thorins. If you drive south out of Romanèche on the D86, you can turn right onto the D32 which will lead you straight into Fleurie. Or, from Chénas, drive south on the D68: a beautiful road with a wonderful view of the village as you approach it.

Fleurie is a peaceful village. Life centres on the square with its stores, cafés and restaurants. One shop, La Cave Vigneronne, sells wines. There is a market here on Saturdays.

On the first weekend after November 1 (All Saints' Day), the peacefulness that reigns for most of the year gives way to hustle and bustle when a large wine fair is held here with wines from Beaujolais, the Mâconnais and the Chalonnais: Fleurie is then invaded by thousands of winegrowers, wine-lovers and wine merchants.

Fleurie, the wine, is one of the best-selling Beaujolais *crus*. A good one has lively, fresh fruitiness, with an elegant firmness and a seductive aroma of red fruits and spring flowers.

CHIROUBLES

Leave Fleurie on the D68 travelling south. After about 2kms there is a turning to the right onto the D119 to Chiroubles. Do not turn off this road, but follow it as it climbs the hillside with the village visible on the slopes to the left. The road continues up the hill and turns almost through 180 degrees at the top. At the crossroads, turn left onto the D86 and descend towards the village.

This small village – home to the *cru* of the same name – is situated at a height of 400 metres. Here the southeast-facing vineyards with granite-based soils give a light, tender Beaujolais which is usually best to drink within a year of bottling.

The village has a small, 19th-century domed church and next to it is a bust of Victor Pulliat, the brilliant researcher who found a remedy against the gluttonous grape aphid phylloxera: grafting onto American rootstock. The local cooperative – with tasting room – is close by. There is also a tasting room in a chalet, La Terrasse du Beaujolais, on the hillside high above the village, where you can taste many wines from the area and eat well in the restaurant, with its superb panoramic view.

MORGON

The vineyards of the Morgon *cru* lie within the commune of Villié-Morgon. To reach the village of Villié-Morgon drive out of Chiroubles heading south on the D86.

The villages of Villié and Morgon became one municipality in 1867. Since then, the border has been situated at Mont du Py, the 352-metre high remains of a

Jean Mortet
Oak-matured, strong, fruity wines. The best is Les Rouchaux.
Château du Moulin-à-Vent
Fine, generous, quality Moulin-à-Vent.

PLACES OF INTEREST

There is a Touroparc amusement park near Romanèche-Thorins which has a zoo, a swimming pool, roller-coaster, miniature train, and even a cave boat trip.

FLEURIE

HOTEL

Les Grands Vins
Tel: 04 74 69 81 43
Modern hotel, 20 peaceful rooms (from about FF350). Small swimming pool.

RESTAURANT

Auberge du Cep
Tel: 04 74 04 10 77
A bistro specialising in regional cuisine and a pleasant place to linger. Menus from FF135. Attractive wine list with the accent on Beaujolais wines – naturally.

RECOMMENDED PRODUCERS

Domaine Bernard
Excellent Fleurie, well-balanced.
Domaine Chantreuil
Balanced Fleurie, beautifully rounded.
Michel Chignard
Medal-winning Fleurie Les Moriers.
Alain Coudert
Relatively powerful, fragrant Fleurie Clos de la Roilette.
Domaine de la Grand' Cour
Fruity, juicy Fleurie with a firm backbone.

CHIROUBLES

RESTAURANT

Chez Marc et Annick
Tel: 04 74 04 24 87
Cosy inn in the centre of the village. For less than FF100 you can eat very well.

RECOMMENDED PRODUCERS

Domaine Bouillard
Distinctive, lively, elegant wine. Drink young.
Domaine Cheysson-les-Farges
Award-winning, distinctive Chiroubles.
Domaine de la Combe aux Loups
Aromatic wines, complex and lengthy.
Bernard Méziat
Sturdy, fruity wines.
Alain Passot/Domaine de la Grosse Pierre
Fresh, fruity Chiroubles; delicious young.
Francis Tomatis & Fils
Family estate for excellent Chiroubles listed at some of France's best restaurants.

Left *The Fleurie landscape, one of the most popular Beaujolais crus: wines with a delicious fresh fruitiness.*

Above and right *Aspects of life in the Beaujolais region: harvesting, barrel-cleaning – and beautiful surroundings.*

MORGON

HOTEL

Château de Pizay
Tel: 04 74 66 51 41
62 modern, well-decorated rooms, from FF565. Excellent, regional cuisine served in a vaulted dining room. Menus from FF200. Swimming pool. Also a wine estate.

RECOMMENDED PRODUCERS

Domaine de la Chanaise
Leading property producing powerfully bouqueted Morgon.
Louis Claude Desvignes
Morgons: good fruit and rich tannins.
Domaine des Pillets
Well-made Morgon, ageing two years.
Domaine Pierre Savoye
Attractive, supple Morgon Côte du Py, with intense colour and flavour.

BROUILLY

HOTEL

Le Mont Brouilly
Quincié
Tel: 04 74 04 33 73
30 rooms (about FF300). Peaceful at the rear, with a view of Mont Brouilly.

RESTAURANTS

Monique et Jean-Paul Crozier
Saint-Lager
Tel: 04 74 66 82 79
Welcoming, unpretentious; good for wholesome food. It also has a bar.
Christian Mabeau
Odenas
Tel: 04 74 03 41 79
The best restaurant of both the *crus*. On weekdays the menu costs about FF115. Terrace overlooking vineyards.

volcano, with Villié on the north side of the hill and Morgon on the south side. Mont du Py and Charmes are two of the best vineyards of the Morgon appellation. Underlying schistous rock helps produce a substantial, generous wine. In fact, it has been said of Morgon's wine that it has '*Le fruit d'un Beaujolais, le charme d'un Bourgogne*' (the fruit of a Beaujolais and the charm of a Burgundy). A classic Morgon is distinguished by its aroma of wild cherries, and there is frequently a substantial core of alcohol.

Morgon's winetasting room is one of the most visited of the region. It is housed in the arched cellars of a castle near to the village centre.

BROUILLY AND COTE DE BROUILLY

From Villié-Morgon, follow the D68 south towards the Côte de Brouilly and the village of Brouilly itself.

The entrance to southern Beaujolais is dominated by the 483m Mont Brouilly, an extinct volcano. The vineyards growing on its slopes have their own appellation, that of the *cru* Côte de Brouilly. Wines from this appellation are usually large, mouthfilling and light in alcohol, thanks to the optimum levels of sun which hit these hillside slopes. At the same time, the wines have a refined aroma, often with hints of violets and raspberries.

The vineyards surrounding the volcano belong to the Brouilly appellation, which has the biggest yield of all the Beaujolais *crus*. The appellation is made up of parts of the communes of Cercié, Charentay, Odenas, Quincié-en-Beaujolais, Saint-Etienne-la-Varenne and Saint-Lager. Differences in the soil and the large number of producers mean that there are many styles of Brouilly, but fruit and firmness are the prevalent characteristics.

All the villages of Côte de Brouilly and Brouilly have their own charm. Follow the D68 to Cercié with its ancient chapel, then travel on to Saint-Lager, where you will find several small châteaux and the Cuvage des Brouilly (the tasting room of both *crus*). At Saint-Lager, the D68 splits in two, with the D68-e continuing straight on and the D68 turning left. Take the latter road, turning left after about 1km (still the D68) to Charentay. Here you can see the ruins of the castle of Arigny and (along the road to Odenas) the 19th-century Tour de Belle-Mère.

Close to the village of Odenas are two castles: the 17th-century Château de Pierreux to the north and the much grander Château de la Chaize to the west.

If you drive south out of Odenas on the D62 you will come to Saint-Etienne-la-Varenne, a picturesque village built in terraces which is pleasant to stroll around.

Quincié-en-Beaujolais is situated northwest of Mont Brouilly on the D9. Here, there is a cream-coloured church, a large cooperative and the imposing 15th-century castle of Varennes (along the road to Marchampt).

REGNIE

In 1988, the nine existing Beaujolais *crus* were joined by a tenth, Régnié, lying west of Morgon and Brouilly. The wine is colourful, expressive, very fruity and fairly firm. To get to Régnié from Odenas, take the D43 heading north, turn left onto the D37 and then, after 1km, turn right onto the D9, which takes you into the village.

The most impressive building in Régnié-Durette is the church with two tall towers; nearby is the local tasting - room. Outside the centre lies the striking Domaine de la Grange-Charton, belonging to the Hospices de Beaujeu: it is an enormous courtyard, surrounded by houses and cellars, and has an immense underground vaulted cellar. There are two castles near the village: Châteaux de la Pierre and des Vergers.

RECOMMENDED PRODUCERS

Domaine Ruet (Cercié)
Usually exquisite: lively and full of fruit.
Bernard Champier (Odenas)
Tiny estate for strikingly good Brouilly.
Château Thivin (Odenas)
Excellent Côte de Brouilly and Brouilly.
Laurent Martray (Saint-Etienne-la-Varenne)
Try the Brouilly Cuvée Vieilles Vignes.

REGNIE

RESTAURANT

Auberge la Vigneronne
Tel: 04 74 04 35 95
Rustic, inexpensive country restaurant.

RECOMMENDED PRODUCERS

Desplace Frères/Domaine du Crêt des Bruyères
Award-winning, pure and fruity Régnié.
Domaine de la Gérarde
Firm Régnié; pleasing amount of fruit.
Domaine Passot les Rampaux
Good Régnié and a Morgon.
J-P Rampon
Lively, elegant Régnié.

SOUTHERN BEAUJOLAIS

HOTELS

Hostellerie Saint-Vincent
Salles-Arbuissonnas
Tel: 04 74 67 55 50
This hotel has a park, swimming pool and tennis court. The rooms are comfortable (starting at about FF300) and you can eat well here: *confit de canard maison, suprême de caille,* etc. Menus start at around FF140.
Le St-Romain
Anse
Tel: 04 74 60 24 46
Pleasant hotel with some 25 rooms (starting at approximately FF200). Decorated classically, but with modern facilities. Peacefully situated a few kilometres from the exit of the *autoroute*. It also has a restaurant.

Below *The grand architecture and grounds of the 19th-century Château Lacarelle, the largest wine estate in Beaujolais.*

SOUTHERN BEAUJOLAIS

The southern part of Beaujolais consists of both flat and pronouncedly hilly areas. The wines produced here are given the appellations Beaujolais-Villages and ordinary Beaujolais (in red, white and rosé), but, apart from wine, the region has a lot to offer the tourist. It is worth the effort of exploring this beautifully varied and unspoilt countryside with its attractive golden-stone *(pierres dorées)* villages by taking the following route.

It begins with a short excursion to Beaujeu, which is to the west of the Côte de Brouilly, along the D37. The centre consists of a long street, which runs past the church of Saint-Nicolas (a good place to park). Nearby you will find the tasting room of Beaujolais-Villages: the Temple of Bacchus. Next to it is the town hall, which houses the Syndicat d'Initiative (tourist office) and the Musée des Arts et Traditions Populaires. Across from the church there is a pretty half-timbered building which now serves as the Maison du Pays de Beaujeu et Haut-Beaujolais – an exhibition space and a shop.

Returning east along the D37 from Beaujeu, and turning south onto the D43, you will come to the village of Odenas (*see* page 128) and, further along the same road, you'll arrive at Saint-Etienne-des-Ouillières with its 19th-century Château de Lacarelle, which is the largest wine estate of Beaujolais.

Take the D62 west out of Saint-Etienne-des-Ouilliéres and, at the crossroads, turn left onto the D133 to Le Perréon, where you can taste wine in the cellars of the Château des Loges (also a hotel-restaurant). Just south of Le Perréon is the village of Vaux-en-Beaujolais, on the D49. This charming hilltop village was the backdrop for the novel

Southern Beaujolais

—·—·— Département boundary

▬▬▬▬ Limit of Beaujolais region

FLEURIE Beaujolais Grand Cru commune

PRUZILLY Beaujolais-Villages commune

<u>BEAUJEU</u> Main merchant centres

▢ Crus Beaujolais

▢ Beaujolais-Villages

▢ Beaujolais

[122] Area mapped at larger scale on page shown

▬▬▬ Wine route

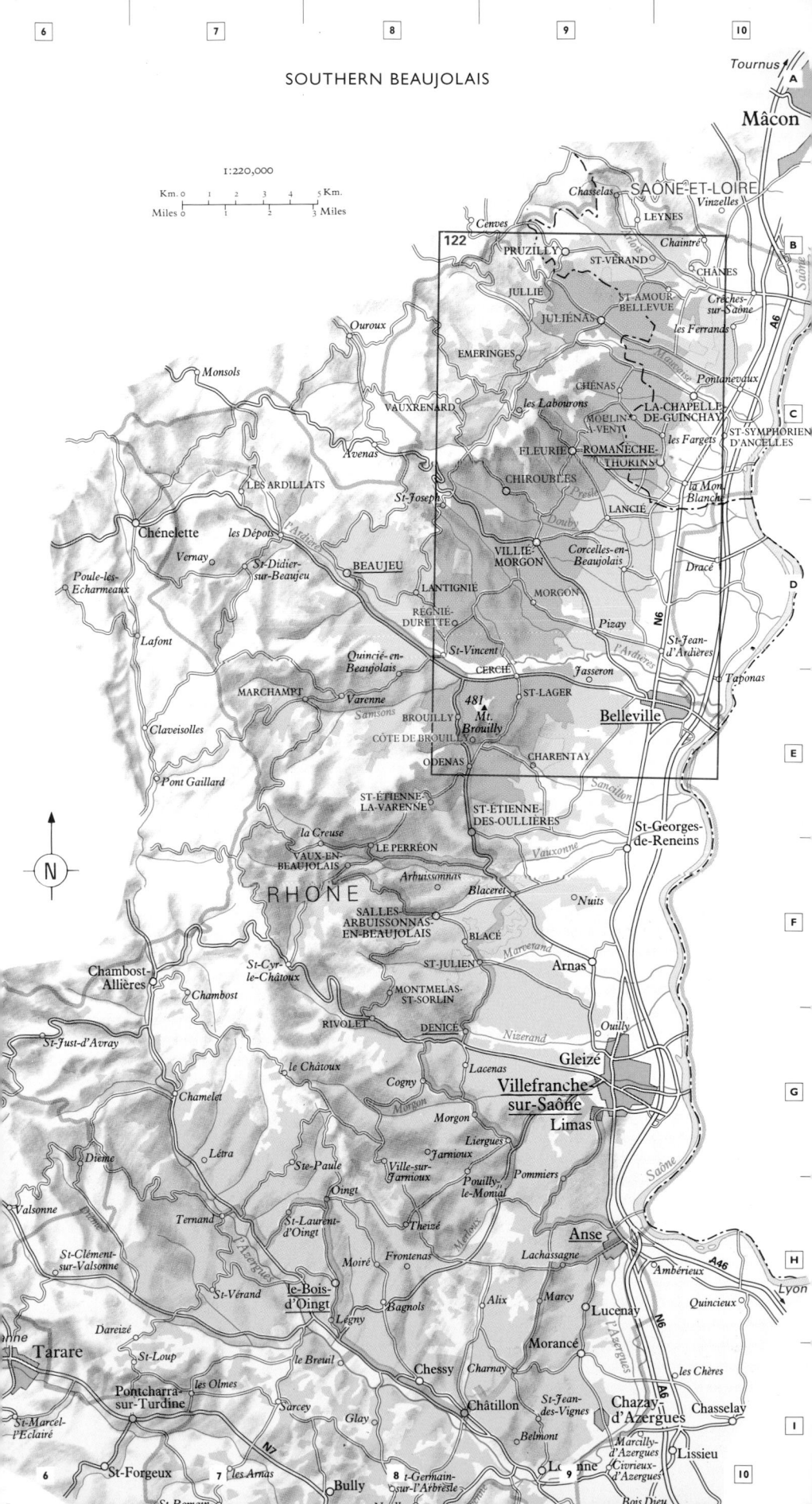

SOUTHERN BEAUJOLAIS

1:220,000

Km. 0   1   2   3   4   5 Km.
Miles 0   1   2   3 Miles

Clochemerle by Gabriel Chevallier. Near the village church is the subject of Chevallier's book: a urinal. You will find another one near the Musée Viticole et Agricole (in a side street next to the church). Black, metal signs point out the way to shops and craftsmen in Vaux.

From Vaux, travel along the D35 road southeast. As you travel along this marvellous, winding road to Salles-Arbuissonas, along the way there are some spectacular views over the surrounding countryside. In the village, park near the town hall and walk under a gateway to the church and the 10th-century monastery, founded by the monks of Cluny. There are wonderful frescos in the chapter house and next to the church is a fine, peaceful cloister.

To the east of Salles, Blaceret has a good restaurant serving regional dishes. Also worth visiting are Blacé with its 19th-century castle (follow the D19), and the village of Cogny, again on the D19, where the church is built from the ochre-coloured *pierres dorées* so characteristic of southern Beaujolais. Lierques is the next stop. This little village has a good wine cooperative as well as an interesting church to see, with frescos and stone statuettes of craftsmen and winegrowers decorating the walls.

Carry on to Pommiers by driving east out of Cogny on the D84. Turn right at the crossroads onto the D76 and continue until you reach the D38. Turn right onto the D38, travelling south for about 2kms and then turn left and left again to reach the village of Pommiers. Here in the 15th-century church, there are curious stone animal heads to be seen.

Now drive south on the D70, turning left after 1km to Anse, which has Roman mosaics in the Château de Tours. Then, stopping briefly at Lachassagne on the D39, for the view and the art gallery La Cuvée, go back onto the D70 to Charnay.

RESTAURANTS

Anne de Beaujeu
Beaujeu
Tel: 04 74 04 87 58
Tasty regional cooking (*poulet de Bresse à la crème légère*). The most inexpensive menu – with the speciality of the day – costs less than FF125. There are also seven hotel rooms, with variable bathroom facilities. There is a car park in front and a larger one 60 metres further up the road.

Auberge de Clochemerle
Vaux-en-Beaujolais
Tel: 04 74 03 20 16
Rural inn with regional specialities (terrines, *coq au vin*), fresh fish and a few surprises. Menus start at FF100.

Auberge de Liergues
Tel: 04 74 68 02 02
Large portions, keen prices (menus begin under FF100) at a café on the church square. Cuisine is mainly regional.

Restaurant du Beaujolais
Blaceret
Tel: 04 74 67 54 75
An ivy-covered restaurant with terrace. Many attractive dishes. A *pot au feu* is usually on the menu one day a week. Menus start at about FF130.

Above *Vaux-en-Beaujolais, setting of the famous novel, Clochemerle.*
Right *Vines near the village of Vaux-en-Beaujolais.*
Far right *Cloisters in southern Beaujolais.*

Above *A house with vines in Oingt, a beautiful little town dating from the medieval period.* Below *View over the village of Jarnioux.*

Le Donjon
Oingt
Tel: 04 74 71 20 24
Pleasant restaurant with a terrace and fine views. Rural dishes such as *confit de canard*. Menus start around. FF100.

Le Savigny
Blacé
Tel: 04 74 67 52 07
Stylish, classic, delicious cuisine. Menus start at about FF150. It is also a small hotel (nine rooms starting at FF300).

La Terrasse des Beaujolais
Buisante
Tel: 04 74 65 05 27
Dining room with magnificent view.

 PLACES OF INTEREST

There is a golf club near Lucenay, south of Anse. Called *Le Golf du Beaujolais* it has a 9-hole and an 18-hole course.

 RECOMMENDED PRODUCERS

Louis et Hélène Deschamps
Elegant Beaujolais with plenty of fruit and exhilarating freshness.

Paul Gauthier (Blacé)
Ordinary Beaujolais-Villages and Beaujolais as well as the *primeur* versions have a lot of fruit and a pure, balanced taste.

Georges Texier & Fils (Blacé)
Attractive Beaujolais-Villages.

La Folie (Blaceret)
Good reputation for fruity Brouilly.

Gobet (Blaceret)
Négociant with Beaujolais of various qualities. Top Domaine des Grandes Tours.

There are 'golden stones' galore here, as well as a church (with a giant, multicoloured statue of Saint Christopher) and a château (also the town hall).

From here the D70-e, a beautiful road, runs south down to Châtillon-d'Azarques, which is dominated by its large château with interesting wall paintings in one of its chapels. Now travel northwest, along the D485 to the fortified

Left *A vine-covered outbuilding in Jarnioux reflects the timeless, rustic peacefulness of Beaujolais.*

Charmet (Le Breuil)
Prize winning wines. Red Beaujolais Cuvée la Centenaire is one of the best in the district, with excellent fruitiness and flawless quality. Also very good white.

Les Vins Mathelin (Châtillon-d'Azergues)
Reliable *négociant*, with delicious, supple, fruity wines. The best are labelled with their estate names.

Cave Coopérative (Liergues)
Good cooperative with modern equipment for delicious Beaujolais. The white is also worth tasting..

Château des Loges (Le Perréon)
Label for good Beaujolais-Villages wines made by the local cooperative.

René et Christian Miolane (Salles-Arbuissonas)
Large estate exclusively for Beaujolais-Villages, usually of excellent quality, style, depth, fruit and refinement. There is also a small wine museum here.

Château de Lacarelle (Saint-Etienne-des-Ouillières)
The largest Beaujolais estate and one of the oldest. Much Beaujolais Nouveau. The ordinary Beaujolais-Villages is generally lively and fruity.

village of Le Breuil. Turn right, a little further on, to Le Bois d'Oingt, the 'city of roses', and then take the beautiful D120 northwest to medieval Oingt. One of the best ways to appreciate this charming little place is to climb the central tower in the village and enjoy the marvellous view.

To round off the tour of Beaujolais take the D96 southwest again and turn right onto the D485 to the ancient hilltop village of Ternand. The archbishops of Lyon once had their summer residences here and there are frescos from the Carolingian era in the crypt of the 15th-century church.

At this point you have reached the southernmost fringes of Beaujolais, and your tour of Burgundy is complete.

GAZETTEER

Abbaye de Morgeot 82 E2
Aigrots, les 64 H5
Allots, aux 48 F4
Aloxe-Corton 10 D5, 35 E7,
    60 C4, 87 E9
Aluze 93 C8
Amoureuses, les 45 C8
Angles, les 70 G3
Anse 131 H9
Arbresle, l' 131 I10
Arbues, les 79 B7
Ardillats, Les 131 C7
Argillas, aux 48 G5
Argillières, les,
    Chambolle-Musigny 45 C8
Argillières, les,
    Prémeaux-Prissey 49 F10
Arlot, Clos 49 F10
Arnas 131 E3
Arvelets, les, Fixin 40 G4
Arvelets, les, Pommard 65 H8,
    70 H1
Athées, aux 48 E5
Athets, les 45 B7
Audignac, Clos d' 70 H4
Aussy, les 70 F4
Autun 10 E4
Auxerre 10 A2, 29 C6
Auxey-Duresses 10 D5, 35 G6,
    71 I7, 87 F8
Avallon 10 B3
Avaux, Clos des 64 G4
Avaux, les 64 G4
Babillères, les 45 B7
Banc, le 79 F9
Baraques 41 F7
Baraques de Gevrey-Chambertin,
    les 41 E7
Barbières, les 70 H5
Banzey 93 F8
Barottes, les 45 C8
Barraults, Clos des 93 D9
Barre Dessus, la 71 F6
Barre, en la 71 F6
Barre, la 70 G3
Barrières, aux 48 F4
Bâtard Montrachet 79 B7
Battaudes, les 82 E3
Baudes, les 45 C6
Baudines, les 82 G3
Baulet, Clos 44 C5
Beauder, Clos 70 G2
Beaujeu 131 D8
Beaumonts, les 60 B5
Beaune 10 D5, 35 F7, 64 E3, 87 E9
Beauregard 82 F4
Beaurepaire 82 G5
Beauroy 22 E5
Beaux Bruns, aux 45 B7
Beaux Fougets, les 65 F6
Beaux Monts Bas, les 48 G1
Beaux Monts Hauts, les 48 G2
Beaux Monts Hauts
    Rougeots 48 G1
Beaux Monts, les Hauts 48 G2
Bel Air 122 E4
Bel-Air 41 G9, 44 D2
Bélissand 64 F4
Belle Croix 49 E7
Belleville 123 H7, 131 E10
Benoites, les 82 E2
Bergerie, la 79 B8
Bernot, Clos 79 B9, 82 F1
Bernouil 29 A9
Berthet, Clos 60 E2
Bertins, les 70 G2
Berzé-la-Ville 106 F2
Berzé-le-Châtel 106 E2
Bessay 123 A6
Beugnons 22 G5

Beuttes, les 79 B8
Biaune, la 122 D5
Bidaude, la 44 C5
Bienvenues Bâtard
    Montrachet 79 B7
Bievaux 82 H5
Billard 41 F7
Bissey-sous-Cruchaud 93 H8
Bissy-la-Mâconnaise 106 B4
Blacé 131 F8
Blagny 78 C5
Blagny, Sous 78 C5
Blanc, Clos, Pommard 65 G8, 70 G1
Blanc, Clos, Vougeot 45 B8
Blanchards, les 44 B5
Blanches Fleurs 61 C8, 64 G1
Blanches, les 70 H4
Blanches, les 71 F8, 78 C2
Blanchisserie, la 64 F3
Blanchot 23 F7
Blanchot Dessous 79 B8
Blanchot Dessus 79 B7
Boiches, les 64 F2
Boichot, en 82 F5
Boirettes, les 82 F3
Bois de Blagny, le 78 D4
Bois de Chassagne 82 F3
Bois de Noël et Belles Filles,
    Sous le 60 E3
Bois-d'Oingt, le- 131 H8
Bondues, les 79 B8
Bonnes Mares, les 45 C6
Bons Feuvres, les 65 F6
Borne, la Grande 82 F3
Borniques, les 45 C8
Bossière, la 41 I8
Bossières 48 E2
Botaveau 83 H6
Bottière, la 123 B7
Bouchère, la 70 G3
Bouchères, les 71 F9, 78 C2
Boucherottes, les 65 G6
Bouchots, les 44 C5
Boudières, les 40 G5
Boudots, aux 48 F3
Boudrières, les 79 B6
Boudriotte 82 F2
Bougros 23 E6
Boulmeau 60 B4
Boulotte, la 60 B4
Bourg-Bassot 93 D9
Bourg-en-Bresse 11 H6
Bourgeots, les 61 C7
Bourgneuf-Vallée-d'Or 93 D9
Bousse d'Or 70 G3
Bousselots, aux 48 F5
Boutières, aux 60 C5
Boutières, les 60 C4
Boutoillottes, aux 40 F5
Boutonniers, les 71 H7
Bouzeron 93 B9
Brazey, les 45 B6
Brelance 79 B6
Brescul, en 65 H7
Bressandes, les, Aloxe-Corton 60 C2
Bressandes, les, Beaune 64 H2
Bréterins, les 71 I7
Brevau 82 H5
Breynets, le 123 D7
Brins, les Hauts 70 H4
Brochon 41 G6
Brouillards, les 70 G3
Brûlées, aux 48 G2
Brûlées, les 49 F8
Brunelle, la 41 F7
Brunettes et Planchots, les 60 B4
Brureaux, les 123 B6
Brussonnes, les 82 F3
Bruyères, les, Aloxe-Corton 60 B3

Bruyères, les, Beaujolais 122 G5
Bucherats, les 123 B6
Buisson Certaut, le 71 F9, 78 B3
Bully 131 I8
Burgy 106 C5
Bussière, la 45 B6
Bussières, Beaujolais 122 I5
Bussières, Mâconnais 106 G2
Bussières, les 45 B6
Butteaux 22 H5
Buttes, les 70 F3
Buxy 93 I8
Cailleret 79 B9, 82 F1
Cailleret Dessus, les 70 G5
Cailleret, en 70 G4
Cailleret, le 79 B6
Cailles, les 49 F8
Caillettes, les 60 B4
Calouère 44 C5
Canet, Champ 78 C5
Canière, la 79 B9
Caradeux, en 60 E3
Cardeuse, la 82 E3
Carelles Dessous 70 F4
Carelle-sous la Chapelle 70 G4
Carougeot 41 F8
Carquelin, le 123 D6
Carré Rougeaud, le 41 F7
Carrés, les 40 F5
Carrières, les 45 C7
Casse-Têtes, les 71 G8, 78 C2
Cassière, la 83 H6
Castets, les 79 F8
Cave, la 70 H4
Cazetiers, les 41 H7
Cazetiers, Petits 41 G7
Cellier aux Moines 93 H9
Cellier, Sous le 70 H5
Cents Vignes, les 64 G2
Cercié 122 H5, 131 E9
Cercot 93 G8
Cercueils, les 41 F8, 44 C1
Chabiots, les, Chambolle-Musigny 45 C8
Chabiots, les, Morey-St-Denis 44 C5
Chablis 10 A2, 23 F7, 29 C8
Chaboeufs, les 49 F8
Chaffots, les 44 C3
Chagny 10 E5, 35 H6, 87 H8, 93 A10
Chaignots, aux 48 F4
Chaillots, les 60 B3
Chaînes Carteaux 49 F9
Chainey, le 83 I7
Chaintré 10 G5, 106 I3
Chalandins, les 48 E1
Chaliots, les 49 F8
Chalon-sur-Saône 10 E5
Chalumeaux, les 78 C5
Chambertin 44 C3
Chambertin Clos de Bèze 41 G9, 44 C2
Chambolle-Musigny 10 D5, 35 C8, 45 C7, 54 C3
Chambost-Allières 131 F7
Chambres, les 79 A8
Chamirey 93 D9
Champagne de Savigny 61 C8, 64 G1
Champans, en 70 G4
Champeaux 41 G7
Champerrier du Bas 41 F7
Champerrier du Dessus 41 F7
Champlains, les 93 E10
Champlots, les 79 E6
Champonnet 41 G8
Champs, En 41 G7
Champs, les Grands,
    Auxey-Duresses 71 I7
Champs, les Grands, Puligny 79 B6
Champs, les Grands, Volnay 70 F3
Champs, les Petits Grands 79 B6
Chânes 106 I3, 131 B10
Chanière, la 65 I7, 70 H1
Chaniot, au 79 B6

Chanlin 70 H3
Chanlins-Bas, les 70 G2
Chanlins-Hauts, les 70 H2
Chanoriers, les 122 B5
Chapelle Chambertin 41 F9, 44 C2
Chapelle-de-Guinchay, La- 131 C10
Chapelle des Bois 122 D5
Chapelle, Petite 41 F9, 44 C2
Chapelle Reugne, la 71 I7
Chapelle-Vaupelteigne, la 22 C5
Chapelot 23 F8
Chapître, Clos du, Fixin 40 G5
Chapître, Clos du,
    Gevrey-Chambertin 41 G8
Chaponnières, les 70 G2
Charbonnières 106 E5
Charbonnières, les 49 F9
Chardannes, les 45 B6
Chardonnay 106 A5
Chardonnereux, les 64 F5
Chardons, aux Champs 61 C6
Chareau, Clos 82 F3
Charentay 122 I5, 131 E9
Charmes, aux 44 C4
Charmes Chambertin 44 C3
Charmes Dessous, les 83 H7
Charmes-Dessous, les 78 B4
Charmes-Dessus, les 78 B4
Charmes, les, Chambolle-Musigny 45 B7
Charmes, les, Puligny 78 B4
Charmes, les Champs des 40 F5
Charmois, le 79 C8
Charmois, les 49 G6
Charmots, les 65 H7
Charmotte, la 48 F5
Charmotte, la Petite 48 F5
Charnay-lès-Mâcon 106 H4
Charnières, les 60 E5
Charolles 10 G4
Charreux 41 F7
Charrières, les, Chassagne 79 A7
Charrières, les, Morey-St-Denis 44 C4
Charron, en 83 I6
Charrons, les Grands 71 G8, 78 C2
Charrons, les Petits 71 G7
Chassagne 79 B9, 82 G1
Chassagne du Clos St-Jean 79 C9
Chassagne-Montrachet 10 E5, 79 B8
Chasselas 106 H2
Chasselay 131 I10
Châtains 22 G5
Château
    Bellevue, de 122 E4
    Briante, de 122 H5
    Capitans, des 123 A6
    Chaize, de la 122 I3
    Fleurie, de 122 D5
    Jean Loron, de 123 C7
    Juliénas, de 123 A6
    Pierreux, de 122 I4
    Poncier, de 123 C6
    Pres, les 122 E5
    Thivin 122 I4
Chatelots, les 45 C7
Chatenay 122 D4
Chatenière, la 79 D7
Châtillon 131 I8
Chaume de Talvat 22 I4
Chaumées, les 79 C8
Chaumes de Narvaux, les 71 G9, 78 C3
Chaumes des Casse-Têtes 71 G8, 78 C2
Chaumes de Narvaux 71 G8, 78 C2
Chaumes et la Voierosse, les 60 D4
Chaumes, les, Aloxe-Corton 60 D4
Chaumes, les, Chassagne 79 B10, 82 E2
Chaumes, les, Côte Chalonnaise 93 E9
Chaumes, les, Meursault 78 C4

Chaumes, les, *Vosne-Romanée* 48 F3
Chazay-d'Azergues 131 I9
Chazière 41 G7
Cheilly 10 E5
Cheminots, aux 40 F4
Chénas 10 H5, 123 C6, 131 C9
Chénelette 131 D7
Chênes, Clos des 70 G5
Chênes, les, *Beaujolais* 122 E5
Chênes, les, *Chassagne* 79 B9
Chenevery, Bas 44 B5
Chenevery, les 44 B5
Chenevières, les 40 F4
Chenevières, les Basses 40 F5
Chenevottes, les 79 C8
Chenôve 35 A9, 54 A3
Chenys, Champs 44 B3
Cherbaudes 41 F9, 44 C2
Chers, les 123 A6
Cheseaux, aux 44 B4
Chessy 131 I8
Cheusots, aux 40 G5
Chevagny-lès-Chevrières 106 G3
Chevalières, les 71 G7
Chevalier Montrachet 79 C7
Chevret, en 70 G4
Chichée 23 H8
Chilènes, les 61 C8, 64 G2
Chiroubles 10 H5, 122 E4, 131 C9
Chitry 29 D7
Chiveau, en 70 H1
Chouacheux, les 64 F5
Chouillet, au 48 F5
Citernes 60 E4
Claude, les Champs 82 E3
Clavoillon 79 B6
Clémentert 40 G4
Clessé 10 G5, 106 D4
Climat du Val 71 I7
Clomée, en 40 F5
Closeau, au 41 F8, 44 C1
Closeaux, les 71 I8
Clos, les 45 D7
Clos, Les 23 H7
Clos, les Grand 82 F2
Clos, les Petits 82 F2
Clou des Chênes, le 70 H5
Clous, aux 61 F6
Clous Dessous, les 71 H8, 78 D2
Clous Dessus, les 71 G8, 78 D2
Clous, les 71 I6
Clous, les 93 B9
Collan 29 B9
Colombière, la 48 E2
Combards, les 79 C9, 82 G1
Combe, au Bas de 48 F3
Combe au Moine 41 H7
Combe Brûlée 48 G2
Combe Danay, la 70 I5
Combe de Lavaut 41 H8
Combe d'Orveau, la 45 C9
Combe du Dessus 41 G7
Combe Roy, En 40 G4
Combes Dessous, les 70 F2
Combes Dessus, les 70 G2
Combes du Bas 41 F7
Combes, les, *Aloxe-Corton* 60 C4
Combes, les, *Beaujolais* 122 I5
Combes, les, *Chassagne* 79 C7
Combes, les, *St-Aubin* 79 C7
Combes, les, *Volnay* 70 G3
Combettes, les 78 B5
Combotte, la 70 H2
Combottes, aux,
  Chambolle-Musigny 45 B7
Combottes, aux,
  Gevrey-Chambertin 44 C4
Combottes, les 45 C7
Commaraine, Clos de la 65 G8,
  70 G1
Comme Dessus 82 G4
Comme, la 82 F3
Communes, aux 48 E3
Condemennes, les 45 B7
Connardises, ez 61 D6

Corbeaux, les 41 F8, 44 C1
Corbins, les 71 F6
Corcelles-en-Beaujolais 123 F7
Cornières, les 83 H6
Corton Charlemagne 60 D3
Corton, le 60 C2
Cortons, les 79 D7
Corvées, aux, *Gevrey-Chambertin* 41
  F8
Corvées, aux, *Prémeaux-Prissey* 49
  F10
Coteau des Bois, le 49 F6
Côte de Bréchain 23 H8
Côte de Brouilly 10 H5,
  122 H4, 131 E8
Côte de Fontenay 23 D6
Côte des Prés Girots 23 F10
Côte Rôtie, *Beaujolais* 122 E4
Côte Rôtie, *Morey-St-Denis* 44 C5
Côtes de Beaune, Hautes 34 H4,
  87 G7
Côtes de Nuits, Hautes 35 D7,
  54 C2
Coton, en 40 G5
Coucherias, aux 64 G4
Cour, Champ de 123 C6
Courgis 22 I4
Courthil, Sous le 78 C5
Courts, les sous 71 H6
Craipillot 41 G8
Crais, les, *Fixin* 40 F5
Crais, les, *Santenay* 83 H6
Crais, les Petits 40 G5
Crapousuets, les 60 B4
Cras, aux, *Beaune* 64 G4
Cras, aux, *Nuits-St-Georges* 48 F3
Cras, les, *Aloxe-Corton* 60 B4
Cras, les, *Chambolle-Musigny* 45 C7
Cras, les, *Meursault* 70 G5
Cras, les, *Pommard* 70 F2
Crâs, les, *Vougeot* 45 B8
Cras, les Grands 122 G5
Cravant 29 F7
Crays, les 71 H6
Crechelins, en 40 F5
Crèches-sur-Saône 106 I4
Créole 40 G5
Créot, le 41 G6
Créots, les 79 E7
Crètevent 41 F6
Crets, ez 79 B9
Creusot, le 10 E4
Creux Baissants, les 45 C8
Creux de la Net 60 D4
Creux de Tillet 71 I7
Criots, les, *Chassagne* 79 B7
Criots, les, *Meursault* 70 F5
Croisettes, les 41 G6
Croix, aux 45 B7
Croix Blanche, la, *Fixin* 40 F5
Croix Blanche, la, *Pommard* 65 G7
Croix Blanche, la, *Vosne-Romanée*
  48 E4
Croix Noires, les 70 G2
Croix Planet, la 70 F2
Croix Rameau, la 48 F2
Croix Rouges, aux 48 E5
Croix Sorine 83 H6
Croix Viollette, la 41 G6
Cromin, le 71 G6
Cros Martin 70 F4
Crotots, les 71 F9, 78 B2
Crots, aux 49 F7
Crottes, ez 82 F2
Croyen, Champ 78 B5
Cruots ou Vignes Blanches,
  les 48 F1
Cruzille 106 B4
Damodes, aux 48 F4
Danguerrins, les 45 C8
Dannemoine 29 A10
Davayé 106 H3
Déduits, les 123 D6
Denicé 131 G8
Dents de Chien 79 C7

Dérée, en 41 G7
Derrière, Champ 79 B8
Derrière chez Edouard 79 F8
Derrière la Grange 45 C7
Derrière la Tour 79 E6
Derrière le Four, *Auxey-Duresses*
  71 I7
Derrière le Four,
  Chambolle-Musigny 45 C7
Derrière le Four, *Vosne-Romanée*
  48 F2
Derrière les Crais 83 H6
Devant, Clos 79 B8
Dezize 10 E5
Didiers, les 49 F9
Digoine l'Hermitage, la 93 B9
Dijon 11 C6, 35 A9, 54 A4
Doix, les Bas 45 B8
Doix, les Hauts 45 B8
Dominode, la 61 D7
Dommartin 131 I9
dos d'Ane, Sous le 78 C4
Douby 122 E5
Dressoles, les 71 F6
Ducs, Clos de 70 H3
Duresses, Bas des 71 H6
Duresses, les 71 I6
Durots, les 70 F5
Echaillé 79 F8
Echanges, aux 45 B7
Echards, ez 70 F4
Echézeaux, aux 44 B4
Echézeaux du Dessus 48 F1
Echézeaux, les 45 C8
Echézeaux, les Grands 48 F1
Ecu, à l' 61 D9, 64 I12
Ecusseaux, les 71 H6
Embrazées, les 82 F3
Emeringes 122 B5, 131 C9
Enseignères, les 79 B6
Entre Deux-Velles, les 40 G4
Epenotes, les 65 F6
Epenots, les Grands 65 G7
Epenots, les Petits 65 G7
Epinottes, les 23 G6
Epointures, les 41 F9, 44 B2
Ergot, en 41 F9, 44 C2
Escolives-Ste-Camille 29 D6
Essarts, les 79 B9, 82 F1
Estournelles 41 H8
Etelois, aux 41 F10, 44 C3
Etroyes 93 D9
Evêque, Clos l' 93 D9
Evocelles, les 41 H6
Faconnières, les 44 B5
Fairendes, les 82 F2
Fairendes, les Petites 82 F2
Famines, les 70 F3
Farges, les 122 E5
Faubard, Clos 82 G4
Faubourg de Bouze 64 F4
Feguine, Clos de la 64 G4
Feusselottes, les 45 C7
Fèves, les 64 H2
Fichots, les 60 D4
Fiétres, les 60 C4
Fixin 10 C5, 35 B8, 40 G5, 54 B3
Fleurie 10 H5, 123 D6, 131 C9
Fleurières, les 49 F7
Fleurieux-sur-l'Arbresle 131 I8
Fleurville 107 C6
Fleys 23 F10, 29 C9
Folatières, les 79 C6
Fondemens, les 40 F5
Fontaine de Vosne 48 E3
Fontaine de Vosne, la 48 E3
Fontaine Sot 79 A7
Fonteny 41 G8, 44 C1
Forêts, les, *Chablis* 22 H5
Forêts, les, *Prémeaux-Prissey* 49 F9
Forges, les 71 G6
Fortune, la 93 A9
Fosses, les 71 H7
Fouchères, les 45 C8
Foulot, en 83 I6

Foulot, le 64 F3
Fourchaume, la 23 D6
Fourches, aux 61 D6
Fourneaux, aux 60 D5
Fourneaux, les, *Chablis* 23 E9
Fourneaux, les, *Santenay* 83 H7
Fournières, les 60 C3
Francemont 82 F3
Fremières, les,
  Chambolle-Musigny 44 C6
Fremières, les, *Morey-St-Denis* 44 C5
Fremiers, les 70 G2
Fremiets, les 70 G3
Frétille, Sous 60 E2
Frionnes, les 79 E7
Froichots, les 44 C4
Fuées, les 45 C7
Fuissé 10 G5, 106 H3
Fulliot, les Champs 70 G5
Fyé 23 E8
Gain, Champ 79 C6
Gain, les Champs 79 B9, 82 F1
Gamaires, les 45 B6
Gamay 79 E6
Gamay à l'Est, le Bas de 79 D7
Gamay, Sur 79 D6
Gamets, les 71 H6
Gamets, les Petits 70 F4
Garanches 122 I5
Garenne, Clos de la 78 C5
Garenne ou sur la Garenne, la
  79 C6
Gargouillot, en 70 F5
Garrants, les 123 D6
Gaudets, les 122 F5
Gaudichots ou la Tache, les 48 F3
Gauthey, le Clos 70 H5
Genaivières, aux 48 E3
Genavrières, les 44 C4
Genet, Clos 83 G6
Genêt, en 61 C8, 64 G1
Genevrières Dessous, les 78 B3
Genevrières Dessus, les 78 C3
Genevrières et le Suchot, les 60 C4
Germolles 93 E9
Gevrey-Chambertin 10 D5, 35 B8,
  41 G8, 54 C3
Gibassier, les 40 F4
Gigotte, la 70 F3
Gimarrals, les 123 C7
Givry 10 E5, 93 F9
Gleizé 131 G9
Godeaux, les 60 E5
Godeaux, Petits 60 E5
Gorges de Narvaux, les 71 G9,
  78 C3
Goudins, Champs 48 E3
Gouin, en 79 E7
Goujonne, la 79 A9, 82 E1
Goulots, les 41 H7
Gouttes d'Or, les 71 F8, 78 C2
Gravains, aux 61 E6
Gravières, les 82 F4
Grenouilles 23 E7
Grésigny 93 C9
Grèves, les, *Aloxe-Corton* 60 C3
Grèves, les, *Beaune* 64 G3
Grèves, sur les 64 G3
Grevilly 106 A4
Grillés, les Champs 123 A6
Griotte Chambertin 41 F9, 44 C3
Groseilles, les 45 C7
Gruenchers, les,
  Chambolle-Musigny 45 C7
Gruenchers, les, *Morey-St-Denis*
  44 C5
Gruyaches, les 78 B4
Guerchère 82 E2
Guérets, les 60 C4
Guéripes, les 45 C8
Guetottes 61 F6
Guettes, aux 61 F6
Gueulepines, les 41 F6
Guillattes, les 123 D7

Guinelay, En 123 B7
Hameau de Blagny 78 C5
Hâtes, les 82 G5
Hautés, les 71 H8
Herbues, aux, *Fixin* 40 G5
Herbues, aux, *Nuits-St-Georges* 48 E4
Herbues, les 45 B6
Herbuottes, les 44 B4
Hervelets, les 40 H5
Homme Mort, l' 22 C5
Houillères, les 79 A7
Hurigny 106 F4
Igé 106 E3
Irancy 10 B2, 29 D7
Jachères, aux 48 E2
Jacques, les 123 D7
Jacquines, les 48 E4
Jambles 93 F8
Jarolières, les 70 G2
Jarrons, Hauts 61 D7
Javernière 122 F5
Jendreau, Champs 82 F2
Jeunelotte, la 78 D5
Jeunes Rois, les 41 G6
Jouènes, les 71 H6
Jouères, les 70 F4
Jouise 41 F8, 44 B1
Journaux, les 41 F6
Journoblot, en 79 B7
Juliénas 10 G5, 123 B6, 131 B9
Jullié 122 A5, 131 B9
Jully-lès-Buxy 93 I8
Justice, la 41 E7
Jutruots, les 45 D8
Ladoix-Serrigny 10 D5
Laize 106 E4
Lambots, les 70 G3
Lambrays, Clos des 44 C5
Lancié 123 E6, 131 D9
Landry, Clos 64 G5
Languettes, les 60 C3
Lantignié 131 D8
Largillière, en 65 G8
Larrets, les 44 C5
Latricières Chambertin 44 C3
Lavaut Saint Jacques 41 H8
Lavières, aux 48 F4
Lavières, les 60 D5
Lavrottes, les 45 C7
Léchet, Côte de 22 F5
Lèvrier, Champ 122 G5
Levière, la 65 F7
Levrons, les 78 B5
Leynes 106 I3, 131 B9
Liards, aux Grands 61 D6
Liards, aux Petits 61 E6
Liards, les Bas 61 D6
Lignorelles 22 B3
Ligny-le-Châtel 29 A8
Limas 131 G9
Limozin, le 78 B3
Lissieu 131 I10
Loachausses, les 48 F1
Loché 106 H3
Lolières, les 60 B1
Lombardes, les 79 A9, 82 G6
Longecourts, les 49 F8
Longères, les 70 I5
Longvic 35 A9, 54 B4
Lozanne 131 I9
Lucenay 131 H9
Luchets, les 71 H7
Lugny 10 G5, 106 C4
Luraule, en 71 F8, 78 C2
Lurets, les 70 F4
Lyon 10 I5
Lys, les 22 F5
Macabrée, la 71 H7
Ma Carrées, les 45 B7
Macherelles, les 79 B8
Mâcon 10 G5, 106 H4, 131 A10
Maison Brûlée 44 C5
Maizières Basses 48 F1
Maizières, Hautes 48 F2
Maladière, la 82 H5

Maladières, les 45 B7, 49 F7
Malconsorts, au Dessus des 48 G3
Malconsorts, aux 48 F3
Maligny 22 B5, 29 B8
Malpoiriers, les 71 F6
Maltroie, la 79 B9
Marchais, les 41 G8
Marchampt 131 E7
Marconnets, Bas 61 D7
Marconnets, Dessus de 61 D8, 64 H1
Marconnets, les 61 D8, 64 H1
Marconnets, les Hauts 61 D7
Mareau, en 70 H1
Maréchaudes, le Clos des 60 B2
Maréchaudes, les 60 B2
Mariages, les 64 G3
Marinot 79 F8
Marissou 93 B9
Marsannay 11 C6
Marsannay-la-Côte 35 B8, 54 B3
Masures, les 79 B9, 82 F1
Mazeray, Clos de 71 F8, 78 B2
Mazière, la, *Fixin* 40 G4
Mazière, la, *Gevrey-Chambertin* 41 F6
Mazis Chambertin 41 F9, 44 C2
Mazoyères 44 D3
Mazoyères Chambertin 44 C3
Meix au Maire, le 41 F6
Meix-Bas Champ 41 G6
Meix Bas, le 45 C8
Meix Bataille, le 70 H5
Meix Chavaux, les 71 H7
Meix, Clos des 79 B6
Meix de Mypont, le 71 H6
Meix des Duches 41 G8
Meix-Fringuet 41 F6
Meix Gagnes, les 71 F8, 78 B2
Meix Garnier, le 71 H6
Meix Goudard, les 79 B8
Meix, les, *Aloxe-Corton* 60 C4
Meix, les, *Puligny* 79 B6
Meix Pelletier 79 A6
Meix Rentier 44 C5
Meix Tavaux, le 71 G6
Mélinots 22 G5
Mellecey 93 E9
Mercurey 10 E5, 93 D9
Meursault 10 E5, 35 G6, 71 F7, 87 F8
Méville 41 G8
Michelons 123 C6
Micot, Clos 70 G2
Mignotte, la 64 G4
Millandes, les 44 C5
Milly 22 F5
Milly-Lamartine 106 F2
Mitans, les 70 G3
Mochamps, les 44 C4
Mombies, les 45 B7
Monchenevoy, Dessus de 60 F5
Monéteau 29 B6
Monim, le Bas de 79 E9
Montagne, la Grande 79 C9, 82 G1
Montagne Saint Désiré 65 H6
Montagny 10 F5
Montagny-lès-Buxy 93 I8
Montaigus, Clos des 93 D9
Montbellet 106 B5
Montceau, en 79 E6
Mont de Milieu 23 F8
Montée de Tonnerre 23 F8
Montée Rouge 64 H4
Monthelie 10 D5, 70 H5
Montmains 23 G6
Montmelas-St-Sorlin 131 F8
Mont-Rachet, le 79 B7
Montrevenots, les 65 H6
Monts, les Petits 48 G2
Monts Luisants 44 C4
Morais, les 60 B3
Morancé 131 I9
Morand, la 60 D2
Morein 23 E9

Morey-St-Denis 10 D5, 44 C5
Morgeot 82 F2
Morgon 10 H5, 122 F5, 131 D9
Morichots, les 79 A9, 82 E1
Moriers, les 123 C6
Morjot, Champs de 82 E2
Moroges 93 G8
Motrot, en 41 G8
Mouchère, Clos de la 78 B5
Mouches, Clos des 82 F5
Mouches, le Clos des 65 G6
Mouchottes, les 79 B9
Mouille, la, *Fixin* 40 F4
Mouille, la, *Gevrey-Chambertin* 41 G6
Moulin-à-Vent 10 H5, 123 C7, 131 C9
Moulin Cruottes Moyne, aux 61 E6
Moulin Landin, au 71 G7
Moulin, le 122 D5
Moulin Moine, le 71 H7
Mousse, le Clos de la 64 F4
Moutier Amet 61 D6
Mues, Dessous les 79 A8
Murées, les 79 A9
Murger de Monthélie, au 71 H6
Murgers, aux 48 F4
Murgers des dents de chien, les 79 C6
Murs, les Grands 45 C7
Musigny, les 45 B8
Musigny, les Petits 45 C9
Napoléon, Clos 40 H5
Narbantons, les 61 D7
Narvaux-Dessus, les 78 C3
Narveaux-Dessous, les 78 C3
Nazoires, les 45 B8
Noirets, les 60 E3
Noirots, les 45 C7
Noizons, les 65 H7
Noizons, les Petits 65 H7
Nolay 34 G4, 87 G7
Nosroyes, les 78 B5
Nosroyes, les Petits 78 B5
Nuits-St-Georges 10 D5, 35 D8, 49 E6, 54 D3
Odenas 122 I4, 131 E8
Ormeau, en l', *Chassagne* 82 E2
Ormeau, en l', *Volnay* 70 G3
Orme, en l' 61 D8, 64 H1
Orme, les Clos de l' 45 B7
Ormes, aux 48 E2
Ormes, Clos des 44 B4
Ouvrées, Clos de 60 70 G5
Ozenay 106 A5
Pallud, en 41 F8
Paquiers, aux 83 H7
Parantoux, Clos 48 G2
Parterre, le 79 C9
Pas de Chat, les 45 C7
Pasquelles, les 79 C8
Pasquiers, les 70 F4
Passetemps 61 D7
Paulands, les 60 B2
Paules, les 64 F5
Paupillot, au 78 B5
Pave, le 122 H5
Pelles-Dessous, les 71 F8, 78 B2
Pelles Dessus, les 71 F8, 78 B2
Perchots, les 71 F6
Perclos, les 79 B8
Perdrix, aux 49 F9
Perdrix, aux Champs 48 G4
Pernand-Vergelesses 10 D5, 60 E3
Pérolles, les 83 G6
Pèronne 106 D4
Perréon, Le 131 F8
Perrière, la, *Fixin* 40 H5
Perrière, la, *Gevrey-Chambertin* 41 F8, 44 C2
Perrière Noblot, en la 48 F4
Perrières, aux 78 C4
Perrières, Clos des 78 C4
Perrières Dessous, les 78 C4
Perrières Dessus, les 78 C4

Perrières, les, *Aloxe-Corton* 60 C3
Perrières, les, *Beaune* 61 D8, 64 H2
Perrières, les, *Meursault* 78 C4
Perrières, les, *Nuits-St-Georges* 49 F8
Perrières, les, *Pommard* 65 F7
Perrières, les, *Puligny* 78 B5
Perrières, les, *St-Aubin* 79 E8
Perriers, les Champs 41 F7
Pertuisots 64 G5
Peuillets, les 61 C7
Peutes Vignes, les 70 F5
Peux Bois 79 C6
Pézerolles, les 65 G7
Picotins, Grands 61 B6
Picotins, les Petits 61 B6
Pièce Fitte, la 70 H5
Pièce sous le Bois, la 78 C4
Pied d'Aloue 23 F8
Pierreclos 106 G2
Pierre, la 123 D7
Pierres, les 79 A8
Pierreux 122 I5
Pierre Virant 44 D4
Pimentiers, les 61 C6
Pimont, En 79 C8
Pimonts, Champs 64 G4
Pince-Vin 41 F7
Pinchons, les 123 C6
Pirolette 123 A7
Pitangeret 79 C8
Pitois, Clos 82 F3
Pitures Dessus 70 H3
Pizay 123 G6
Places, les 79 B8
Planchots de la Champagne, les 61 C7
Planchots du Nord, les 61 B7
Plante du Gaie 79 B8
Plantes au Baron 49 F9
Plantes, les, *Chambolle-Musigny* 45 C7
Plantes, les, *Monthelie* 70 I5
Plantes Momières, les 82 E3
Plantigny ou Issart 41 G8, 44 D2
Plateaux, les 49 F6
Platière, la, *Chassagne* 79 B10, 82 E2
Platière, la, *Pommard* 65 H7
Plâtre, le 122 E5
Plice, la 82 F4
Pluchots, les 70 F4
Plures, les 71 G6
Poinchy 22 E5
Point du Jour, le 122 D5
Pointes, aux 61 E6
Pointes d'Angles 70 G3
Pointes de Tuvilains, les 64 F5
Poirets, les Hauts 49 F7
Poirets Saint-Georges, les 49 F8
Poirier du Clos, le 79 A9
Poisets, les 49 F8
Poisot, le 70 F2
Poisots, les Grands 70 F3
Poisots, les Petits 70 F3
Poissenot 41 H8
Pommard 10 D5, 35 F6, 65 G8, 70 G2, 87 F9
Poncey 93 F9
Pontcharra-sur-Turdine 131 I6
Pontigny 29 A7
Porlottes, les 45 D8
Porroux, les 45 B6
Portes Feuilles, les 40 G5
Portes Feuilles ou Murailles du Clos 48 E1
Porusot Dessus, les 71 F9, 78 C3
Porusot, le 71 F9, 78 C2
Pot Bois 79 C9, 82 G1
Potets, les 83 G7
Pougets, les 60 D3
Pouilly 106 H3
Pouilly-Fuissé 106 H2
Pouilly-Loché 106 H3
Pouilly-Vinzelles 106 I4
Poulaillères, les 48 G1
Poulettes, les 49 F8

Poutures, les 70 G2
Poyebade, la 122 I3
Prarons-Dessus, les 82 E4
Préau 40 G5
Pré de la Folie, le 48 E2
Pré de Manche, le 71 G6
Prémeaux-Prissey 49 F10
Preuses 23 E6
Prévaux, les 61 C6
Prévoles, les 64 F5
Prieur-Bas, Clos 41 F9, 44 C2
Prieur, Clos 41 F9, 44 C2
Prissé 106 G3
Procès, les 49 F7
Pruliers, les 49 F7
Pruliers, les Hauts 49 F7
Pruniers, aux Champs des 61 C6
Pruzilly 106 I2, 123 A6, 131 B9
Pucelles, les 79 B6
Puits, le 79 F8
Puits Merdreaux 79 B9
Puits, Sous le 70 D5
Puligny-Montrachet 10 E5, 35 H6, 79 A6, 87 G8
Quartiers de Nuits, les 48 F1
Quartiers, les 60 D2
Quatre Vents, les 122 D5
Queue de Hareng 40 H5
Raignots, aux 48 F2
Ranché, en la 79 E7
Ratausses, les 61 B6
Ratosses, les 61 B6
Ravelles, les 78 D5
Raviolles, aux 48 E4
Réas, aux 48 F3
Réas, le Clos des 48 F3
Rebichets, les 79 C8
Réchaux, la 40 H5
Redrescut 61 D7
Refène, la 65 G8, 70 G1
Referts, les 78 B5
Régnié 122 F3
Régnié-Durette 122 G4, 131 D8
Reland, le Clos 79 B9, 82 F1
Remigny 82 E3
Remilly, en 79 C7
Renardes, les 60 C2
Reulle-Vergy 35 C7, 54 C2
Reversées, les 64 F4
Richarde, en la 79 C6
Richebourg, le 48 F2
Richemone, la 48 F4
Riotte, la 44 B5
Riottes, les, Monthelie 70 H5
Riottes, les, Pommard 65 F7
Rivaux, les 70 I5
Rivière, au dessus de la 48 E3
Rivolet 131 G8
Robardelle 70 F4
Roche, Clos de la 44 C4
Rochegrés 123 C6
Rochelle, la 123 C6
Rochepot, la 34 G5, 87 G7
Roche, Sous la, St-Aubin 79 D6
Roche, Sous la, Santenay 82 H5
Roches, Sur 70 H3
Roche-Vineuse, La 106 F2
Rognet-Corton, le 60 C1
Roichottes 60 E5
Roi, Clos du, Aloxe-Corton 60 C3
Roi, Clos du, Beaune 61 C8, 64 G1
Roilette, la 123 D6
Romagniens, en 70 I5
Romanèche-Thorins 123 D7, 131 C10
Romanée Conti, la 48 F2
Romanée, la, Chassagne 82 F2
Romanée, la, Gevrey-Chambertin 41 H8
Romanée, la, Vosne-Romanée 48 F2
Romanée St-Vivant 48 F2
Ronceret, le 70 F4
Roncière 49 F7
Roncières 22 G5
Ronds, les Champs 70 H5

Roquemaure, la 82 F2
Rosey 93 H8
Rougeots, les 71 G7
Rougeotte, la 70 G3
Rouges du Bas, les 48 G1
Rouges du Dessus, les 48 G1
Rousseau, Grand Clos 83 I7
Rousselle, la 78 B5
Rouvrettes, les 61 D7
Ruchots, les 45 C6
Ruchottes du Bas 41 G9, 44 C2
Ruchottes du Dessus 41 G9, 44 D2
Ruchottes, Grandes 82 F2
Rue au Porc 70 F2
Rue aux Vaches, la 79 B6
Rue de Chaux 49 F6
Rue de Vergy 44 C6
Rue de Vergy, en la 44 C6
Rue, la Grande 48 F3
Rue Rousseau 79 B6
Rugiens-Bas, les 70 G2
Rugiens-Hauts, les 70 I I2
Rully 10 E5, 35 I6, 87 H8, 93 B9
Russilly 93 F9
Ruyère 122 F4
St Albain 107 D6
St-Amour 10 G5, 123 A7
St-Amour-Bellevue 123 A7, 131 B10
St-Aubin 10 E5
St-Bris 10 A2
St-Bris-le-Vineux 29 D7
St-Denis, Clos, Morey-St-Denis 44 C5
St Denis, Clos, Vougeot 48 F1
St-Denis-de-Vaux 93 E8
St-Désert 93 G9
St-Étienne-des-Oullières 131 E8
St-Étienne-la-Varenne 131 E8
Ste-Vertu 29 D10
St-Forgeux 131 I6
St Gengoux de Scisse 106 C3
St-Georges-de-Reneins 131 F9
St-Georges, les 49 F8
St-Gervais-sur-Couches 34 H4, 87 G6
St-Jacques, le Clos 41 H8
St-Jean, Clos 79 C8
St-Jean-d'Ardières 123 G7
St-Jean-de-Vaux 93 E8
St-Joseph 122 E3
St-Julien 131 E8
St-Lager 122 H5, 131 E9
St-Mard-de-Vaux 93 E8
St-Martin-Belle-Roche 106 E5
St-Martin-sous-Montaigu 93 E9
St-Maurice-de-Satonnay 106 D4
Saints Jacques, aux 48 F4
Saints Juliens, aux 48 F5
St-Symphorien 49 F6
St-Symphorien-d'Ancelles 131 C10
St-Véran 106 I2, 131 B9
Salle, La 106 D5
Salles-Arbuissonnas-en-Beaujolais 131 F8
Salomon, Clos 93 F9
Sampigny 10 E5
Sance 106 G5
Santenay 10 E5, 34 H5, 82 G5, 87 G7
Santenay, Bas 83 G6
Santenay, Haut 83 H6
Santenots Blancs, les 70 G5
Santenots Dessous, les 70 F5
Santenots du Milieu, les 70 G5
Sarottes, les 40 F4
Saucours, les 61 E7
Saules, aux 48 E2
Saulieu 10 C3
Saunieres, les 83 H7
Saussilles, le Bas des 65 H6
Saussilles, les 65 G6
Savigny 10 D5
Savigny-lès-Beaune 35 E6, 61 F7, 87 E9

Sceaux, les 64 F4
Séchet 22 G5
Seignelay 29 A6
Senozan 106 E5
Sentier du Clou, Sur le 79 E7
Sentiers, les 45 C6
Serpens, les 70 F3
Serpentières, aux 61 E6
Seurey, les 64 G4
Sionnières, les 44 B6
Sizies, les 64 G5
Sologny 106 F2
Solon, Clos 44 B5
Solutré-Pouilly 10 G5, 106 H2
Sombernon 10 C5
Songe, en 41 G7
Sorbé, Clos 44 C5
Sorbés, les 44 C5
Sordes, les 45 B7
Sorgentière, la 40 G5
Suchot, en 40 H5
Suchots, les 40 I2
Sylvie 41 F7
Tache, la 48 F3
Taille Pieds 70 G4
Talmettes, les 60 E5
Tamisot 41 F7
Tarare 131 I6
Tart, Clos de 44 C5
Taupe, la 45 C9
Taupine, la 70 G5
Tavannes, Clos de 82 F3
Tavannes, les 65 F7
Tellières, les 40 G5
Terres 71 F8, 78 C2
Terres Blanches, les 49 F10
Terres, les Grandes 82 E3
Tesson, le 71 G8, 78 C2
Tête de Clos 82 F3
Têtière, la 79 A8
Teurons, les Bas des 64 G3
Teurons, les 64 F4
Thorey, aux 48 G5
Thorins, les 123 C7
Tillets, les 71 G9, 78 C3
Tions, les Champs 40 F5
Tirant, Champ 79 F9
Toisières, les 70 G5
Tonnerre 29 B10
Topons, les 49 F9
Toppe Marteneau, la 60 D4
Tour du Bief, la 123 C7
Tournus 10 F5
Toussaints, les 64 G2
Travers de chez Edouard, les 79 F8
Travers de Marinot, les 79 F7
Traversins, les Champs 48 G1
Très Girard 44 B5
Treux, les 48 F1
Trézin, le 79 D6
Triblanourg 49 F7
Troêsmes 22 E4
Trois Follots 70 H2
Truffière, la 78 C5
Tuvilains, les 64 F5
Tuyaux, aux 48 E5
Uchizy 107 B6
Vache, la 70 H2
Vaillons 22 G5
Vallerots, les 49 F8
Valmur 23 E7
Valozières, les 60 B3
Varoilles, les 41 H8
Varot 93 B9
Vaucoupin 23 G9
Vaucrains, les 49 F8
Vaudésir 23 E7
Vau de Vey 22 F4
Vaugiraut 23 G7
Vaulorent 23 E6
Vaumuriens-Bas, la 70 H2
Vaumuriens-Hauts, les 70 H2
Vaupulent 23 D6
Vaux Dessus, les 83 G6
Vaux, en 70 H3

Vaux-en-Beaujolais 131 F8
Vauxrenard 131 C8
Vellé, au 41 G7
Velle, Sous la 71 H7
Velle, Sous le 71 I7
Velle, Sur la 70 H5
Vercots, les 60 C4
Vercots, les Petits 60 C4
Vergelesses, Basses 60 D5
Vergelesses, Ile des 60 D4
Vergelesses, les 60 D4
Vergelesses, les Basses 60 D4
Vergennes, les 60 B2
Verger, Clos de 65 H8, 70 G1
Vergers, les 79 C8
Vergisson 10 G5, 106 H2
Vermarain à l'Est, Bas de 79 F7
Vermarain à l'Ouest, Bas de 79 F7
Vermenton 29 E8
Véroilles, les 45 C6
Vérottes, les 64 F4
Verrillats, les 123 C7
Verroilles ou Richebourgs, les 48 G2
Verseuil, en 70 G4
Verzé 10 G5, 106 E3
Vide Bourse 79 B7
Vigne au Saint, la 60 C4
Vigne Blanche 82 F2
Vigne Derrière 79 B9, 82 F1
Vigne Rondes, aux 48 F4
Vignes aux Grands, les 40 G5
Vignes Belles 41 F9, 44 B2
Vignes Blanches, les 70 F5
Vignes Franches, les 64 G5
Vignes, les Grandes, Auxey-Duresses 71 H7
Vignes, les Grandes, Prémeaux-Prissey 49 F10
Vignes Rondes, les 70 H5
Vigness Moingeon 79 E7
Vigncux 18 E2
Vignois 41 F6
Vignois, aux 40 G5
Vignots, les 65 I7
Vignottes, les 48 F1
Village, Gevrey-Chambertin 41 F8
Village, Pommard 65 F8
Village, Vosne-Romanée 48 F2
Village, au 71 G7, 78 B2
Village, le, Aloxe-Corton 60 C4
Village, le, Chambolle-Musigny 45 D7
Village, le, Morey-St-Denis 44 C5
Village, le, Pernand-Vergelesses 60 E2
Village, le, Puligny 79 A7
Village, le, St-Aubin 79 E8
Village, le, Santenay 83 G6
Village, le, Savigny-lès-Beaune 61 F6
Village, le, Volnay 70 G3
Village, le, Vougeot 45 B8
Villefranche-sur-Saône 10 H5, 131 G9
Villié-Morgon 122 E5, 131 D9
Villy 22 B4
Vinzelles 10 G5, 106 I3
Violettes, les 48 F1
Vionne, la 40 G5
Viré 10 G5, 106 C5
Vireuils Dessous, les 71 H8, 78 D2
Vireuils Dessus, les 71 H8, 78 D2
Vireux, les 71 H8
Virondot, en 82 G2
Vivier, le 123 D6
Voillenot Dessous 79 B8
Voillenots Dessus, les 79 B8
Voitte 79 B6
Volnay 10 D5, 70 G3
Vosger, Champs de 40 F5
Vosgros 23 H7
Vosne, en 41 G7
Vosne-Romanée 10 D5, 35 D8, 48 F2, 54 D3
Vougeot 10 D5, 45 B8
Vougeot, Clos de 45 B9, 48 F1
Vougeots, les Petits 45 B8

139

INDEX

Indexer's note: Names of vineyards and wines are often the same and are indexed together eg Bonnes Mares 44, 46 where 44 refers to vineyard and 46 to wine. Towns are given in brackets for hotels and restaurants.

Accad, Guy 50, 51
Agneux 95
Aligoté grapes 15, 59, 86, 91
Aloxe-Corton 52, 59
Amandier, L' (Mâcon) 115
Amboise, Domaine Bertrand 52
American camps 69
Amiot-Bonfils, Domaine Guy 81
Amiot et Fils, Domaine Pierre 43
Amoureuses 46
Ampeau et Fils, Robert 77
André Ziltener, Château (Chambolle-Musigny) 46
Angerville, Domaine du Marquis d' 73
Angles 72
Anne de Beaujeu 132
Années Vins, Aux (Buxy) 103
Anse 132
appellations 12
Brouilly 128
Chalonnais 91
Mâconnais 107
Arcenant 57
Arfentière, Domaine de l' 111
Arigny castle 128
Arlaud Père et Fils, Domaine 43
Arlot, Domaine de l' 52--3
Armand, Comte 72
Arnoux, Robert 50
Arts et Terroirs (Gevrey-Chambertin) 42
Arts, Les (Meursault) 76
auberges see under individual names
auctions, wine 67, 69
Auvenay, Domaine d' 75
Auvigue-Burrier-Revel 110
Auxerre 27
Auxey-Duresses 74, 76
Auxey-le-Petit 74
Avaux 69
AXA Millésimes 52
Azé 111, 112
Azenay, Domaine de 111

Bachelet, Domaine 43
Bachelet, Jean-Claude 84
Bachelet & Ses Fils, Domaine 85
Bailly, Caves de 28
Ballot-Millot & Fils, Raymond 77
Banée de Meursault 77
Batacchi, Philippe 43
Bâtard-Montrachet 80, 81
Bauderon 119
Beaujeu 130
Beaujeu, Hospices de 129
Beaujolais 11, 120--35
Beaujolais, Hôtel du 115
Beaujolais-Mâconnais, Relais (Leynes) 118
Beaujolais Nouveau 123
Beaujolais, Restaurant du (Blaceret) 132
Beaune 9, 35, 64--9
Beaune, Hospices de 67, 69, 75
Beauregard 82
Beauregard, Château de 117
Beines 23
Belin, Jules 52
Belland, Adrien 84
Belland, Roger, Domaine 84
Bellecroix, Hostellerie du Château de (Chagny) 94
Belle Epoque (Beaune) 66
Bellevue (Mâcon) 114
Bénéton, Le (Beaune) 66
Berchère 51

Bernard, Domaine 127
Bernollin, Pierre 103
Bersan & Fils, Domaine 28
Bertagna, Domaine (Vougeot) 47
Berthaut, Vincent et Denis 42
Bertheau, Domaine 46
Berthe au Grand Pied 59
Berzé-la-Ville 110, 111
Berzé-le-Châtel 112
Besançenot-Mathouillet, Domaine 68
Beursaudière, Auberge La (Nitry) 27
Bévy 57
Bèze, Clos de 42--3
Bichot, Albert 25, 68
Bief, Auberge du (Ligny-le-Chatel) 27
Bienvenue, Léon 31
Bienvenues-Bâtard-Montrachet 80, 81
Billaud-Simon, Domaine J 24
Billebaude, Auberge de la (Givry) 98
Billoux, Jean-Pierre (Dijon) 37
Bissy-la-Mâconnaise 111
Bistro Bourguignon, Le (Beaune) 66
Bistrot, Le (Chalon-sur-Saône) 101
Bize & Fils, Simon 63
Blacé 132
Blaceret 132
Blagny 80
Blain-Gagnard 81
Blanche, La Maison (Moulin-à-Vent) 126
Blanches, Domaine des Pierres 69
Blanchots 21
Bleu Marine (Beaune) 66
Bocquenet, Marcel 51
Boillot et Fils, Lucien 43
Boillot, Jean-Marc 72
Boillot, Pierre 77
Bois d'Oingt, Le 134--5
Bois de la Salle, Château du 124
Boisset, Jean Claude 51
Bongraine, Domaine de la 111
Bonhomme, Domaine André 110
Bonneau du Martray, Domaine 62
Bonnes Mares 44, 46
Bonnet, Château 125
Bonnot-Lamblot 63
Bordeaux-Montrieux, Domaine 97
Bouchard Aïné 96
Bouchard Père et Fils 69
Bouchères, Les 77
Boudriotte, Clos de la 81
Bougros 21
Bouillard, Domaine 127
Bourgeon, René 99
Bourg Neuf, Le 123
Bourgogne (Cluny) 116
Bourgogne, Le (Chalon-sur-Saône) 101
Bourgogne Aligoté 13, 27, 34, 54, 94
Bourgogne Aligoté de Bouzeron 15
Bourgogne Côte Chalonnaise 91
Bourgogne Irancy 31
Bourgogne Passe-Tout-Grains 11, 13, 15, 91
Bousse d'Or, Clos de la 72
Boussey, Denis 73
Bouvier, Christian 39
Bouzeron 15, 91, 94, 95
Bouzerotte, La (Bouze-lès-Beaune) 89
Brançion 108
Brelière, Jean-Claude 95
Breuil, Le 134
Briday, Michel 95
Brintet, Luc 97
Brocard, Jean-Marc, Domaine 24

Brochon 42
Brosse, Claude 105
Brouillards, Les 72
Brouilly 121, 128
Bruck, Lionel J 51
Brureaux, Domaine des 125
Bruyère, Domaine de la 126
Buissière, Domaine de la 85
Buisson-Battault, A. 77
Buisson, Domaine Henri et Gilles 75
Burgonde, Le (Nolay) 89
Burguet, Alain 43
Burgundy, Dukes of 64, 67
Burgy 109
Buxy 103, 108
buying wines 19

Caesar, Julius 64, 124
cafés see under individual names
Cailleret Dessus 73
Caillerets 72, 81
Calvet et Cie, J 69
Camp Romain, Auberge du (Chassey-le-Camp) 94
Camus, Père & Fils 43
Cantin, Bernard 31
Capron-Manieux 63
Carillon, Louis & Fils 80
Carnot, Lazare 89
Carnot, Sadi 89
casinos 82
Cassis, Crème de 17, 55
Castel de Très Girard (Morey-St-Denis) 43
Cauvard Père & Fils, Domaine 69
caves coopératives 12; see also individual names
Cellier-Expo 112
Cellier Volnaysien, Le (Volnay) 72
Centre, Hôtel du (Lugny) 108
Centre, Hôtel du (Meursault) 76
Cent Vignes 68
Cep, Auberge du (Fleurie) 127
Cep, Le (Beaune) 66
Cercié 128
Cerve, Manoir de la 119
César grapes 15, 31
Chablis
area 20--3, 26--8
town 24--5, 36
wine categories 21
Chablis-Bar, Le 24
Chablisienne, La 25
Chagny 91, 92, 94
Chaintré 119
Chaize, Château de la 128
Chaley, Yves 57
Chalonnais 11, 90--103
Chalon-sur-Saône 91, 100--2
Chambertin 34
Chambertin-Clos de Bèze 43
Chambolle-Musigny 44, 46, 53
Chamirey 98
Chamirey, Château de 97
Champagnon, Domaine 125
Champans 72, 73
Champier, Bernard 129
Champs Fulliots 73
Champy Père & Cie 68
Chanaise, Domaine de la 128
Chancerons 116
Chandon de Brailles, Domaine de 62
Chânes 119, 123
Change 86, 89
Chanson Père & Fils 68
Chantreuil, Domaine 127
Chanzy Frères Domaine de l'Hermitage 94
Chapeau Rouge (Dijon) 36
Chapelle-Chambertin 43
Chapelle-de-Guinchay, La 124
Chapelle-Vaupelteigne, La 26
Chapître, Clos du 40
Chapuis, Maurice 62
Chardonnay, Au 42
Chardonnay, Coopérative de 110
Chardonnay, Domaine du 25

Chardonnay grapes 14, 21, 54, 91, 103, 107
Chardonnay (village) 108
Charentay 128
Charlemagne 59
Charlemagne, Le (Pernand-Vergelesses) 62
Charles & Fils, Domaine François 89
Charles, Frédéric 97
Charleux, Maurice 85
Charlopin-Parizot, Domaine 42
Charmes (Chambolle-Musigny) 46
Charmes (Meursault) 77, 78
Charmes (Morgan) 128
Charmes-Chambertin 43
Charmes, Les (Meursault) 76
Charmet 135
Charmois 81
Charnay 132
Charnay-lès-Mâcon, Coopérative 110
Charriat, René 31
Chartron et Trébuchet 80
Chassagne, Le 81
Chassagne-Montrachet 80--1, 82
Chasselas 119
Chassey-le-Camp 94, 101
Château, Auberge du (Cruzille) 108
Château, Auberge du (Val-de-Merry) 27
Châtillon-d'Azarques 134
Chauvenet, Jean 51
cheese 16, 51, 110
Cheilly, La Cave de 85
Cheilly-lès-Maranges 85
Chénas 121, 124, 125, 126
Chênes, Clos des 72
Chenôve 39
Chers, Domaines des 125
Chervin, Domaine de 110
Chevalier-Montrachet 80
Chevalier Père & Fils 53
Chevaliers du Tastevin 47
Chevallier, Gabriel 121, 132
Chevannes 57
Chevillon, Robert 51
Chevrot, Fernand, Domaine 85
Cheysson-les-Farges, Domaine 127
Chez Denise (Evelle) 86
Chez Jeanette (Fixin) 42
Chez Jean-Pierre (St-Amour) 124
Chez Joël D (Beaune) 66
Chez Marc et Annick (Chiroubles) 127
Chez Marianne see Sports, Café des
  (Marsannay-la-Côte)
Chez la Rose (Julienas) 125
Chignard, Michel 127
Chiroubles 121, 127
Chitry 27, 28
Choffliet-Valdenaire, Domaine 99
Chorey, Château de 63
Chorey-lès-Beaune 63
Ciboulette, La (Beaune) 66, 67
Cinq Tours, Château des 109, 110
Citeaux 51
Citeaux, Hôtel de (Beaune) 67
Clair, Bruno 42
Clair, Joseph 39
Clair, Michel 85
Clarion, Villa Louise 62
Clerget, Domaine Yvon 73
Clerget, Georges 47
Clerget, Michel 47
Clerget, Raoul 84
Clessé 109
Clessé, Coopérative 111
climate 13
Clochemerle 121, 132
Clochemerle, Auberge de (Vaux-en-
  Beaujolais) 132
Clos (Chablis) 21, 26
Clos, Hostellerie des (Chablis) 24
Clous 94
Cluny 105, 112, 132
Coères 103
Colin, Marc 84
Colinot, Robert & Fils 31
Collanges-lès-Bévy 57
Collin et Bourisset 110
Collongette 111

Combe aux Loups, Domaine de la 127
Comblanchien 52, 53, 57
Comme, La 82, 84, 85
commune wines 13
Côte d'Or 34
Condé, princes of 37
Confrérie, Clos de la 84
Confuron, Domaine Jean-Jacques 52
Contat-Grangé, Yvon et Chantal 85
Coopérative, Cave 135
coopératives see under individual names
Copeau, Jacques 60
Copiaux, Les 60
Coq au Vin, Le (Juliénas) 123, 124
Coquines, Les (Prémeaux-Prissy) 52
Corgoloin 52, 53, 57
Cormatin 108
Corton 59, 60
  white wines 63
Corton-André, Château 59
Corton-Bressande 63
Corton-Charlemagne 59
Corton Grancey, Château 69
Côte de Beaune 35, 52, 58--89
Côte de Brouilly 121, 128
Côte Chalonnaise see Chalonnais
Côte de Léchet 26
Côte de Nuits 35, 38--57
Côte d'Or 11, 12, 32--7
  wine categories 34
  see also Côte de Beaune; Côte de Nuits
Côte d'Or, La (Nuits-St-Georges) 51
Côte de Troesmes 25
Couches 94
Coudert, Alain 127
Coulanges-la-Vineuse 27, 31
Courgis 26, 28
Coursel, Domaine de Mme Bernard de 72
Cras 69
Crêches-sur-Saône 112
Crémaillière, La (Auxey-Duresses) 74
Crémant de Bourgogne 11, 13, 27, 28, 91,
  96
Crêt des Bruyres, Domaine du 130
Creusefond, Gérard 74
Criots-Bâtard-Montrachet 81, 84
Croix Senaillet, Domaine de la 118
crosses, stone 48, 72
Crotet, Jean 67
Crozier, Jean-Paul 128
Cru St-Amour, Caveau du 123
Cruzille 112
cuisine 16, 17
Curtil-Vergy 56
Curveux, Louis 117
Cuverie, La (Savigny-lès-Beaune) 63

Daguerre, Louis 100
Dame d'Aquitaine, La (Dijon) 37
Damoy, Pierre, Domaine 43
Dauvissat, René et Vincent 25
Davayé 119
Defranc, Robert et Philippe 30
Delalogue, Roger 31
Delorme, André 95
Demoiselles 81
Denon, Dominique 101
Deschamps 124
Deschamps, Louis et Hélène 134
Desplace Frères 130
Desvignes, Louis Claude 128
Desvignes, Propriété 99
Deux Roches, Domaine des 119
Dezize-lès-Maranges 85, 86
Diconne, Jean-Pierre 74
Dijon 9, 36--7, 39
Diligence, Relais de la (Meursault) 76
Dime, Maison de la 124
district wines 13
documentation centres, wine 69
dolmens 56
Donjon, Le (Oingt) 134
Donzy-le-Pertuis 112
Doudet-Naudin, Maison 63
Dracy, Le (Dracy-le-Fort) 98
Dracy-lès-Couches 94

Droin, Jean-Paul 25
Drouhin, Joseph 67, 69
Drouhin-Laroze, Domaine 43
Duboeuf, Georges 126
Duboeuf, Roger & Fils 117
Dubois, Robert & Fils 52
Dubreuil, Bernard 62
Dubreuil-Fontaine, Domaine 62
Ducs, Clos des 72
Ducs, Domaine des 124
Dujac, Domaine 43
Du May, Seigneur 81
Dupont & Ses Fils, Guillemard 89
Dupuis, Raymond 31
Duresses 74
Dureuil-Janthial, Raymond 95
Durup, Jean 25

Eau-Vive 110
Echézeaux 48
Ecusson, L' (Beaune) 66
Eglantière, Domaine de 25
Epeneaux, Clos de 72
Epenots, Grand Clos des 72
Epenottes 89
Ermitage Corton, L' 63
Escolle, Château d' 110
Estrées, Gabrielle d' 99
Etang-Vergy, L' 57
Eveneaux, Clos des 69
exchanges, wine 92

Fairchild, Robert 85
Fairendes 82
fairs, wine 112, 127
Faiveley 96
Falaises de Cormot 89
Falveley, Joseph 51
Ferme de Rolle (Hameau de Rolle) 56
festivals
  village 61
  wine 27, 31, 77
Fête Raclet 125
Fête du Sauvignon 31
Feuillette, La (Chalon-sur-Saône) 102
Fèves, Clos des 69
Fèvre, Bernard 75
Fevre, William 26
Fief, Domaine du Clos du 124
Fin Bec, Au (Leynes) 118
Fiscentix see Fixin
Fixey 40
Fixin 40
Flagey-Echézeaux 48
Flammarion 69
Fleurie 121, 126--7
Fleurville, Château de 108
Florent de Mérode, Prince 53
Florilège, Le (Chalon-sur-Saône) 101
Foire aux Sauvagines 100
Folie, Domaine de la 95
Folie, La 134
Fontaine, Guy 94
Fontenay-près-Chablis 25
Forêts, Clos des 53
Fort, Domaine 30
Fortune, Clos de la 94
Fouquerand Père & Fils, Domaine 89
Fourchaume 25, 26
Framboise, Crème de 17, 55
François Frères 75
Frantin, Clos 68
Fremiets 89
Fribourg, Domaine Marcel et Bernard 57
Frionnes 81
frost, vines damaged by 13
Fuissé 118
Fuissé, Château 117
Fussey 57

GAEC des Vignerons 94
Gagnard, Jean-Noël 81
Gamay 81
Gamay grapes 15, 81, 86, 121, 123
Ganoux, Domaine Michel 72
Garenne, La (Dracy-le-Fort) 98

Garnerot, Château de 97
Garnoux, Michel, Domaine 72
Gaulois, Relais (Nantoux) 94
Gauthey, Emile 99
Gauthier, Paul 134
Gelin, Domaine Pierre 42
generic wines 13
Genièvres (Meursault) 77
Gentilhommière, La (Nuits-St-Georges) 50
Gérarde, Domaine de la 130
Germain Père & Fils, Domaine 75
Germolles 96, 99
Gevrey-Chambertin 34, 42--3
Gilly, Château de (Gilly-lès-Citeaux) 47
Girandin, Vincent 85
Girardot (Buxy) 102
Giroud, Camille 69
Gisors, Guy de 116
Givry 91, 98--9, 103
Glantenay, Bernard 73
Gobet 134
Goisot, Ghislaine et Jean-Hugues 30
golf courses 67, 102, 134
Gorge du Bout du Monde 89
Gouges, Domaine Henri 51
Gourmandin, Le (Beaune) 66
Gourmets, Les (Marsannay) 42
Goutte d'Or, La 77
Goyard, Domaine 111
Grand Blue, Le (Beaune) 67
Grand' Cour, Domaine de la 127
Grand Cru wines 13
   Chablis 13, 21
   Côte d'Or 34
Grande Rue 49
Grandes Tours, Domaine des 135
Grands Crus Blancs, Cave de 117
Grands Crus, Les (Gevrey-Chambertin) 42
Grands Crus, Relais des (Chénas) 125
Grands Echézeaux 48, 100
Grands Vins, Les (Fleurie) 127
Grange-Charton, Domaine de la 129
Grange du Bois, Auberge de la 118
Grange du Bois, La 118
grapes
   picking 62
   varieties 14--15
Gras, Alain 75
Gravières 82, 84
Grégoire, Henri-Lucius 119
Grenouilles 21
Greuze, Hostellerie de (Tournus) 109
Griotte-Chambertin 43
Grivot, Jean 50
Gros, Domaine Jean 50
Grosse Pierre, Domaine de la 127
Grossot, Domaine Corinne et Jean-Pierre 25
Guffens-Heynen, Domaine 117
Guide de Marloux, Le (Mercurey) 96
Guillemot-Michel, Pierrette et Marc 112
Guyon, Domaine Antonin 63
Guyot Père & Fils 75

Halle, Hôtel de la (Givry) 99
Hautes-Côtes 35
Hautes-Côtes de Beaune 86, 89
Hautes-Côtes, Maison des (Marey-lès-Fussey) 57
Hautes-Côtes de Nuits 54--7
hot air balloon trips 69
Hôtel-Dieu (Beaune) 67--8
hotels 18--19; see also individual names
Hôtes du Domaine Bouzereau-Gruère, Chambres d' 81
Huchette, La (Replonges) 114
Hudelot-Noëllat, Alain 47
Hudelot-Verdel, Domaine Bernard 57
Hugo II, Duke of Burgundy 36
Huguenot, Père & Fils, Domaine 42

Ibis 24
Igé 111
Igé, Château d' 108
Igé, Coopérative 111

Ile St-Laurent 102
ingredients, regional 16--17
inns see individual names
Irancy 27, 31
Isle Bleue, L' (Chalon-sur-Saône) 101

Jacob, Domaine Lucien 89
Jacques, Château des 126
Jacqueson, Henri et Paul 95
Jadot, Louis 69
Jaffelin 51, 69
Jambles 98, 99
Janodet, Jacky 126
Janroux 124
Jardin des Remparts, Le (Beaune) 67
Jayer-Gilles 57
Jayer, Henri 75
Jefferson, Thomas 72
Jessiaume Père & Fils 85
Jobard, François 77
Joblot, Jean-Marc et Vincent 100
John of Chalon, Prince of Orange 80
Joliot, Domaine 89
Juillot, Michel 96
Juliénas 121, 123--4
Juliénas, Château de 125
Jully-lès-Buxy 103

Labouré-Roi 51
Labry, Domaine André et Bernard 74
Lacerelle, Château de 130, 135
Lachassagne 132
Ladoix 53, 59
Ladoix-Serrigny Capitain-Gagnerot 53
Ladoucette, Patrick de 26
Lafarge, Domaine Michel 73
Lafarge, Henri 111
Laferrère, Hubert 112
Lafon, Domaine des Comtes 77
Lafouge, Jean et Vincent 74
Lagelée, Denise 89
Laleure-Piot, Domaine 62
Lamartine, Alphonse de 112, 114, 119
Lamartine, Domaine de la Cave 124
Lamartine, Relais (Bussières) 109
Lambrays, Clos des 44
Lambrays, Domaine des 46
Lameloise (Chagny) 94
Langres, Clos des 52
Laroche, Domaine 24, 25
Larochette, André 119
Latour, Henri 74
Latour, Louis 69
Latricières-Chambertin 43
Leclerc, Philippe 43
Leflaive, Domaine 75, 80
Leflaive Frères, Olivier 80
Lejeune, Domaine 72
Lequin-Rousset, Domaine 85
Leroy 74
Leroy, Domaine 50
Leroy family 49
Levernois, Hostellerie de 67
Leynes 118, 119
Liergues, Auberge de 132
Lierques 132
Lignier, Domaine Hubert 46
Lignier et Fils, Georges 46
Ligny-le-Châtel 25
Loché 119
Loché, Château de 119
Loges, Château des (Le Perréon) 130, 135
London, Château 111
Long Depaquit, Domaine 25, 68
Losset (Flagey-Echézeaux) 47
Louis XI, King of France 72, 80
Louis XIV, King of France 72, 105
Louis XV, King of France 72
Lud' Hotel (Savigny-lès-Beaune) 63
Lugny 111, 112
Lugny, Coopérative 111
Lumpp Frères 99
Lycée Viticole de Davayé 119
Lys, Les (Chablis) 24

Mabeau, Christian 128

Mâcon 107, 114--16
Mâconnais 11, 12, 104--19
Mâconnaise des Vins, Maison 116
Mâconnais, Le Relais de 109
Ma Cuisine (Beaune) 66
Magnolias, Les (Meursault) 76
Maladière (Santany) 84
Maladière, Domaine de la (Chablis) 25
Malandes, Domaine des 25
Maligny 25
Manassès, Hôtel le (Curtil-Vergy) 56
Mancey, Coopérative 111
Manciat-Poncet, Domaine 111
Mandelot 89
Manoir des Chailloux (Jully-lès-Buxy) 102
Manoir de la Perrière (Fixin) 42
Maranges 11, 33, 85
Marc de Bourgogne 16
Marchampt 128
Maréchal, Jean 96
Marey, Etienne-Jules 67
Margerand, Domaine Jean-Pierre 125
Maritonnes, Les (Moulin-à-Vent) 126
markets 77, 100, 126
Maronniers, Domaine des 25
Marsannay 33, 39--40
Martin & Fils, André 31
Martin, Jean-Jacques 119
Martin, René 86
Martray, Laurent 129
Martray, Réné de 61
Maufoux, Prosper 85
Maume, Domaine 43
Mavilly-Mandelot 89
Mazilly Père & Fils 89
Mazis-Chambertin 43
Melin 74
Meloisey 89
Melon de Bourgogne grapes 15
menhirs 116
Méo-Camuzet, Domaine 50
Mercey (Côte de Beaune) 85
Mercey (Mâconnais) 109
Mercey, Domaine du Château de 85
Mercure-Bord de Saône (Mâcon) 114
Mercurey 91, 96--7, 98, 99
Mestre Père & Fils 85
Meuilly 57
Meunier, Sophie et Alain 53
Meursault 72, 76--7, 78
Meursault, L'Hôpital de 77
Meursault, Château de 77
Méziat, Bernard 127
Micaude 53
Michel & Fils, Louis 25
Michel, Bernard 103
Michelot, Alain 51
Michelot-Buisson 77
Millésimes, Les (Gevrey-Chambertin) 43
Millot, Raymond & Fils 77
Milly 26
Milly-Lamartine 112
Miolane, René et Christian 135
Miotte, Auberge de la 52
Moillard 51
Moine-Hudelot, D 46
Momessin 43
Monassier, Armand 96
Monceau, Château de 119
Monette, Domaine de la 97
Mongeard-Mugneret 50
Monnet, Jean-Marc 125
Monnier, Domaine René 77
Monnier et Fils, Domaine Jean 77
Montagne de Brançion, Le 108
Montagne des Trois Croix 86
Montagny 91, 102--3
Montagny, Le Relais du (Buxy) 102
Montagny-lès-Buxy 103
Montbard 36
Montbellet, Domaine de 111
Mont Blanc 72
Mont Brouilly, Le 128
Montcuchot 103
Mont du Milieu 25, 26
Mont du Py 128

Monthelie 73
Monthelie, Château de 73
Montille, Hubert de 73
Montmains 26
Montmartre, Relais de (Viré) 109
Mont Mélian, Le (Meursault) 76
Montpierreux, Domaine de 27
Montrachet 34
Montrachet, Le (Puligny-Montrachet) 80
Montrevots 72
Monts Battois 69
Moreau & Fils, J 26
Moreau, Christian 26
Moreau, Jean 85
Morey, Marc 81
Morey, Pierre 77
Morey-St-Denis 43--5
Morgeot 82
Morgon 121, 127--8
Moriers 127
Mortet, Domaine Denis 43
Mortet, Jean 127
Mouches, Clos de 85
Moulin aux Canards, Auberge du
    (Aubigny-en-Plaine) 51
Moulin-à-Vent 121, 126
Moulin-à-Vent, Château du 127
Moulin de la Coudre, Le (Vency) 27
Moulin de Martorey 101
Mugnier, Jean-Paul 94
Mugnier, J F Domaine 47
Munier, Bernard 47
Mûre, Crème de 17
museums 56, 68, 85, 101, 112, 115, 130,
    132
Alphonse Lamartine 114--15
archaeology 37, 50, 111, 117
fine arts 37
François Rude 37
historic tools 112
Napoleon 40
open air 110
photographic 67, 100
transport 62
wine and wine artefacts 31, 40, 47, 67,
    84, 111, 135
wooden towers 125
Musigny 34, 46
Mussy, Domaine 72
Muzard, Lucien, et Fils 85
Naigeon-Chauveau 43
Nantoux 89
Napoléon, Clos 40
Naudin-Ferran, Henri 57
négociants-éleveurs 12, 33, 50
Nielion, Michel 81
Niellon, Michel 81
Nièpce, Nicéphore 100
Noir, Domaine Clos 43
Noisot, Claude 40
Nolay 86, 89
Nord (Mâcon) 114
Notre-Dame de Bonne Espérance chapel
    60, 61
Nudant & Fils, Domaine André 53
Nuits-St-Georges 33, 35, 48--51, 52

Obédiencerie, L' 24, 25
Odenas 128, 129, 130
Oingt 135
Opéra, Paris 53
Orches 89
organic wines 50, 57
Orly airport 53
Ouillette, L' (Santenay) 84

Paix, Hostellerie de la (Beaune) 67
Panorama des Clos 24
Panthéon, Paris 28
Paradis, Auberge du (St-Amour) 124
Parc de la Colombière (Dijon) 36
Parc, Le (Beaune) 66
Parc Noisot 40
Parent, Domaine 72
Parigot Père & Fils 89
Passetemps 82

Passe-Temps, Château du 84
Passot, Alain 127
Passot les Rampaux, Domaine 130
Patriarche Père et Fils 67, 69
Paulée de Meursault 77
Pavelot, Domaine 63
Pérelles, Domaine des 119
Pernand-Vergelesses 60--1
Pernin-Rossin, A 50
Perrachon, Pierre 123
Perréon, Le 130
Perret, Denis 66
Perrière 51
Perrière, Clos de la 40
Perrières 77
Perrier, Laurent 97
Petit Blanc, Le (Mercurey) 96
Petit Chablis 23
Petits Clos, Les 82
Philip the Bold, Duke of Burgundy 37, 84,
    96
Philippe de Valois 72
Philippe-le-Hardi 96
Philippe le Hardi, Château 84
phylloxera 118, 127
Picq & Ses Fils, Domaine Gilbert 26
Pierre, Château de la 129
Pierreclos 112, 116
Pierre (Mâcon) 115
Pierreux, Château de 128
Pillets, Domaine des 128
Pillot, Paul 81
Pinot Blanc grapes 15
Pinot Gris grapes, 15
Pinot Noir grapes 14, 31, 39, 54, 91
Pinson, Domaine 26
Pizay, Château de (Morgon) 128
Place, Café de la (Marsannay-la-Côte) 39
plagues (1347) 95
Plâtre-Durand 123
Podor, Jean 31
Poinchy 26
Poire William 89
Poisson d'Or, Le (Mâcon) 115
Poitevin, André 124
Pommard 33, 70, 72, 89
Pommard, Château de 70, 72
Pommiers 132
Poncey 98, 99
Ponnelle, Pierre 51
Ponsot, Domaine 46
Pont, Café du (Pommard) 72
Porrets 51
Porte Noël (Chablis) 24
Poruzots, Les 77
Potin Gourmand, Le (Cluny) 116
Pouilly 118
Pouilly-en-Auxois 36
Pouilly-Fuissé 11, 107, 112, 116--19
Pouilly-Fuissé, Au (Fuissé) 116
Pouilly-Loché 107, 117, 119
Pouilly-Vinzelles 107, 117, 119
Pousse d'Or, Domaine de la 73
prehistoric caves and settlements 74, 75--
    6, 94, 111, 116, 117
Préhy 26
Prémeaux, Château de 52
Prémeaux-Prissy 51, 52--3
Premier Cru wines 13
Chablis 21
Côte d'Or 34
Preusses 21
Prieur-Brunet, Domaine 85
Prieur, Domaine Jacques 77
Prieuré, Domaine du 95
Prissé 119
Prissé, Coopérative 119
Pruliers 51
Prunier, Michel 74
P'tiote Cev, Domaine de La 94
Puligny-Montrachet 78, 80
Puligny-Montrachet, Château de 78
Pulliat, Victor 127

Quincié-en-Beaujolais 128
Quintaine 109

Raclet, Benoît 125
Ragot, Domaine 99
Ramonet, Domaine 84
Rampon, J P 130
Rapet Père & Fils, Domaine 63
Ravenau, François en Jean-Marie 26
regional wines 13
Côte d'Or 34
Regnard, A & Fils 26
Régnié 121, 129
Reine Pédauque, Caves de la 62
Reine Pédauque, La 52, 67
Relais Sainte-Vincent, Le (Ligny-le-Châtel)
    27
Remparts, Domaine des 30
Renarde, Domaine de la 95
Renardes 53
Renardière, La (Marsannay) 42
restaurants 19; see also individual names
Reulle-Vergy 56
Richebourg 49
Rion & Fils, Domaine Daniel 53
Roally, Domaine de 111
Robin (Chénas) 125
Roche, Clos de la 43, 44
Rochepot, Château de la 89
Rochepot, La 89
Rocher de Cancale (Mâcon) 115
Roches, Hôtel-Restaurant les (St-Romain)
    75
Roche Vineuse, La 110
Rodet, Antonin 85, 96, 97
Roi, Clos du (Chenôve) 39
Roi, Clos du (Corton) 63, 100
Roilette, Clos de la 127
Rolin, Nicholas de 67
Rolle 56
Romanèche-Thorins 125, 126
Romanée 49
Romanée-Conti 48--9
Romanée-Conti, Domaine de la 50, 75
Romanée-St-Vivant 49
Ropiteau Frères 51, 77
rosé 39--40, 89
Rôtisserie du Chambertin, La (Gevrey-
    Chambertin) 42
Roty, Joseph 43
Rouges, Domaine des Pierres 119
Rournier, Domaine G. 47 spelling correct
    ??????????????????
Rournier, Hervé 47 spelling correct see
    old edition ??????????????????
Rousseau Père & Fils, Domaine Armand
    43
Roy, Dominique et Vincent 74
Roy Frères 74
Roy-Thévenin, Alain 103
Ruchottes-Chambertin 43
Rude, François 37
Ruelée, Auberge la (Curtil-Vergy) 56
Ruet, Domaine 129
Rugiens 72
Rully 91, 95--6
Rully, Château de 95, 96
Russilly 99

Sacy grapes 15
Sagy 112
St-Amour 119, 121, 123
St-Amour, Château de 123
St-Aubin 81
St-Bris-le-Vineux 27, 28
Ste Claire, Domaine 26
St-Denis, Clos 44
St-Denis de Vaux 98
Sainte-Denis, Domaine 112
St-Etienne-des-Ouillières 130
St-Etienne-la-Varenne 128
St-Gengoux-de-Scisse 111
St-Gengoux-le-National 105
St-Georges 51
St-Georges (Chalon-sur-Saône) 100
St-Jean 84
St-Jean (Chalon-sur-Saône) 101
St-Jean, Clos 81
St-Jean de Vaux 98

St-Lager 128
St-Laurent, La (Mâcon) 115
St-Louis, Domaine du Clos 40
Sainte-Marie, Hôtel (Nolay) 86
St-Martin-sous-Montaigu 98
St-Maurice-lès-Couches 94
St-Maurice de Satonnay 109
St-Pierre (Lugny) 109
St-Régis (Chalon-sur-Saône) 100
St-Romain 75--6, 89
St-Romain, Le (Anse) 130
St-Ugezon, Caveau (Nuits-St-Georges) 50
St-Vallerin 103
St-Véran 107, 119
St-Vérand 119
St-Vincent, Hostellerie (Salles-Arbuissonnas) 130
St-Vincent, Le Relais (Chablis) 24
Salins, Guigone de 68
Salles-Arbuissonas 132
Salomon, Clos 99
Sampigny-lès-Maranges 85, 86
Sanglier, Le (Nuits-St-Georges) 50, 56
Sangoy Côte Cour (Gevrey-Chambertin) 43
Santenay 33, 82, 84--5, 86
Santenots, Clos des 72
Sarazinière, Domaine de la 112
Sassangy, Château 102
Satonnay 110
Saule, Château de la 103
Saulx, Relais de (Beaune) 68
Sauvignon Blanc grapes 15, 27
Sauvignon de St-Bris 27
Sauzet, Etienne, Domaine 80
Savigny, Le (Blacé) 134
Savigny-lès-Beaune 61--2, 64
Savoye, Domaine Pierre 128
Savy, Domaine de 124
Senard, Domaine Daniel 62
Serveau et Fils, Domaine B 46
Simonnet-Febvre 26
soils 13, 21
Solutré 115, 116--18, 119
Sorin, Luc 30
Sports, Café des (Marsannay-la-Côte) 39
spring waters, medicinal 82
Steinmaier & Fils, Veuve 103
Syracuse, Le (Chablis) 24

Table d'Olivier Leflaive, La 80
Tâche, La 49
Talmard, Domaine Philibert et Gérard 111
Tart, Clos de 43, 46
tasting wines 19, 56
Taupenot-Merme, J 46
Taupenot Père & Fils 75
Tavanne, Clos de 84--5
Temple of Bacchus 130
Ternand 135
Ternant 56
Terrasse des Beaujolais, La (Buisante) 134
Terrasse du Beaujolais, La (Chiroubles) 127
Terroir, Le (Santenay) 84

Tête, Michel 125
Teurons 69
Texier & Fils, Georges 134
theatre groups 60
Thénard, Domaine 99
Theurons 68
Thévenet, Jean 111
Thévenin-Monthelie & Fils, Domaine René 75
Thévenin, Roland 76
Thévenot-Le-Brun & Fils, Domaine 57
Thibert (Dijon) 37
Thivin, Château 129
Tilleuls, Auberge des (Vincelottes) 28
Tire Bouchon, Le (St-Vérand) 118
Toison d'Or, La (Dijon) 37
Tollot-Beaut & Fils 63
Tomatis & Fils, Francis 127
Tonnerre 36
Tontons, Les (Beaune) 67
Touches 97
Tour de Belle-Mère 128
Tour, Château de la 47
Tour du Doyenné 102
Tour, La 103
Tournus 107
Touroparc 126
Tour Rouge 103
Tours, Château de 132
Toute Petite Auberge, La (Vosne-Romanée) 47
Tremblay, Gérard 26
Trénel Fils 111
Tressot grapes 15
Trichard, Georges 124
Trois Glorieuses, Les 69
Trois Greniers, Maison aux 101

Uchizy 109

Vachet, Jean 103
Vaillons 26
Val d'Or, Hostellerie du (Mercurey) 96, 97
Valanges, Domaine des 119
Val, Clos du 74
Val de Vergy, Domaine du 57
Valmur 21, 26, 27
Valois, Dukes of 37
Varennes castle 128
Varoilles, Domaine des 43
Varoux, Domaine de 27
Vauchignon 89
Vaucoupins 25
Vaucrains 51
Vaudésir 21, 26
Vau de Vey 26
Vaudon, Domaine de 26
Vau Lignau 26
Vauroux, Domaine de 26
Vaux-en-Beaujolais 121, 130
Vendangerot, Le (Rully) 95
Vendanges de Bourgogne, Aux (Gevrey-Chambertin) 42
Vendanges, Les (Coulanges-la-Vineuse) 27

Vercingetorix 117
Verdet, Alain 57
Vergelesses, Les 60
Vergers 81
Vergers, Château des 129
Verget 117
Vergisson 112, 116
Vermots 84
Vernoy, Clos du 99
Verre Galant, Le (Chalon-sur-Saône) 101
Verzé 110
Vieille Eglise, Cellier de la 124
Viénot, Charles 51
Vieux Moulin, Le (Chablis) 24
Vieux Pressoir, Auberge du (Évelle) 89
Vignaud, Michel 24
Vigne Blanche, La (Fuissé) 116
Vigneronne, Auberge la (Régnié) 129
Vignerons de Buxy, Cave de 103
Vignes, Auberge des (Volnay) 72
Vignes, Hôtel des (Juliénas) 124
village festivals 61
village wines 13
Côte d'Or 34
Villaine, A et P de 94
Villars-Fontaine 56
Ville, La 123
Villié Morgon 127
Vincelottes 31
Vins de la Côte Chalonnaise, Maison des 91, 101--2
Vins Mathelin, Les 135
Vinzelles 119
Vion, Jacky 94
Viré 109
Viré, Coopérative 111
viticulture and wines 12--13
Voarick, Michel 62
Vocoret, Domaine 26
Vogüé, Domaine Comte Georges de 47
volcanoes 128
Volnay 72
Vosne-Romanée 47, 48--9
Vougeot 46--7
Vougeot, Château de 47
Vougeot, Clos de 34, 46--7, 53

walking routes 89, 112
wall inscriptions 62
Wilson, Hôtel (Dijon) 36, 37
wine categories 12--13
wine events 77, 125
auctions 67, 69
exchanges 92
fairs 112, 127
festivals 27, 31, 77
wine regions 11

Yonne 29--31

Ziltener, André 44, 46

PICTURE CREDITS